Praise for the British edition:

"In the final analysis, we may describe Patwant Singh as a romantic, perhaps one of the last great romantics. But for this reason alone, his book is a must. We still have much to learn from dreamers, most especially when they are as cultivated as this writer." —Juliet Reynolds, *The Pioneer*

"*Of Dreams and Demons* is an eloquent expression of [Singh's] intense involvement in India's destiny. It is an emphatic declaration of his faith in India's people and the fundamental values they chose for themselves when they made 'a tryst with destiny' in the stirring days of 1947. . . . Patwant Singh's abiding faith in the India of his dreams has been severely buffeted but refuses to be quenched. He takes on the 'demons,' who are out to extinguish Auden's 'affirming flame,' with characteristic robustness. If so far it has been 'a rendezvous with renegades,' in his sharply etched phrase, there is still hope. He recalls Gandhi's beautifully elegant words: 'Everything appears muddy on top, but underneath it is crystal-clear and calm. The mud goes to the sea of itself, and the rivers mingle and flow clear and pure.' His memoir is an eloquent testament of hope, disillusionment, though in the end not despair, but a sustaining faith in India's people." —John Lall, *Financial Express*

"The strange combination of connoisseur of art and fighter for lost political causes takes us on wondrous journeys around the world, to Armi Ratia, the founder of Marimekko and great Finnish fabric and dress designer in Finland, to . . . the Bauhaus in Germany, and [Singh's] . . . own magazine *Design*. It is this natural mix of Indian with foreign, whether it is ideas or people, that Patwant brings out with poise and sophistication in his book. . . . I feel that anyone interested in contemporary India will find this a valuable assessment of current events and recent history, by a man who has no political axes to grind, but is typical of the cultivated, concerned, and decent Indian." —Amita Malik, *The Hindustan Times*

Also by Patwant Singh

India and the Future of Asia
The Struggle for Power in Asia
The Golden Temple
Gurdwaras in India and Around the World

Of Dreams and Demons

A Memoir of Modern India

With a new Preface by the Author

Patwant Singh

KODANSHA INTERNATIONAL
New York • Tokyo • London

Kodansha America, Inc.
114 Fifth Avenue, New York, New York 10011, U.S.A.

Kodansha International Ltd.
17–14 Otowa 1-chome, Bunkyo-ku, Tokyo 112, Japan

Published in 1995 by Kodansha America, Inc.
by arrangement with the author.

First published in 1994 by Gerald Duckworth & Co. Ltd, London.

This is a Kodansha Globe book.

Library of Congress Cataloging-in-Publication Data
Singh, Patwant, 1925–
Of dreams and demons : a memoir of modern India / Patwant Singh.
p.   cm. — (Kodansha globe)
Includes index.
ISBN 1-56836-086-X
1. Singh, Patwant, 1925–   . 2. India—Politics and
government—1919–1947. 3. India—Politics and government—1947–
I. Title. II. Series.
DS481.S554A3   1995
954.04'092—dc20
[B]   95-2163

Printed in the United States of America

95 96 97 98 99   Q/FF   10 9 8 7 6 5 4 3 2 1

Contents

To Meher

with my
love, gratitude and admiration

Preface to the North American Edition

JAWAHARLAL Nehru, Mahatma Gandhi's political heir and independent India's prime minister, had this to say to the West about his country: "Try to understand and appreciate that something magnificent and colossal is happening in India."

This book tells the story of what has happened during India's turbulent journey from colonial rule to republican statehood to the present day. From the thirties to the nineties. It sifts rhetoric from reality and presents India as she is today, neither glossing over the disgraceful conduct of dishonest politicians nor her unique achievements. I have not pulled punches when recounting India's trials and travails, because I believe that truth may help pragmatism and decency prevail over opportunism and deceit. This belief is reinforced by the fact that we have held together as a nation for forty-eight years since independence, and taken gigantic strides toward industrialization and self-sufficiency in food. Huge plants all across India now produce an astonishing variety of manufactured goods, such as steel, locomotives, automobiles, aircraft, ships, heavy machinery, and much else, and provide equipment to oil refineries, hydroelectric projects, and atomic power stations.

I am proud of our dramatic breakthroughs, but ashamed at the manner in which the out-of-work and the poor — the three hundred million Indians who live below the poverty line — are excluded from civil society and seen as an embarrassment and burden on the earth. The number of those neglected continues to grow even as we proudly point at our expanding middle class.

My effort in this book has been to place things in perspective, to show that if political waywardness occupies so prominent a place in our lives today, so does dissent. Many countervailing forces are beginning to oppose those who are destroying traditional decencies in India's social and political life. In describing our momentous journey from that profoundly moving night of August 14, 1947, when colonial rule ended and India became an independent state, to the present time, I have avoided negative

v

criticism and have tried instead to show that, like all epoch-making journeys, this one has also faced turbulent weather. With over nine hundred million hopeful, diverse, and impatient people on board, the boat continues to be rocked. Which scarcely means our journey is futile; if anything, what is fueling India's drive for a place under the sun is faith in the future, in our "tryst with destiny," which Nehru described so movingly on the night we achieved our independence.

The only way to keep our tryst is to make sure that in rushing to embrace new technologies we do not neglect the poor in the decades ahead. Interestingly, even curiously, this need was underscored by some very perceptive comments in a personal letter to me from Michael Spindler, head of Apple Computers. Even though his observations relate to the United States they are equally – if not more – relevant to India: "Some 150 years ago, all economic activity was basically geared toward producing food. That's today less than 3 percent of the working and voting population. With the increase in automation and productivity gains through technology, there may be only an additional 10–15 percent of the working population necessary to produce all products there is a market for. So the question is: what do we do with the other people? We are drifting towards a model where certain people will never work in their lives. Are we ready for this chaos in any civilized society? I suggest we are not."

Nor are we. Although sophisticated technology may help India compete in the market places of the world, it will certainly not provide work for the hundreds of millions who need to be included – and employed – as enthusiastic participants in the nation's productive processes.

If the paradoxes of India are endless, so are the problems she has to grapple with. Which is understandable since one-sixth of the world's population exists in the complex mosaic of her different faiths, languages, customs, creeds, and castes and each group prefers its own religious, scholastic, and philosophical beliefs. But these differences should excite the imagination, should make the effort of understanding India more challenging, as there is so much to assimilate, savor, and experience. Seeking to know India is an unending quest that leads to an appreciation of her achievements in the arts, architecture, sciences, and mathematics as well.

India's accomplishments in these fields were no doubt a result of her people's inherent genius, but they were also an outcome of her wide contacts with the ancient civilizations of Rome,

Greece, Egypt, Arabia, Persia, China, Japan, and Central Asia. As my friend and fellow writer H. Y. Sharada Prasad puts it: "To all of them India was a land of wisdom and wealth. It is no accident that the only ocean to be named after a country is the Indian Ocean. Finding a passage to India, geographically and philosophically, has been a major undertaking in the annals of mankind, leading to unexpected discoveries, like the finding of the Americas."

I have described some of India's architectural masterpieces in this book. As for her contribution to mathematics and its impact on mankind, Georges Ifrah, the author of *Universal History of Figures*, tells of his world travels in search of the origins of the zero and its first uses, and how his search ended in India. He found that her mystics, looking for a way to define the extent of the universe and the age of Brahma, had discovered the notion of zero, as a means of giving specificity to infinity. The discovery of the zero also enabled them to deal with very large figures, since for centuries Indians who had contemplated abstract ideas of time and space wanted to make the measurement of them possible — which the zero finally permitted. Algebra and other mathematical systems followed. While the Arabs soon adopted the Indian notation, Europe took a thousand years to accept it. Ifrah believes that "the zero is one of the most brilliant manifestations of human intelligence, almost as important as the discovery of fire."

The spectrum of knowledge spanned by Indian scholars and savants in their search for understanding of the universe and answers to the mysteries of life is vast. Yet India and other descendants of centuries-old civilizations continue to be described as "third world" countries. This denigrates them. It ignores their past, mocks their struggle to rebuild their ravaged societies, and creates stereotyped images. The term *third world* was once used to identify nations that belonged neither to the capitalist nor communist world but belonged instead to the uncommitted third world. Yet it has, through continuous misapplication, come to represent backwardness and worse. I have heard it argued that it still means the politically unaligned, but I am unconvinced. Because in that event, Switzerland and Sweden too should belong to the third world, but they are seldom described as such. I also wonder why the blighted areas of the Bronx and Brooklyn are compared to the third world since neither their politics nor foreign policy is involved. Even a liberal American commentator like Noam Chomsky falls into this trap when he writes critically of his country's march towards "a two-tiered society with striking third world features." Unmindful of the irony, many Indians also, parrotlike, use this term when referring to their country. Clearly, invidious repetition can blunt not only people's perceptions of others but also of themselves.

There is much Indians and Americans have in common: diversity, democratic systems, an astonishing mix of religions, races, and cultural overlays, and a natural, warm, unaffected outgoingness. And yet, these peoples are still uninformed about each other. Because few American books offer an inside account of the first forty-seven years of our independence, I have tried to provide insights into life in India before and after British rule, about her archaeological and artistic past, her modern social environment, and her predicaments and potential. It is not easy to pack all this in a single book, but I have tried.

Indira Gandhi, at a dinner in the White House on March 28, 1966, said: "The present-day world offers the possibility of bringing together one people with another. The young men and women of your Peace Corps are well known and well loved in our country. Every endeavor to sustain and enlarge this people-to-people partnership is a good effort and is welcome."

I hope this book will help such endeavors.

New Delhi
January 1995

Prologue

A NOTHER memoir amidst proliferating autobiographies, reincarnated lives and compulsive recollections may seem excessive. But it may perhaps be justified if the writer has witnessed the wanton hijacking of an entire country by politicians unburdened by principles and moral rectitude, and if he has seen them experience a perverse thrill through disruption, death, violence and waste. It would be dishonest not to expose the misdeeds of such men, whose idea of democracy is to use frenzied mobs for genocidal attacks against fellow-citizens; who engender enmities between religions and caste groups to gain votes, and who undermine the institutions established to ensure the rule of law.

One way of exposing them would be to join the political 'mainstream' – which is how we laughingly call it in India – and start a new movement for clean government. Another would be to join whichever party is in power with the declared intention of reforming it from within. Several of my friends have used this perfectly respectable excuse to explain their haste in scrambling on to one or other of the bandwagons which happen to be passing by with room on board for them. Yet another route which desperate people driven to the wall are beginning to take is that of armed uprisings with bombs and blazing AK-47s.

My course has been to write a book – not an impersonal and academic account, but a story of the first forty-six years of our independence told in the form of a personal memoir and in the hope that it may help build up public opinion against the usurpers. I felt it had to have an immediacy which can only come from an individual's personal expectations, enthusiasms, experiences – and perhaps even too romantic a vision of his own society. I wanted it to strike a responsive chord in countless people everywhere who have also, in their own way, aspired and striven for similar goals.

The story begins with the carefree days of my childhood, continues through freedom's advent and ends at the present time. I have written about momentous events, each of which marks a change of course from our original ideals and goals, to a rudderless, wayward journey into a shadowy world, without moral compass, humane concerns, or decencies in public life. The contrast between where we started and where we are now could not be more poignantly highlighted than by an event in the life of Mahatma Gandhi. During his travels on foot through the villages of Bihar, Gandhi stopped by a hut one day and knocked on the door. When a woman's voice asked him his business he told her who he was. She replied that, much as she wanted to meet him, she could not come out, because she and her husband had only one *dhoti* between them and he had gone out wearing it. A deeply-moved Gandhi vowed that he too would wear only a *dhoti* from then on.

Contrast this with the chosen lifestyle of India's Prime Ministers. Take their travels abroad in the refurbished Jumbo jets complete with imported table-linen, stemware, Turkish towels, a double-bed with electronically operated headrests, specially printed menus et cetera. In India, streets are cleared of all traffic to enable them to drive around in peace. They nod approvingly at proposals for building 5-star hotels, while the sick and dying spill out on the capital's pavements because there is no room for them inside its hospitals.

Have these extravagant priorities earned greater respect for India's leaders, or increased their self-esteem? Far from it. Jumbos are not known to provide iron in the spines of men without backbone. As for self-respect, all Indians are debased by our cringing attitude to Western statesmen. Prime Minister P.V. Narasimha Rao, for instance, saw nothing odd in what he said to a meeting of civil servants at the end of visits by John Major and Boris Yeltsin to New Delhi in January, 1993. Their visits, he said had 'given us some confidence after a good deal of adverse publicity, reaction, suspicion and misgivings ...' (this was after the demolition of the Babri mosque a few weeks earlier), adding for good measure that they had helped put India 'back in the reckoning'. What price national self-esteem when we try to distract attention from anarchy and mismanagement, with certificates of good conduct by visiting houseguests?

While their testimonials may give comfort to a faltering leadership, they are nothing more than diplomatically correct statements made by men whose own national self-interest required it. When they praise us and our democracy, they are not unaware of how it has been eroded by repeated amendments to the Constitution, and by making it impossible for countless men and women – without party affiliations – to contest elections, since vast sums of money are now needed to run for public office. This is not a problem for those who wield power at the Centre and have made corruption into a national cult, collecting kickbacks on massive government spending with funds provided by smugglers, black-marketeers and other racketeers. An additional element making a mockery of the electoral process is the use of hired hoodlums to intimidate voters and capture polling booths. Established political parties – who have mobs on call – field them wherever needed. With their money and muscle-power, these parties have cornered the democratic domain.

Such is Indian democracy today.

The story which follows will irk many who are in politics and those in the communications business who level unfounded charges at large segments of Indian society but are too squeamish to let the world see us the way we are. They would rather India was interpreted as a large, happy family of different faiths, beliefs, languages and cultures; admittedly difficult to manage at times, but gamely marching on to a promising future. I see it differently.

For me India's present state is that of a cultural amputee severed from all that is best in her by criminals masquerading as law-makers and by some media-men who extend the media's support to them. They played a particularly notorious role in Punjab in the eighties, widening the communal gulf through biased and inflammatory editorials, analysis and reporting. Government patronage, assiduously sought and subtly extended, had a hand in it. In India it takes many forms. Editors have been known to land top jobs through a Prime Minister's kindly intercession with obliging newspaper owners. Even diplomatic assignments can be acquired. There are countless other congenial ways of keeping newsmen happy and, if power corrupts, proximity to power is equally corrupting.

Therefore, it came as an agreeable surprise to see – with some exceptions – the balanced and remarkably unbiased coverage in the aftermath of the Babri Masjid's demolition at Ayodhya in December 1992 and the massacres which followed it. I see the media's stand as an 'affirming flame'. As I do the honorable conduct of those members of the permanent executive who stand up to political pressures and uphold their statutory responsibility to protect life and property. The inherent and traditional decency which makes people transcend blinding passions and extend a helping hand to one another is yet another affirming flame. Then there are the increasing number of individuals, non-governmental organisations and voluntary agencies who resist the erosion of human rights, environmental conservation, women's rights, press freedom and the very concept of the rule of law.

The challenge is to ensure that these flames are not extinguished by the stormy winds which are sweeping across India.

Acknowledgments

IT IS difficult – even for Indians – to come to grips with the bewildering reality of India without the advice and help of many friends. I am particularly indebted to those whose personal involvement with events and helpful advice made the distillation of my own experiences possible. Many, for understandable reasons, I cannot name. But among those I can, and do so with warmth and gratitude, are:

Ameena Ahuja, Lt. Gen. J.S. Aurora, Wing Commander Ravi Badhwar, Rasil Basu, Lt. Gen. J.S. Dhillon, C. Gopalan, Harold Harris, Rajni Kothari, Jack Masey, Inder Mohan, Saeed Naqvi, F.S. Nariman, Justice R.S. Narula, Padam Rosha, Narinder Saroop and R.S. Sodhi.

Marjorie and Tom Dove, whom I have known since the early fifties when I arrived to live in Bombay, and who confirmed me in my decision to write this book during our drive from Prague to Cologne in May 1990.

Satjiv Chahil for his introduction to that miracle worker, the Macintosh PowerBook. Without it, I would have taken another decade to finish this book.

Kamal Capoor, my invaluable colleague, who not only scored an eagle with the word processor and researched, revised and edited the manuscript, but who also came perilously close to taking over the actual writing herself.

I could not have known while writing this book that my friend Harold Harris – who had edited all my books since he commissioned me to write one for Hutchinson in 1970 – would not live to see it published. His friendship and wise counsel had enriched me for twenty-five years. Fifi Oscard, my literary agent in the United States, was unstinting in her support and spectacular in her style – qualities that were both reassuring and very endearing.

April 1995
New Delhi

Patwant Singh

Of Dreams and Demons

Chapter 1

The Thirties: Years of Awakening

He was discovering ... the world of the emotions that are so lightly called physical.

Colette, *Le Blé en herbe* (Ripening Seed)

THERE WAS no doubt about it. I was desperately in love. I had found in Miss Wynant the great love of my life. Tall, shapely, with the face of an angel – it was all too much. It was obvious that she too felt the stirrings of a grand passion for me. Why else would she smile at me, give me toffees and pat me on the head once in a while?

I was eight years old and the school where Miss Wynant was a teacher was the Convent of Jesus and Mary in New Delhi, where my sister Rasil and I – she was a year and a half older – were admitted in 1932. It could have been on another planet from our own familiar Indian household. We looked with astonishment at the nuns in their strange cowls and long black habits, and at our predominantly English classmates. We had to grow accustomed to differences in discipline, in rituals, routine, food, language and customs, not to mention the knives and forks.

I had a rougher time than Rasil, though I did not yet appreciate the causes. The awareness that colour and religion can create deep divisions between people of different pigmentations and persuasions came later. But the jibes at my turban – which I had trouble winding anyway – led to frequent fist fights which left me the worse for wear, since I took on boys who were more settled and older. I did gradually earn their grudging approval, and in time a few of us Indian boys ganged up to defend ourselves, which also helped. But what turned my head completely were the appreciative looks I got from Miss Wynant. She had seen me get thrashed and, so I fondly believed, had been vastly impressed by my staying powers. Her occasional smile would leave me disoriented for days, and when she gave me a toffee I would hold on to it as a precious memento, until it was a sticky mess.

There were, however, other distractions. Our convent was a co-educational school, and I could not quite believe my luck at being

1

deposited in the middle of so many bouncy, beautiful classmates of the opposite sex. Unfortunately, the word sex was to get me into serious trouble. The school authorities decided to end co-education and moved the boys to what would later become the nearby Columbus School. Through a happy oversight I was left with the girls until the day when we were all told to assemble in the big hall for the visit of an important dignitary.

We stood in two long rows, one for the boys' school and the other for the convent girls. Naturally I stood with the girls, and this was my undoing. As the reverend mother and her aides walked past us for a last minute inspection she came to a shuddering halt when she saw me.

'What sex are you?' she asked in a withering voice.

Having no idea what the word meant, I assumed it was short for section, and said, 'Miss Wynant's', which brought the house down.

Turning to me in a towering rage, she demanded, 'How dare you?'

'Dare what?' I asked innocently. That did it. I was turned out of the hall and sent home. Indeed, as I learned later, I came perilously close to being expelled from the school altogether.

Born in 1925, I grew up in New Delhi in a Sikh household at peace with itself, which can be said for most of India in the twenties and early thirties. My father, Manohar Singh, owned a large construction firm which took him travelling a great deal to his different building projects across the country. The head office of the firm was in New Delhi, and indeed he, and my uncle, Ram Singh Kabli, belonged to the small band of builders responsible for putting into effect Sir Edwin Lutyens's architectural plans for the transformation of India's capital. But his contracts in other parts of the country kept him from us for months at a time, and he became an endearing though elusive presence in the lives of Rasil and myself. We were confident of his love for us, but we missed not having him around all the time. Our quiet, sensitive and caring mother, Gyan Kaur, with a steadfast moral core and amazing reserves of inner strength, did all that she could to make up for his absence, though a better understanding of her influence in those early years would come much later.

My parents were very different from each other. My mother was inward-looking and easily hurt, especially by the insensitivity of people she cared for, though her refined nature seldom allowed her to show it. My father was the opposite. Robust and outspoken, he would get things off his chest without wasting time, while she was thoughtful and reflective before giving an opinion.

Their different backgrounds had much to do with this contrast. Her family had lived for generations in Amritsar, where her father

1. The Thirties: Years of Awakening

was a District and Sessions Judge under the British. His family lived further north, in Rawalpindi, and his father was a merchant who wanted his eldest son to become a lawyer. Indeed, my father obtained a law degree at Lahore, but he devoted his working life to building.

My mother was the youngest of three children. Her brother Harnam Singh, the eldest, had passed his law exams at London's Inner Temple at the turn of the century to become a barrister. Her sister Harnam Kaur, who doted on her, was ten years older. Marriages in those days were arranged – as they mostly are even now – with the help of relatives and friends who brought families with eligible sons and daughters together. So it was that my aunt married a remarkable man, Ram Singh Kabli, whose family had long settled in Kabul, which accounted for his surname. He was an imposing figure, tall, dignified and charismatic, who had come to India to make his fortune at a very young age and had established his own thriving construction enterprise in Punjab.

My mother's side of the family was close-knit, and Kabliji (*ji* signifies both affection and respect) and my father had fitted into it easily, partly because we all lived in Delhi, except for my mother's older brother who lived in Amritsar. But he still played an important role, influencing many of our family's decisions, including our schooling. He even chose our names, selecting them from the holy book of the Sikhs. Another person they all looked up to with profound respect was my mother's cousin, Bhai Vir Singh, one of the truly great Punjabi poets.

The most cherished recollection of my childhood is the happy atmosphere of our home, for I cannot remember a single instance of my parents ever raising their voices at each other. They had been brought together by sheer chance. How then to allow for their deep and enduring bond of affection? I believe it arose from their absolute commitment to the Sikh faith which had taken root during the stormiest period of Indian history, when Nanak (1469-1539), its founder, set about trying to synthesise the subcontinent's two warring religions, Hinduism and Islam. As word spread of his harmonious quest, people came to listen, and many stayed on. His followers were called Sikhs, which is derived from *sikhia* – a variation of the sanskrit word *shishya*, meaning 'disciple' or 'devoted follower'. After Nanak came nine other 'gurus', a term which was not meant to signify divinity but was simply a way of addressing a teacher.

The fifth guru, Arjan Dev, convinced that the dynamics of Sikhism could not be sustained without a strong magnetic core, set about compiling the Granth, or Sikh scriptures. He also built the Har-

3

mandir (or the Golden Temple, as it is more popularly known) and in 1604 installed the first copy of the Granth in it. The Harmandir and the holy city of Amritsar, where it is located, are the heart and soul of Sikhism. The tenth guru, Gobind Singh, ended the office of living gurus for all time, enjoining Sikhs to look upon the Granth as the supreme guru of their faith after him. The Guru Granth, which is how it has been addressed ever since, includes not only the writings of Sikh gurus but also the works of Hindu and Muslim scholars and saints. Written in Gurmukhi, the script of the Punjabi language, each copy of the Granth is 1430 pages long. It occupies a place of honour in every Gurdwara, the Sikh house of prayer. And as modern techniques of printing have made it easier to acquire copies, an increasing number of Sikhs set aside a special room in their homes for it, reading passages from it with profound respect. Its very presence in the house is an act of consecration.

One of my earliest memories is of the Gurdwara in our own home, lovingly filled with flowers, adorned with carpets, a beautiful over-head velvet canopy, and a pedestal draped with many squares of fine silks on which rested the Guru Granth. Deep reverence was accorded to this space hallowed by the holy book from which there were morning and evening readings every day. Rasil and I joined in these prayers which were central to the very existence of our family.

Yet I cannot recall any effort made by our parents to influence us into disregarding the essential goodness of other religious beliefs. For them, their own faith was a life-line without which they could not live. They felt that similar sentiments, entertained by other people, for their faiths, must be respected. By the same token, there could be no compromise with the requirements of our own religion – such as Sikhs wearing their hair long, as a sign of respect for the god-given form, and the turban identifying all Sikhs which evolved as a means of managing long hair. Its colours, and the art of tying it, provide scope for individual ingenuity. I was six when I first started tying my own turban (of fine muslin and, initially, three yards in length) and I daresay the results of my early efforts were far from perfect.

My mother was deeply committed to ensuring that Rasil and I develop a closeness which would endure throughout our lives, just as her relationship with her own brother and sister – especially her sister – had. But it was hard work living up to her expectations, as Rasil and I were at each other's throats at least once a day, though usually the score was higher. With not much difference in our ages, we were fiercely competitive although devoted. Rasil was given to introspection, to working on her dreams within the security of her

1. The Thirties: Years of Awakening

inner world. My world was the outer one, to which I would announce whatever was on my mind. One dissimilarity between us, which I found most irksome, was the seriousness with which she took her studies. It led to unhealthy comparisons. But the unchanging constant in our relationship was the intensity with which we missed each other when not together.

We were the only children, at a time when four or more children were the norm, and my mother's brother and sister were childless. But, although our immediate family was small, the extended family on my father's side more than made up for it. His two brothers and four sisters had quite out-distanced him in the size of their families, and I was awed by the sheer number of our cousins who periodically descended on Delhi for family occasions such as weddings. But the distance between Rawalpindi, where most of them lived, and Delhi, where we were, was not very conducive to close contacts. Initially, we found our childhood companions among the children in our family's circle of friends. Entirely new possibilities of friendship opened up once we started going to school.

Our five years in the convent school were landmark years. We luxuriated in its beautiful surroudings and the warmth of new friendships, many of which have endured over the years.

The thirties were heady years to be growing up in. We lived in an environment in which people felt secure, and respect for the law was mandatory. The rulers set the example by observing proprieties in public and administrative life. But beyond the security of our home, and the pure pleasure of a carefree childhood, the mood of India was changing. Although the thirties were witnessing a gradual strengthening of the resolve to rid the country of British rule, my family had not been drawn into the political struggle which was under way. Nor had several of our friends and relations who were not politically inclined either.

This was not unusual. To countless people British rule represented a just system and an orderly way of life. It provided a stable government, administered by a confident leadership with a welcome sense of fair play, even if their privileged position was unchallengeable under the Raj. Other Indians, infuriated by the racial arrogance of the colonial rulers and their patronising attitude towards the descendants of civilisations far older than their own, were actively involved in the independence movement, though my family was not a participant in that struggle.

But one man's name kept coming up with increasing frequency in conversations between my parents and their friends whenever they talked of India's future. Mohandas Karamchand Gandhi seemed to have fired the Indian imagination with his demand for freedom from British rule. His message transcended the people's regional and religious differences and awakened their dormant sense of pride and self-esteem. He was, without doubt, destined to become an inspiring symbol of nascent Indian nationhood.

Even those who did not endorse Gandhi's struggle were moved by the incongruity of this slightly-built man, dressed in the traditional dhoti (material draped from the waist down) and a cotton wrap, throwing the gauntlet down to rulers obsessed by a sense of their own paramountcy.

Gandhi was anathema to a few of those who gravitated to our house, not as a person but as a symbol of the policy of non-violence he advocated. They were contemptuous of his political strategy which in their view would emasculate Indians already enfeebled by their prolonged enslavement. Some even saw Gandhi as an unwitting tool of the British since his insistence on peaceful protest helped to insulate the rulers from the nightmarish prospect of violence on a subcontinental scale. Such friends were in favour of an armed struggle.

*

More comprehensible to us at the time was our physical environment. New Delhi's air was crystal clear. The spectacular red ball of the sun went over the edge triumphantly each evening, to be followed by another wondrous sight – the night sky with a million stars. They were the last thing we saw as we went to sleep outdoors on summer nights. Air pollution was not a matter of concern then. Unauthorised encroachments on public or private land were unacceptable, as was bedlam on the roads. There was a quality of dignity, clarity and coherence in everything about us, evidence everywhere of civic grace.

My own growing confidence was typified by the expeditions I made on my beloved Raleigh bicycle – that endearing and cherished symbol of mobility. My friends and I covered enormous (so we thought) distances on our bicycles, often four-to-five and later eight-to-ten miles a day. Delhi was a safe city then. We discovered places and rejoiced in our responses to the life unfolding around us. Everything we experienced was part of a sensory repast we were partaking of without knowing what the feast was about.

The magnificent sweep of this new imperial city which the British were building, with a passion which matched that of India's Mughal rulers was heaven-sent for us. Its wide, tree-lined avenues opened up endless and exhilarating possibilities for our eager and inquisitive minds, as did the gracious vistas of King's Way (now Rajpath) with its broad, well-cut lawns and lines of trees extending as far as the eye could see. Clear watercourses paralleled the grassy expanses on either side of this mile-and-a-half-long ceremonial driveway. At the crest of the hill all these culminated in the Great Place – the vast and spacious plaza with six reflecting pools and fountains, generous in scale and filled to the brim with water.

There were many other elements which had helped to create an awe-inspiring setting for the pomp and pageantry of military parades and ceremonial processions in British India. Behind the Great Place rose the monumental offices of the imperial government. And beyond them was the Viceregal Lodge, home of the Viceroy who ruled India.

We loved watching the pageantry, but we savoured even more the excitement of climbing the shady, fruit-bearing trees in King's Way for the succulent jamun, shatoot and mangoes; or the thrill of sailing smack into the inviting waters of the canals on our bicycles during the sweltering months of May and June; or the sheer wickedness of scaling the low walls which surrounded the bungalows of the British, and exploring their gardens with stealth and cunning. After I had been hotly chased and nearly caught on one occasion, this sport lost much of its appeal. But I continued to entertain a proprietorial feeling towards the new capital because of the role of my father and my uncle in constructing some of its new buildings.

Connaught Place – the great, two-storied, colonnaded circle of elegant shops, restaurants, cinemas and hotels – was a treasure trove of a different kind that excited us each time we arrived there, which was more than once a day since we lived very near. We would gaze wide-eyed at the glittering showrooms with their wondrous wares from around the world, though we gradually learnt that they were mostly from Britain – or Great Britain, as we were urged to call it.

The gleaming Rolls Royces, Bentleys and Sunbeam Talbots stood aloof and inaccessible amid the spit and shine of the Allied Motors showroom. We were riveted by the window displays of gentlemen's outfitters like Rankin and Phelps. We marvelled at the amazing range of silks, cottons and woollens in Lila Ram & Sons, and next to it the shop of Dr. Sahib Singh & Sons – its air heady with the perfume of exotic scents, soaps, talcums and other toiletries. We were astonished even more by the incredible variety of goods in the Army and Navy Stores.

As there was no chance – despite much fantasising – that any of these exotica would find a place in our immediate calculations, my

7

friends and I invariably gravitated to the pastry shops of the two top restaurateurs, Wengers and Davicos. (Our first exciting elevator ride was at Davicos which had installed it to take its patrons up one floor to the restaurant.) There were problems here, too, which had to do with the rather modest allowance of two rupees a month (later increased by my untiring efforts to five), which could hardly underwrite any kind of feasting in those pricey establishments, even after pooling our resources.

But we had found a way out. Wengers was owned by a Swiss couple, and Mrs Wenger after her husband's death had carried on with considerable success. Though daunting in appearance, she had a soft side which provided the breakthrough we needed, not to mention the fact that my family happened to own the building on Parliament Street in which Wengers ran an exclusive hotel. I managed to bargain this tenuous link for the occasional free tuck-in, but it involved a considerable amount of planning and worry. If my mother had caught on, she would have taken a very serious view of my enterprise.

While Wengers was not a steady standby, the weekly mela (fair) at the nearby Hanuman Mandir certainly was. To this temple of Hanuman, the monkey god in the Hindu pantheon, traders from Old Delhi would journey each Tuesday with wares guaranteed to gladden every heart: toys, mouth organs, knives, bangles, beads, necklaces, anklets, embroideries, clothes, cooking utensils. But what we waited impatiently for every week was the Indian food we could buy at the fair. Cutting through the jostling crowds, we would make a beeline for the end where the food stalls were clustered. Paradise was spread before us. The sweet-sellers, chaat-wallahs, pappad-wallahs, the man with the alloo-tikkis simmering on hot iron tawas, the fruit-chaats, namkeens of every description: chanaas, moong-phali, daal, beej, spun-sugar puffs, kulfis, sherbets, lassi, 'English' cold drinks like lemonade, ice-cream soda, Vimto. It was an elevating, unsettling and inspiring sight, enhanced by the lights of the gas lamps, candles and oil wicks; the smoke and smells of the seasonings; the bustling, jostling and cheerful crowds in their colourful clothes; all of this against a mix of sounds as only we Indians know how to make them.

This changing, surcharged world was within our reach without facing financial disaster. The formidable rupee stood at the apex of sixteen annas which were in turn made up of sixty-four paisas, below which were the dhelas and the pies, each of them with their own purchasing power. Even though we could have done with a few more rupees every month, whatever we had in those days did us proud.

Another great draw was the construction work going on in this imperial city in the making and the colourful entrepreneurs, artisans, craftsmen and workers who had converged on the wild and rugged site of the new capital. A great assembly of Indian talent was involved in giving form and substance to imperial convictions, to design concepts conceived, ironically enough, to awe Indians with what the British saw as the civilising genius of the English-speaking races. Every broad avenue, every great square, structure, forecourt, fountain and statue, had to proclaim the sentiment of British sovereignty, of pomp and the processional, of the ceremonial.

My friends and I were in awe of everything around us: not of the rulers' power – we didn't know what it meant – but of the unfolding panorama of people, the masons, stone-cutters, carpenters, joiners, blacksmiths, pipe-layers, plumbers, electricians and construction workers. The magnetic pull of this human mosaic drew us just as surely as the melas and glittering showrooms of Connaught Place. Without realising its deeper significance we were seeing India in microcosm: people from far-apart regions, different in physical appearance, dressed in a variety of styles, speaking a bewildering babel of tongues, yet working together to achieve remarkable results.

We gazed at the gracefully synchronised movements of long lines of men and women as they passed pans of mortar from one end to the other, from the mixing areas to the masons at work. We admired the surefootedness of the latters' helpers as they scaled the lattice-like scaffolding made of bamboo and balli (long wooden poles), which seemed to reach the skies, the supple movements of the carpenters planing planks, the rhythmic beat of the stone-carvers' hammers and the marble-cutters' chisels, the voices of men chanting an ancient song in unison as they hauled a rope which lifted a stone block higher and higher.

And the materials! The quarries of Bharatpur, Agra and Dholpur supplied the red and buff sandstone, just as they had to the great Mughal builder Shah Jahan, and to Akbar before him. Marble of different colours was brought from all over India: white and pink from Makrana and Alwar; green from Ajmer and Baroda; Jaisalmer supplied the yellow, Marwar the gray, and Gaya and Bhaislana the black. While some of the teakwood was imported from Burma, India's own beautifully-grained woods – shisham, walnut, blackwood and others – were also extensively used. Bricks were fired in kilns not far from Delhi.

Although New Delhi was functioning as the capital in the year I was born, it lacked that special pulsating life of a typical Indian city with its kuchhas, katras, and mohallas (traditional neighbourhoods and meeting places); its galis and havelis (lanes and old houses); its tantalising temptations and spaces teeming with life, leavened with history and offering continuity as well as emotional and nostalgic fulfilment. Yet all of this was also within reach and our bicycles often took us to the historic city of Shahjahanabad – the Walled City, as some preferred to call it, while to others it was simply Old Delhi.

It was a few miles north of New Delhi. Its builder, the Emperor Shah Jahan, was one of the world's great patrons of architecture. When he decided to move his capital from Agra to Delhi he decreed that the new city should represent the very best of Mughal culture and rule. Its scale had to be heroic, its architecture unparalleled, its aesthetics exquisite. All this his planners and builders achieved. After the court's move from Agra and the new capital's inauguration in 1648, historians were to say that during his reign the magnificence of his court and the power and glory of the Mughal Empire were at their peak. Delhi's splendour and importance surpassed that of other Asian cities.

This city of ancient lineage was also ours as we were growing up. We would enter it through the Delhi darwaza (gate), the Ajmeri darwaza, or one of the other ancient gateways set in the towering walls which once encircled the old city. If we took the Delhi gate we would pass Daryaganj on our right, and a couple of miles beyond we would see the awe-inspiring Lal Quila (Red Fort) ahead of us. On our left was the Jama Masjid, resplendent in its raiment of rich materials, its superb proportions and the elegance of its magnificent dome and soaring minarets. No wonder it was considered the most striking mosque in the world.

If we turned left we could park our bicycles in the great shadow of the mosque and wander around the stalls with their kababs, tikkas, biryani and roti, or go through the shops that sold second-hand or stolen goods, or turn to the meena-kari shops where master-craftsmen worked at a myriad handicrafts with skills handed down for generations. We could have bicycled around the mosque, but we never did. We always stopped by its gigantic plinth before plunging deep into the lanes and byways at the very core of the old city.

Our Jama Masjid visits provided us with an experience whose importance we would not understand till much later, our first puzzling exposure to the Muslim culture. Brought up in traditional Sikh homes – except for the occasional social mix to which our families took us – we were unfamiliar with a way of life and with attitudes and observances so different from our own. This did not apply so

10

much to the Hindus who were more integrated with the Sikhs: their sons and daughters had married into each other's families, they had shared their joys and sorrows, and enjoyed each other's friendships. But despite our unfamiliarity with Muslims, we found our first contacts with them appealing. Indeed, where the more visible symbols were concerned, Sikhism had more in common with Islam. Neither believed in idol worship and each was a religion of the book – the Koran in the case of Muslims, and the Guru Granth for the Sikhs. Muslims, like Sikhs, treated worshippers as equals in the house of God; none was accorded special privileges on account of caste. Both were non-vegetarians.

There were differences, of course. Most Muslim women wore burquas – head-to-toe veils – and Sikh women did not. When Muslims killed animals for meat, it was a slow and ritualistic process, while Sikhs killed with a single stroke. Nor was circumcision practised among the Sikhs. There was, however, an undeniable vitality and robustness, a directness, about the Muslims which we liked. Not that we found the cream of their culture in the places we haunted then – we would meet it in college and later – but even in those early years we found a rapport at the personal level.

If we did not turn off towards the Jama Masjid and bicycled on, we came to the crossing where a right turn took us to the Red Fort and a left to Chandni Chowk – the historic shopping artery of the Walled City. The Red Fort was yet another celebration of the Mughal passion for pavilions, gardens and waterways; for exquisite inlay, marble and stone work; for open spaces interlocking with halls of audience, the Emperor's quarters and those of his harem, courtiers and staff. It was a city within a city, a perfect setting for us to act out our fantasies, amidst the ghosts of the past, as frolicsome, fierce and indolent emperors by turn.

In contrast to this, Chandni Chowk would be bursting with life, vibrating with the eager enthusiasm of the shoppers, the avariciousness of the shopkeepers, and the quality and competitiveness of the trades that flourished in and around it, and still do. It always conjured up visions of an opulent colourful era – when a water channel lined with trees flowed through its centre and the grandees of the Mughal court, bedecked in their finery, would promenade up and down with the traders waiting to catch their eye and show them exotic jewellery, brocades, silks, cottons, embroideries, shawls, scents, carpets, gold and silver ware, ivory, miniature paintings, pottery and much else. The British, with their astonishing propensity for building Gothic towers in the most unlikely settings, had built

11

one smack in the middle of Chandni Chowk. It was quite a landmark when we were growing up, though it was later pulled down.

Narrow streets and lanes like the tributaries of a river took off from Chandni Chowk, turning and twisting their way through the densely built and populated city. Many of them were named after the trades or skills which flourished there – Meena (crafts) Bazar, Jauhri (jewellers) Bazar, Phool-Ki-Mandi (flower market), Parathewali Gali. This last was our idea of bliss, for this gali specialised in parathas: layers of flat, fried unleavened bread, often done to a crisp and served with pickles and a dish of cooked and heavily spiced potatoes.

Chandni Chowk bore the burden of a tragic past as well, for this street had witnessed the ruthless whims of wayward despots. It had seen a man of deep religious convictions beheaded for scoffing at a bigoted Emperor's offer to convert to Islam. It had witnessed a hundred thousand innocent men, women and children slaughtered in a day to satisfy the perversity of a Persian ruler. It had watched the bodies of the sons and grandson of a captive Mughal Emperor shot by the British and publicly displayed by them to discourage those prone to 'disloyalty and disturbance'.

In the seventeenth century, Tegh Bahadur, the ninth guru of the Sikhs, had challenged the Mughal Emperor Aurangzeb not in defence of his own rights but for the right of Kashmir's pandits (the Brahmin elite) to practise their own Hindu faith instead of being terrorised and forcibly converted to Islam. The guru announced that if Aurangzeb could make him convert to Islam, the pandits of Kashmir would accept Islam as well. Aurangzeb's response to the challenge from this man of conviction and unshakeable inner faith was to have him publicly tortured and executed in Chandni Chowk. That was on November 11, 1675. A hundred and ten years later, in 1785, the victorious Sikh armies conquered the Mughals, entered Delhi and built a gurdwara on the hallowed spot where their great guru had been put to death.

A visit to Sisganj, the name of the gurdwara, was a must whenever we found ourselves in Chandni Chowk. The karah parsad, or sacramental food which is given at all times to anyone who visits a gurdwara, was a greater incentive with us than our religious beliefs at that age.

Chandni Chowk was again the setting for acts of unspeakable human depravity in the eighteenth century. This time the violence was against the Mughals and their Muslim and Hindu subjects. On the morning of March 11, 1739 an affronted Nadir Shah, the Persian conqueror, ordered Delhi to be put to the sword and witnessed the carnage himself from Chandni Chowk's Golden Mosque of Roshanud-daula. According to historians a hundred thousand people were slaughtered in eight hours in the walled city and jewellery, gold, silver, cloth, carpets and much merchandise were taken away to Persia, along with the bullion, gold coins (aasharfis), regal jewels and property in the imperial treasury. The fabled Koh-i-Noor diamond and the Peacock Throne, built on the orders of Shah Jahan, were also taken to Persia.

In the nineteenth century it was the turn of the British to prove that senseless murder is not the prerogative of a particular race but of all those in power. Following the surrender of Delhi at the end of the 1857 Mutiny, the old and ailing Mughal Emperor Bahadur Shah Zafar had taken refuge in Humayun's tomb about seven miles from Shahjahanabad. On September 21, 1857 he and his wife, sons and grandsons were taken into custody by Capt. W.S.R. Hodson of 'Hodson's Horse'. On the way back to the Walled City Hodson shot the Emperor's two sons and grandson in cold blood. To quote his words: 'Seizing a carbine from one of my men, I deliberately shot them one after another. I then ordered the bodies to be taken into the city, and thrown out on the Chiboutra (a raised platform) in front of the Kotwali (police station) .... I am not cruel, but I confess I did rejoice at the opportunity of ridding the earth of these wretches.'

Hodson was also pleased by the applause his action earned him. 'I am much gratified by the congratulations I receive on all sides regarding the capture of the King and the retribution on the Shahzadas [his murdered sons and grandsons].' His concern for sanitation made the good captain order their removal within three days. 'The bodies remained before the Kotwali until this morning (September 24), when, for sanitary reasons, they were removed.'

Many of Delhi's admirers from distant lands had adorned her with buildings and founded cities of rare beauty. There were periods, of course, when sanity deserted those who arrived at her doors and they turned to destruction, but their sane and civilised successors had again restored her to her former pedestal. Long before we knew what an open university was, we were growing up in one, because that is what Delhi was. The city and its environs, before they were destroyed by developers from the 1960s onwards, provided a rare opportunity for learning. In the thirties Delhi was generous to those who respected her physical beauty and her awe-inspiring lineage and acknowledged her incredible magnetism and charm. She taught them about India's chequered past, and they learnt a lot. No capital in the world is built on the site of as many legendary cities of old as Delhi.

We lived in the Delhi designed by the British, the eighth Delhi. Within its parameters and around it were relics of seven other cities, the first of these, Indraprastha, going back to the Vedic period, quite possibly the tenth century BC. The Mahabharata, India's epic poem, tells of the founding of Indraprastha by Yudhisthira during the great conflict between the Pandavas and the Kauravas. For 2,500 years Indraprastha was to remain obliterated by time, until in the sixteenth century the Mughal Emperor Humayan built Dinpanah, the sixth Delhi (later known as Purana Qila), on a hillock below which Indraprastha lay buried and which India's archaeological authorities have excavated.

It was not archaeology but curiosity, and a boyhood sense of adventure, that sent us clambering over the crumbling ruins of these ancient cities. Lal Kot, the second Delhi, was a favourite. A fortress city, it was built in the eleventh century by the Rajput King, Anang Pal. An earlier city had existed on the same site, though very little evidence of it has survived. It was founded by the Hindu Raja Dillu around the first century AD, and Delhi, so historians believe, derives its name from Raja Dillu. Lal Kot provided us with endless fascination because of the Iron Pillar which Anang Pal had installed there in the fourth century. The Iron Pillar is seen by some as the standard of the god Vishnu, but it is a mystery how, when and from where it was brought by Anang Pal. Many of Delhi's conquerors tried to destroy it but failed. Our favourite sport, as of thousands of other visitors, was to press our backs against the Iron Pillar and, encircling it with our arms – in a reverse embrace as it were – to try to touch our fingertips. Few succeeded, and failure was very mortifying.

A hundred yards or so from the Iron Pillar stood the Qutab Minar, which was an altogether different experience. This soaring tower of victory, which rises 242 feet from the ruins of old Lal Kot, was started at the end of the twelfth century by Qutb-ud-din, a general of the Afghan invader Mohammed of Ghor, who annexed Delhi (or Lal Kot) in 1191. While he ended a thousand years of Hindu rule over this once flourishing city, his successor, Altamish, made Delhi for the first time the capital of India's Muslim rulers. It became from then on a major political, economic and cultural centre. He also completed the Qutab Minar.

Climbing to the top of the Qutab and seeing the whole world spread at our feet – which is what it seemed to us as we looked down from that dizzy height – was always an amazing experience. Around us we could see the remnants of once great cities, the gateways and battlements of old fortresses, domed pavilions over the graves of dead nobles, and much else.

The foundations of Siri, the third Delhi, or the Abode of the Caliphate, were laid in 1303 by Ala-ud-din of the Khilji rulers who had overthrown the dynasty of Qutb-ud-din. Very little of Siri survived, though the exciting complex of buildings at Hauz Khas, near Siri, exist to this day. After the Khiljis it was the turn of the Tughlaqs – representatives of the Turkish Sultans – who built Tughlaqabad, the fourth Delhi, in the fourteenth century. We felt somewhat let down by it, not because it was mostly in ruins, but because it had been located too far away for us to bicycle there too often. Hundreds of monkeys held sway over the ruins. They were aggressive, demanded their share of our picnic fare, took affront at not getting it, and rallied within minutes around those we had the temerity to tease.

Ghiyas-ud-din, the founder of Tughlaqabad, completed its construction in four years, for a population twice the size of the medieval city of London, and its life span was almost as brief. Within five years Ghiyas-ud-din was assassinated by his son, Mohammed Tughlaq, who first abandoned the city to go south, then changed his mind and returned to Delhi to settle in the Siri – Lal Kot area. He built walls to link the two, naming the place Jahanpanah, but it does not rank among the nine Delhis.

Mohammed Tughlaq's son, Feroz Tughlak, not content with the cities he had inherited, built his own, which he called Firozabad, or Firoz Shah Kotla, as this fifth Delhi is better known. It was a flourishing city overlooking the Jamuna river and given to the pursuit of pleasure and prosperity. It was known for its civilised way of life, and Lane Pool described it as 'the Windsor of Delhi'. Feroz Tughlak's reign lasted thirty-seven years and, as proof of his sagacity, he installed one of Ashoka's pillars in his capital with the Buddhist ruler's message engraved on it. Silhouetted against the evening sky, the ruins of Feroz Shah Kotla, destroyed by the Mughals, were a dramatic sight whenever we visited them at dusk.

Much of my later life would be influenced by the impact of this rich architectural heritage in which I grew up. Because it was easy to reach from where we lived, and because of its heroic location on a hillock, the Purana Qila (or Dinpanah) drew us often. The founder of the Mughal Empire, Babur, had entered Delhi on April 24, 1526 and, while he made Agra his capital, his son, Humayun, preferred Delhi. Khondamir, a chronicler of Humayun's reign, describes the emperor's vision of the sixth Delhi: 'To found near the capital of Delhi a large city … Also in this city to erect a magnificent palace of seven storeys, surrounded by delightful gardens and orchards, of such elegance and beauty that its fame might draw people from the remotest corners of the world for its inspection. That the city should be the asylum of wise and intelligent persons, and be called Din-panah.'

Humayun's dream city was only partly completed in 1538 when the unpredictable winds of war intervened. Defeated by the Afghan Sher Shah Sur, Humayun withdrew to Persia leaving Sher Shah to build many of the fine buildings in Purana Qila. He was a patron of architecture, and it is said of his craftsmen that they 'laid out their buildings like giants and finished them like goldsmiths'. Humayun recaptured Delhi in 1555 and completed the next phase of Dinpanah in the following year – the year, in fact, of his death.

A long ramp led up to the massive bastions of Purana Qila's Western gate. There were usually no people inside as we entered, nor did it resemble paradise any more. But it was always still and serene, as if the ghosts of the past had found the peace denied them in their lifetime. Although Purana Qila, too, had been vandalised, there was a grandeur about its ruins, and a majesty mirrored in its magnificient ramparts. We would climb up on them to see the sweeping vista of King's Way culminating in the Great Place and the buildings beyond. The British planners had used the old monuments to provide visual appeal to some of their main axes and thus the once formidable fortress of Purana Qila was placed at one end of King's Way with the Viceroy's House and imperial offices at the other. We got a special thrill from looking at these from the ramparts of the Purana Qila – from a height where we didn't feel dwarfed by them. There was an oddly moving quality in the siting of these two centres of power: one a mere relic of a proud emperor's dream, the other a symbol of the English Raj's hold on India.

Humayun's successor, Akbar, moved the Mughal capital back to Agra. Delhi, in eclipse once again, had to wait until Akbar's grandson, Shah Jahan, built Shahjahanabad, the seventh Delhi. In contrast to the cities desolated by time, this survived as a vital city. When our group joined college a few years later, old Delhi would become even more a part of our lives since our colleges lay beyond it and we had to go through or past it all the time.

*

Before joining college in 1940, I had to leave my beloved Delhi for a while. In 1934 the province of Bihar was devastated by a terrible earthquake. My father decided to work on the reconstruction there, and to take his family with him. We moved to Bihar in 1936, in a town

16

on the banks of the Ganga (Ganges) river called Monghyr. I was in two minds about the move, not knowing whether to be excited or upset by it. I was reluctant to leave my many friends and the life I loved, but neither did I want to forgo the long train journey and the thrill of the unknown. The scales in favour of going finally tilted after I was convinced I would be one up on my friends. 'Never mind,' I told them, 'you too might be able to take exciting trips one day.' I was at an age when Monghyr appeared wildly exotic.

This was the first long journey from Delhi that I can remember. We boarded the train for Patna, our first stopover, and the next twenty-four hours, with so much to absorb and assimilate, were magical. The bridges, rivers, ravines, road crossings, villages, cows, bullocks, buffaloes, the alternating stretches of fertile and barren land; the unnerving shriek of the trains as they hurtled past each other; the changing colours of the sky and the contours of the landscape; the different forms of vegetation – an unbelievable panaroma unfolded as Rasil and I watched. Feverishly we noted the names of every small station as we steamed past and admired the big railway stations at which we stopped. Clean, efficient and well-ordered, there was none of the decay about them that became evident in later years. For us there was the prospect – immediately the train pulled in – of waiters ready to take orders for sandwiches, soft drinks, snacks, meals and desserts, or of a quick dash to buy chocolates, sweets and biscuits. Then there were the bookstalls stacked high with papers, magazines, stationery, postcards and, of course, books. My favourites were the adventure storybooks published by Boy's Friend Library which sold for four annas each.

Under their lofty ceilings the railway stations – their floors polished, walls lime-washed, wood and ironwork freshly painted – offered every amenity: rest rooms, retiring rooms, waiting rooms, impeccably catered first- and second-class dining rooms, all managed by trained staff. The joys of train travel in the thirties carried a dawning awareness of India's diversity and scale.

Another impression left on our minds of those journeys was the exclusivity of the British. The dining cars with gloved waiters, gleaming tableware and shaded lamps seemed mostly for them. Indians were not excluded, but looked at pointedly when they entered. We noticed the servility of the railway staff before the white men and women when they came to board their trains. (We caught our trains, they boarded theirs.) The staff stopped anyone scruffy from going near them. They encouraged the impression – with servile Indians reinforcing it at every turn – that each white-skinned person was something special of a race apart. I was puzzled, not disturbed,

17

though that too would come later, with college. But college was still three years ahead.

Monghyr was built on the banks of the Ganga at a point where the river was at its widest. Our house, on the water's edge, had a ringside view, and the river was a daunting sight when in full flow, especially during the monsoon. Depending on the intensity of the rains, floods were frequent and the danger of the Ganga breaking its banks was very real, with its threat to lives, land, cattle, houses and vegetation.

Oddly enough, the Yamuna river had not seemed part of the New Delhi in which we grew up, though some of the previous Delhis – like Indraprastha, Ferozabad, Dinpanah and Shahjahanabad – had been built on its banks. I was mesmerised by the astonishing spread of water in Monghyr, and the life that hundreds of thousands of India's people lived on her rivers and waterways. Monghyr was a great experience in many other ways. I mingled, made friends easily and was vastly impressed by the steadfast attitude of the people who had suffered much during the earthquake. Bihar in the thirties was altogether different from what it is in the nineties. Those from every province in India were made welcome. We neither felt, nor were made to feel, like outsiders because Bihar was free of social and xenophobic tensions, well-administered and law-abiding.

I was in seventh heaven because of the two pets I acquired. Tony was a handsome white pony, swift, sturdy and given to unpredictable swings of mood which usually ended in my getting tossed off his back. Mankoo, the monkey, was an individualist to the core, and quite intolerant of both Tony and King – our big dog who had come with us from Delhi and whom Rasil and I shared. Tony reciprocated Mankoo's dislike by trying to kick him into oblivion, a fate Mankoo avoided with agility and an instinct for survival. King stayed aloof except for an occasional outburst of exasperation at not being able to limber up a tree like Mankoo, or ride on the bar of my bicycle.

Bihar was memorable for other highpoints. Its towns – Bhagalpur, Patna, Jamalpur, Darbhanga – had an air of dignity about them. They seemed orderly and cared for, and did not convey an impression of decay and neglect, very different from what they would become in the coming decades.

The subdivisional magistrate of Madhubani, a part of another Bihar district, was an exceptional man of wit, wisdom and learning with whom I was to enjoy a wonderful friendship almost thirty years later. He was W.G. Archer, of the Indian Civil Service, and he was in court that afternoon of January 15, 1934, when the earthquake hit Bihar. He described it thus:

18

1. The Thirties: Years of Awakening

A normal enough day, mild but crisp. I had noticed, however, a peculiar eerie yellow in the sky and as I had walked the hundred or so yards from my bungalow to the court-house, there was an odd hushed silence. The pleaders were still talking but would not be long, they said. Suddenly I heard a low rumbling and felt a slight shiver ... the noise got louder and louder, the dais on which I sat began to lurch and the court-room walls shook ... and we all dashed for the doors. By then the ground was heaving, everyone stumbled and staggered, great cracks suddenly opened up and the low rumbling became a subdued roar .... The court-house was still standing but I could see the water in a neighbouring pond surging backwards and forwards, the bottom of the pond bare one moment and covered the next.

Bill's own bungalow was intact but 'a bottle of vermouth standing on the mantelpiece had crashed to the ground!' He collapsed after the relief work and was sent to England on a short leave, where he married. He had to retire with the rest of the British ICS when India became independent in 1947. In 1948 he was appointed Keeper of the Victoria and Albert Museum's India Department. This enabled him to return to India often, and it was during one of these visits, in 1968, when he was researching a major two-volume work, *Indian Paintings from the Punjab Hills*, that we were introduced. Bill and his wife, Mildred, wrote several outstanding books on Indian art. His first and last were, interestingly enough, on Indian poetry: *The Blue Grove: Poetry of the Uraons* published in 1940, and *The Hill of Flutes: Life, Love and Poetry in Tribal India* in 1974.

From the late sixties till his death in 1979 I would stay with them whenever I was in London, and they with me on their visits to Delhi. It would be wrong to assume – given the colonial realities of the thirties – that there could ever be a common denominator in our perceptions of Bihar. We were influenced by entirely different experiences, not only the difference in our ages but the racial divide of those times. Philip Mason summed it up later in *The Men Who Ruled India*: 'It is easy to forget the immense gulf between the educated Englishman and the Indians whom he met in a district, even in the twentieth century .... The district officer and his family were one kind of human being, the people of his district another. There was no thought of equality.' And yet, once the changed circumstances of later years brought Bill and Mildred Archer and me together, we discovered the part Bihar had played in our lives and we talked about it with warmth and nostalgia, each from his own experience of it.

Our family left Monghyr in 1938, with memories of a way of life we already knew we would miss very much. I now had some idea of our country's size: 'our country' because that is the only way we had learnt to look at India. Ironically, India's alien rulers – whose rule was being increasingly resented – had provided Indians with the opportunity to travel around their country in safety, and to live wherever they wished.

*

Delhi was as enticing as ever. I was reassured by the ease with which I resumed my friendships, but I did not go back to my old school. Rasil and I had studied with a resident tutor in Monghyr, where she sat for the matriculation examination. I would do so a year later in Delhi. Our school-going days had ended.

As the decade neared its end, talk of war in distant Europe began to dominate thinking in many quarters. While political parties were devising their strategies in the intensifying struggle for independence, the mobilisation of additional forces to fight Britain's war on various fronts would also affect people in India. Ordnance, armament and other wartime plants were expanded, airfields and docks developed. An impressive-looking wireless set was ordered by my father to keep abreast of the gathering crisis. After war broke out in 1939 we were riveted to it for the nine o'clock news every night. I was a little over fourteen then.

That was also the year I sat for my matriculation exam and, miraculously, passed it. It was the last exam I would pass in my academic career. A great deal lay ahead in the forties – college and leaving home to start work in my father's firm. India's independence and the horrors of partition would take the place of our self-absorbed vision of the thirties. With the broadening perspective would come an increasing pride in our own identity, in the recognition that Indians were no less competent, persevering, civilised or sagacious than the colonialists. We were unwilling to believe the tragic literature – all that patronising commentary in newspapers and books – produced by them to humiliate us with our racial and historical inadequacies. We had seen through their game and were ready to show the world that we were strong, unified, committed and unstoppable in our determination to keep our 'tryst with destiny'.

That at least was the ardour, faith and hope which we developed and carried with us through the forties, and which – as we rashly believed at the time – we would nourish forever thereafter.

Chapter 2

The Forties: Tryst with Destiny

What I would personally prefer, would be, not a centralisation of power in the hands of the state but an extension of the sense of trusteeship; as in my opinion, the violence of private ownership is less injurious than the violence of the state.

Mahatma Gandhi

I ENTERED college in 1940 and, heaven knows why, selected physics, chemistry and mathematics as my subjects. It was a disastrous choice. Two years later, in the intermediate exams (half-way to graduation), I failed in all three. After another year of feverish slogging it was examination time again. Mercifully, just days before the fateful date, I went down with pneumonia – an odd thing to happen in early summer, but it was manna from heaven for me. To my immense relief our family doctor vetoed the idea of my appearing for the exams.

My sister Rasil had shown an unnerving tendency to top the entrants of every exam she sat for, and she ended up at the Yale Law School with a scholarship. Unlike her, I was not driven by an urge to have a degree next to my name. I wanted to learn through involvement in the real world.

As my marks in matriculation had not been high enough for me to gain admission to St. Stephen's, I had landed in Hindu College which, given the times, proved a more robust place to be. Students needed to be sturdy, with a finely-honed instinct for survival, in order to co-exist with over twelve hundred others from widely varying social and economic backgrounds. St. Stephen's was the opposite, rather prim and somewhat inbred with fewer than three hundred students, who took themselves much too seriously. The college authorities insulated them from the prevailing political temper and disapproved of their gravitating towards the developing political turmoil.

Hindu College was the opposite. There was an air of *laissez-faire* about the place, which perhaps was inevitable among so many students from such different backgrounds. The group of which I was

21

an informal member was unapologetic about activities outside college. We were influenced not only by the passionate political rhetoric of many student activists, but in addition by the speeches of Congress leaders like Mahatma Gandhi, Jawaharlal Nehru, Maulana Azad, Rajendra Prasad, Acharya Kripalani, Rafi Ahmed Kidwai and many more.

My three years in college, fruitless as they were so far as academic aspirations were concerned, were therefore made unforgettable by the momentous events in the world outside, of which the most important had to do with India's Independence. As news of German victories and British reverses hit the headlines in early 1940, India's main political parties, the Congress Party and the Muslim League, stepped up their demand for an independent India, fortified by justifiable anger at Whitehall's arrogance in committing India to Britain's war without attempting to carry Indian political opinion with it. Not that the sympathies of most Indians lay with the Germans; on the contrary, there was still considerable goodwill for British institutions, endurance and character. But plunging India into a European war without a by-your-leave was seen as a sneer at Indian self-esteem, another example of the growing racial arrogance that was alienating more and more Indians. The breaking point, the Congress Party's Quit India movement, did not come till 1942, but the groundwork had begun in 1940, the year I entered college.

The prospect of India regaining what had been usurped by others and was rightfully hers was heady stuff. The speeches of Congress leaders ignited in us the passionate belief that the British were smothering India's soul and that their departure would rid us of our national shame and lead to India's full flowering. We were overwhelmed by this vision of the future, by the miracles promised once India's resources, skills and countless assets could be used for the welfare of her oppressed people. There would be no outsiders to exploit and demean us, and every Indian would hold his head high.

If our excessive exuberance could be attributed to our age, there were experienced and wiser men who also felt that 'an ancient country which had been the cradle of civilisation and which had gifted many things to the world and contributed to civilisation', would, once free, 'order its life according to its own values and contribute to world civilisation'. That was how J.D. Shukla, a seasoned member of the Indian Civil Service, viewed an independent India.

We believed that public order and efficiency, respect for authority, integrity in office, standards of performance, discipline and much else could only get better once Indians were in charge, free of the shackles of foreign rule. Any disagreement with this view was offensive.

In spite of my fervent belief in these promising vistas, I was not myself drawn to politics. If India became independent, the politicians I listened to would manage the nation's affairs and take India to the eminence which was her birthright. My own hope was that with Independence – still a remote possibility – limitless opportunities would open up for persons with initiative and drive. Since my family had no tradition of sending its sons into government service or politics, such as they were, Independence would not change my plans, which were clear to me. I wanted to join my father's construction firm, and could think of no more beguiling future than one in which buildings figured.

No doubt my decision was influenced by a sense of awe at my father's confident control over the hundreds of men who worked on his construction sites. I admired the verve with which he handled them, his ability to get the best out of them, the effortless ease with which he matched their energies with his own. I wanted to work alongside him, so that one day I too would be like him.

The pace and tempo all around us was changing as India was turned into a gigantic staging-area for the war. Inevitably New Delhi too was changing. We had our first introduction to the Americans, who started arriving in 1943, the year I left college. One- and two-storied simple lime-washed structures, with graceful arches, verandahs, fenestration and façades were being rapidly built on New Delhi's open spaces for British and American army, air force and naval personnel and offices of every description. The exigencies of the war, and the informal and uninhibited ways of Britain's American allies, now crowding the capital, were eroding the city's carefully cultivated imperial ambience.

My father was in Ambala at the time, inundated with war-time construction contracts all over the old, undivided Punjab. My mother was worried by the extent of his labours, and she agreed that I should leave college to join him. I was then eighteen.

*

And so I came face to face with the real world. Once it was decided I could join my father, I had the idea of travelling first-class for the first time. My parents would have had none of it, so I quietly bought a first-class ticket for the train to Ambala, without telling anyone. On a beautiful day in September 1943 I set out to seek my fortune.

My very first move was a complete disaster. No sooner had I

entered the first-class compartment in which I was to travel in style than I was summarily thrown out by two British officers who were clearly unwilling to share it with an Indian. I tried to force my way in, but was advised to get lost, unless I was bent on getting bashed up. Which I was not.

This was my first close encounter with racialism. Just as offensive as the uncivilised behaviour of the two British officers was the squalid attitude of the Indian railway staff, desperately currying favour by defending their right to throw me out. Congress leaders had told us India's soul was being smothered under alien rule and here, as the railway staff cringed, was the evidence.

I spent the next three years rotating between Ambala, Jullundar, Sialkot and Multan, getting on-site training on our different projects, such as airfields, roads, barracks, overhead water towers and the like. The physical landscape was changing before my eyes. No less instructive were my dealings with Punjab's tough construction workers, transporters and material suppliers – our own staff as well as the government agencies and their minions.

My working life in the cantonments (military stations), trying to get used to the rough and tumble of the construction world and to meet completion deadlines, left me with little opportunity to keep up with political events. By the end of the war it had become clear that a victorious Britain was serious about leaving India and that we were nearing Independence. And yet, in another of the unending paradoxes India lives by, she reverted to the dark ages at the very dawn of the freedom we so desperately wanted. The savage blood-letting during the partition of the sub-continent between India and Pakistan was an inevitable outcome of the primitive communal passions whipped up by power-hungry politicians. Muslim fear of Hindu militancy – fanned by the bigotry and ill-concealed anti-Muslim stance of groups like the Arya Samaj and Hindu Mahasabha was matched by the hatred preached by the Muslim League.

The frenzied killings – of both Hindus and Muslims in turn – in Calcutta and Noakhali (in rural Bengal) in August 1946, a year before Independence, were not entirely unexpected, given the open encouragement to violence by the League's leaders. Its President, M.A. Jinnah, told his followers on July 27, 1946, that 'this day we bid good-bye to constitutional methods'. He also asked them to observe August 16, 1946, as Direct Action Day throughout India. On that day S.H. Suhrarwardy, Bengal's Chief Minister and an ardent Leaguer, elaborated on Jinnah's message.

'Bloodshed and disorder are not necessarily evil in themselves, if resorted to for a noble cause,' he proclaimed. 'Among Muslims today, no cause is dearer or nobler than Pakistan ....' This call for 'bloodshed and disorder' came from the man who headed the administration of the province in which Muslims far outnumbered the Hindus, so it was not surprising that the massacres of Hindus in Calcutta followed soon afterwards, with the Hindus retaliating wherever they were in a majority.

In March and April 1947 the communal madness reached Rawalpindi in northern India – a part of the Punjab province in which Muslims once again heavily out-numbered non-Muslims. The pattern of the tragedy was the same, with one difference. According to Alan Campbell-Johnson, who accompanied the Mountbattens for a first-hand assessment of the scene, 'this particular communal orgy involved the destruction of Sikhs and their livelihood by Moslems ...' The brutal attacks on Sikhs by blood-crazed mobs were not confined to Rawalpindi. Massacres were underway elsewhere too in the province: in Lahore, Sheikhupura, Sialkot, Gujranwala and other districts.

*

By good fortune I had returned to Delhi in 1946, so that I escaped by a few months the killing of the Sikhs in West Punjab, which became Pakistani territory after Partition. But I witnessed the viciousness of the retaliatory killings in East Punjab (which remained in India) and Delhi.

Because I lived in Delhi and loved it, the massacres there left a deeper impression on me than the sights I had seen in East Punjab, even though they were a fraction of the terrible toll in that truncated state. The fury of the Hindus and Sikhs, stoked by chilling accounts of the refugees from Pakistan, finally exploded in Delhi on a humid day in September 1947. Within hours communal madness had engulfed the entire capital. Accounts vary as to where and how the first spark was ignited. Some say it was in Paharganj, others that it was in Karol Bagh; still others insist that it was in Sadar Bazar or Sabzi Mandi. Many point to the main railway station where the slaughter of some Muslim porters by Hindus and Sikhs was seen as a sign that they were now out to avenge the massacre of their co-religionists in West Punjab (which remained in Pakistan). By nightfall the capital was in flames, fanned by murderous hate and bands of crazed killers carrying swords, spears, *kirpans* (the short sword carried by many Sikhs), knives and cans of kerosene.

The first intimation of the insanity which had overtaken my safe and civilised Delhi occurred around mid-morning when our two

Sikh servants arrived home with a pile of shoes they had looted from a shop in Connaught Place. (In their haste they had walked off mostly with the left shoes of dozens of pairs scattered on the floor of the ransacked store.) During my parents' dressing-down they confessed that they had joined a mob which broke into the Capital Boot House in Connaught Place, almost adjacent to a big radio and appliances showroom also owned by a Muslim family whose sons, Maqbool and Zafar Hussein, were our great friends. That too, I was told, had been broken into and wantonly vandalised.

These outrageous incidents were far exceeded by what we witnessed late into that night and during the nightmarish days which followed. The lootings had degenerated within hours into an orgy of frenzied killings. As I drove across the city with my friends in my open Baby Austin car, we saw scenes of carnage which are still vivid today – dead bodies on the streets, intestines spilling out of ripped open bellies, blood mixing with the dust and dirt on the ground. Fragments of human flesh, severed tendons, unclaimed limbs, a head with no headless body in sight – these were not just remnants of human beings: they represented a whole social order haemorrhaging before our eyes.

And then, with nightfall, came the twisting, turning, taunting columns of thick black smoke, as if to herald a pointless and pyrrhic victory. The nights also brought the acrid reek of burnt flesh, of human beings torched alive to satisfy the sadistic cravings of killer mobs. Partition seemed to have legitimised the right of the majority to do what it wished with the minority, and it continued to do so with even more sinister interpretations in the years ahead.

Delhi in the grip of communal madness was an affront to every illusion I had nurtured. I had never dreamed that the city in which I had been born and in which I had grown up, whose every avenue, alley, nook and corner I knew, and whose cultivated people I loved and admired, would witness such human depravity. It was my first encounter with this face of Delhi, and it threw me into an inner turmoil. Not only was I buffeted by horror at the cold-blooded killings and the demoniac zest of the killers: even more devastating was my own occasional tendency to justify – even to gloat over – the crimes that avenged our own dead. The confrontational attitude insinuated itself into my own awareness. I was too inexperienced to realise – as I would later – that my country, with its myriad, divisive distinctions of religion, region, caste, customs, language and incomes, rested on fragile foundations of consensus which confrontational and aggressive attitudes would eventually erode and with it dim our hopes of a bright and promising future.

2. The Forties: Tryst with Destiny

The changes caused by the war which had affected Delhi's appearance were as nothing compared to what Partition had in store. Out of nearly six million Sikhs and Hindus who crossed over into India from West Punjab a large number opted for Delhi. Overnight the city became the new home of anguished and bitter refugees. These were not distant people. Many were in our own home – relatives, friends of the family, and their friends. They stayed for months before their efforts at remaking their lives came to fruition. They had to start from new beginnings: shelter, jobs, businesses, professions, schools and colleges for their children, new friendships. Though stripped of everything they had owned, they had not lost their confidence or initiative, nor their self-esteem. There were no beggars from Punjab on Delhi's streets, no outstretched hands. These were not despairing, huddled and beaten refugees, but robust, energetic and zestful people of India's rugged north. Their spirit helped to restore some balance in me.

Delhi, the historic city, was about to enter the most tragic phase of her life, but, it is false to suggest, as is often done, that her decline began with the influx of these refugees. They did not dictate where and how they should be housed. They were not determined to subvert Delhi's civic standards, or to resist the rules of sanitation, hygiene and health. They were willing to accept whatever was demanded of them.

The alien conquerors and colonialists, who had loved the city and lavished their care and concern on it, were already packing their bags to leave. Delhi's tragedy – which would be compounded over the years – is that after the departure of the British, with their insistence on cleanliness of the environment, all we Indians had to offer was our own ingrained indifference to the physical world around us. We showed an habitual disinclination to take civic and municipal laws seriously, and entertained a fatalistic belief that slovenly, stinking and squalid conditions were all that Indians could hope for or expect. This failure to observe minimum civic standards – perhaps our most flagrant flaw – was to become increasingly evident. It was in startling contrast with the assumption that nothing in Delhi would change with the departure of the British and that things could only get better.

*

As it happened, I witnessed the killings of 1947 during one of my frequent visits to Delhi, for I had moved to Poona (now Pune) in the hill ranges south-east of Bombay to work on our construction projects there. It was this that opened my eyes to a disturbing

27

characteristic of Indians – our indifference to what is happening, no matter how calamitous, in distant parts of the country. Was it the number of India's recurring tragedies that was responsible for our reluctance to see them as the concern of the entire nation? Whatever the reason, I had naively assumed that the rest of India would be deeply affected by the events taking place in the North, and I was wrong. Poona could have been in another country for all the difference the blood-crazed killings in the North made to it.

That India's tragedies were caused by caste and religious demagoguery was soon to become all too evident. On Friday, January 30, 1948 I was about to leave a meeting in Kirkee, Poona's twin city, when a distraught secretary burst in on us and announced: 'Mahatma Gandhi has been assassinated.' He had just heard it on All India Radio's six o'clock news. We later learnt that the Mahatma had been shot at seventeen minutes past five, but instead of interrupting its broadcasts to announce his death immediately, AIR had with remarkable foresight not only worked carefully on the wording of the announcement, but also given the government time to take steps to counter possible violence in the wake of the news. The wording of the bulletin at six was: 'Mahatma Gandhi was assassinated in New Delhi at twenty minutes past five this afternoon. His assassin was a Hindu.'

In an atmosphere of communal hate, the mere assumption that the man was a Muslim would have had incalculable consequences. The delay in the broadcast had enabled the government to place the police and armed forces across the country on maximum alert. Driving home from Kirkee towards Poona on the Bombay-Poona road that evening of January 30, I decided to turn right to visit friends in Poona city. You could do it by going across a railway line in those days. The gates of the crossing were closed and, as I waited for the train to pass, I noticed a menacing crowd running in my direction from the other side of the tracks.

I had no reason to assume these people were coming for me, but my instinct was to reverse the car and leave, which was just as well. Even with the assassin's identity clear, some in the city would still have reacted as if Gandhi's killer had been an enraged, uprooted Sikh. But the anger of the swelling mob, which would become a permanent fixture on our political landscape, now turned against the Brahmins, the caste of the killer. By nightfall the flames of Brahmin properties set alight in Poona city could be seen for miles.

This tragedy apart, I enjoyed my life in Poona. I lived in Poona Camp, as it was then called, which was almost the cantonment segment of the old city. Its lifestyle was elegant, a blend of the military and monied classes, who enjoyed the exclusive Turf and Poona Clubs with their racing and sports facilities, dancing and fine dining. And then there were also the deeply traditional families of old lineage and intellectual reputation in the historic Poona City next door. Poona was the stamping ground of Bombay's industrial, professional and entreprenurial elite, many of whom maintained villas there for the racing season and to escape the heat and humidity of coastal Bombay. The journey between Bombay and Poona took three hours on the Deccan Queen, a graciously appointed corridor train which was an institution in itself, with excellent service and everyone on board seemingly known to everyone else.

Best of all was Poona's cosmopolitan mix: Parsis, Gujaratis, Marathas, Punjabis, Anglo-Indians, South Indians. They were all there, and of every religious denomination as well. The British, too, were still present in those waning years of empire. This mix of people contributed to Poona's character, with none claiming proprietary rights. True, there were class distinctions, but otherwise the decencies were observed in accommodating and accepting different political and religious persuasions.

The Poona I lived in was not too obsessed with national politics, although some members of the old families were, no doubt, deeply involved. But politics had not become the all-pervasive preoccupation it was to become later. It was generally agreed that those now in charge in New Delhi had the ability and integrity to make a go of things. There was even a little sadness among some at the dismaying prospect of life without the British. It was too early to talk of the 'good old days', though even that would come. The Parsis, notwithstanding the inspiring leadership many of them had provided in the struggle for Independence, seemed most moved by nostalgia for the old order.

In place of politics, Bombay's elite – which was to an extent Poona's also – was kept at full stretch by its pursuit of profit. The instinct for making money was seen neither as an abnormality nor as an aberration for which people should be apologetic. Old business and industrial families, and many new ones who were emerging, preferred to concentrate their energies on what they knew best. Politics was not high on their agenda.

Their attitude would change, because talents other than entrepreneurial vision and drive would be more in demand in the years ahead. The political class – through its own free-wheeling ways – would often end up making more money than the entrepreneurial. In the late forties and fifties, however, money power, with rare exceptions, was not the goal of that political generation. It had strong moral doubts about reconciling the public weal with amassing personal wealth. Possibly these distinctions in the roles of the different social segments accounted for the buoyant mood of those days, and for the lack of misgivings about the future.

*

If my three years in Poona were far different from life in Delhi, I was due for another experience I could not have imagined in my wildest dreams. In early 1949 a friend asked me if I would go for a couple of years to Koraput, a remote district in the interior of Orissa, which was a state on India's east coast. He had recently signed a major contract with the Orissa government for construction works across the state and he wanted me to handle Koraput. Although I had difficulty finding it on the map, I agreed. It was an Agency Area in those days, which meant it was administered under special rules because of the aboriginal settlements. The aboriginal tribes lived in remote forests and hill areas in states like Assam, Orissa, Bengal, Bihar and Madhya Pradesh.

Orissa would be an entirely new experience for me, though I had lived in Bihar and my father had taken me on a long motoring trip through Assam. Being a deeply religious man, he was particularly keen to visit Dhubri, where a historic gurdwara had been built to commemorate the visit of Guru Nanak in 1505. As for Bengal, though I didn't know it well, we had twice motored through it on our way from Monghyr to Calcutta. But Orissa would be different, because I would not be in transit but living there for two or three years, and that, too, in one of the remotest regions of the country.

The ancient civilisation of Kalinga, from which the Oriyas (inhabitants of Orissa) draw their inspiration, had once flourished in what is present-day Orissa. Clearly the distant rulers of this region, with its spectacular forests, hills, rivers, inland lakes, wild life and a long coast line, were outstanding builders and patrons of the arts. Some of India's finest temples and monuments, literally hundreds of them, still exist in Orissa, as testimony to their genius, together with Emperor Asoka's edicts carved in rock and dating back to 260 BC. It is believed that this remarkable ruler, who had fought many bloody wars in his time, was converted to the gentle, philosophical and non-violent ways of Buddhism after his conquest of Orissa and its peaceful Buddhist population.

Within a century of his death, the Oriyas were taken into the fold of Jainism after Orissa's annexation by the Jain King Kharavela. Jainism – a revolt against the precepts and practices of Hinduism –

was closer to the atheistic beliefs of Buddhism. While acknowledging the existence of gods, Jainism did not accord them a role in the universal scheme since the universe by definition is eternal. Founded in the sixth century BC by the reformer Mahavira, a contemporary of Buddha, though some historians claim greater antiquity for it, it held sway over many parts of India at its peak and was very powerful in Orissa till the second century AD. But it steadily weakened as a result of schisms within the sect, and Orissa – at the end of Jain rule in the second century – reverted to Buddhism for about 400 years before embracing Hinduism.

As the date for my departure from Poona approached, I felt a sense of unreality caused by its remoteness, the long distances involved and the time it would take to reach Koraput. After the short train journey from Poona to Bombay, I embarked on the much longer one across the country to Calcutta, where I spent a couple of days. Then I took the overnight train to Cuttack (the state capital at the time). The state's new capital, Bhubaneshwar, was then under construction.

Orissa, like several other states, still had some British officers in service, although in a year or so they, too, would leave. The Indians in positions of power – whether politicians or civil servants – were confident of their ability to maintain administrative standards. Some of them – including Orissa's first two chief ministers, Hare Krishna Mahtab and Naba Krishna Chowdhury, who was an austere and scholarly Gandhian – were still politicians of the old school with a strong commitment to the public weal. The sub-species of the political nether world had still to surface, but as time went by Orissa would have more than its fair share of them.

I spent several days being briefed by our office in Cuttack, assembling staff, meeting people I would be dealing with, and organising the long journey of nearly 400 miles along poor roads to Koraput. There were unbridged rivers to be crossed by ferry, and I planned to take four days.

I passed the better part of the first day and night at Puri, in the beautiful Railway Hotel on the beach, overlooking the Bay of Bengal. Puri, just forty miles from Cuttack, was home of the Jagannath Temple, one of the holiest Hindu shrines in India. Its great attraction for me was not only its location but even more its sculptures: sensual, sublime, serene.

Just a few miles from Puri were the ruins of the thirteenth-century Sun Temple at Konarak, built to honour the sun-god Surya. Its astonishing structure is an incomparable visual experience as it rises starkly from the sands, its stone weathered black over the centuries. The temple design is conceived as a chariot: seven magnificent horses representing the seven days of the week, 24 wheels for (approximately) the same number of fortnights in the year, and the eight spokes of each wheel representing the ancient division between day and night.

But the most extraordinary feature of this temple is the erotic sculptures that adorn its outer walls. The sexual theme was handled with great sensitivity by the sculptors, who succeeded in conveying through stone the sublime expression on the faces of couples in close embrace. These sculptures also reveal the important role sexual mysticism played in Indian medieval religious thought. Though I was to visit the tenth- and eleventh-century temples at Khajuraho in Central India several times in later years, where the friezes also excel in their sensitive portrayal of the climactic act between the sexes, I still find it difficult to decide which of the two schools of sculpture is more moving. I had not expected to encounter a celebration of the senses in such abundance, and I felt it augured well for the future!

Among the friends who had driven with me to Konarak was the newly-arrived manager of the bank we dealt with in Cuttack. His family, including his two grown-up daughters, came along too. After parking our cars we had walked up to the temple, the men in front and the women some distance behind, when our banker friend sighted the first of the erotic sculptures through his enormous bifocals. His responsibilities as a father galvanised him into action. Raising his right hand high he swung round, sternly told his family to stand back and await his return, and went ahead to reconnoitre. Considering the time he spent examining each of the threatening sculptures, he did not seem to find the chore too onerous. His daughters were not allowed to come anywhere near them.

Next day, after leaving Puri, I joined the coastal highway which runs all the way to Madras and found myself motoring alongside one of the most extraordinary landscapes in this country – the Chilka Lake. Its length of 45 miles, its islands, the thickly forested hills which line one side of it, its fishing, game, wild-life and rare birds invest it with breathtaking beauty. That evening, Oberoi's Palm Beach Hotel at Gopalpur-on-Sea reaffirmed again that the unexpected is the rule rather than the exception in India. This elegant hotel, with its splendid cuisine and rooms opening out to the ocean, was a complete contrast to the neighbouring village of Gopalpur. In the village time seemed to have stood still while the hotel was almost futuristic.

I left Gopalpur early the next morning to cover the 150 miles to Vizianagram. It was considered a long stretch in those days, since the roads were not wide enough for fast driving. After an uneventful night in an old guest house in Vizianagram, I set out next morning for the last leg of my journey – the eighty miles or so to Koraput. As the narrow road wound its way through the hills things began to change, not just the landscape – the lush fields of the coastal districts had given way to the rugged hills of the eastern ghats – but the looks of the people as well. This was a sparsely populated region, but the few people we passed were different from the Oriyas and Telegus. These were the aboriginals – the tribal people of Orissa. They were the original inhabitants of pre-Aryan India who had moved to the hills and other remote regions of the country in the aftermath of the Aryan invasion. They are said to be related to the Australian aborigines, and are identified as of Proto-Australoid strain, but the skin of those in India had certainly lightened and their features softened over the centuries. In these remote settlements with their own customs and traditions, which are judged primitive by the people of the plains, the tribal people had a carefree, uninhibited and spirited way of life in marked contrast to the traditional attitudes engendered by India's all-pervasive caste system. In the last century these people, who were primarily hunters, indulged in occasional human sacrifices and head-hunting, to the dismay of British administrators, who at first tried brutally to suppress them. Later, by persuasion and tactful handling, they managed to reform the people, while protecting their social system and traditions. In continuation of this policy, the Government of India has made specific mention of all Indian aboriginals in the Indian Constitution. I came in contact with hundreds of them every day as they were the unskilled workers most employed on our construction project.

I remember one grisly incident which had a touching human side to it. I was sitting one afternoon with the District Superintendent of Police when his orderly announced that an adivasi (aboriginal) insisted on seeing him. The man was ushered in, a strapping young fellow carrying a bundle. As he wordlessly opened it, out rolled a man's severed head! He had walked twelve miles through the jungle to confess his crime to the police, which was that in a drunken moment he had chopped a man's head off. Then, in deep remorse, he had walked to the police station to report his misdeed.

The aboriginals were hard and enthusiastic workers, easy to deal with, and with an infinite capacity to enjoy themselves, whether at work or leisure. This was in startling contrast to people in the plains of India with rivalries and tensions which were socially inspired and politically manipulated. The aboriginals danced to the rhythmic beat of drums, their arms around one another's waists, in a wide circle with a roaring log fire in the middle, singing and laughing and becoming steadily more animated as they imbibed home-brewed liquor through the evening.

They hunted boar, deer and at times tigers and panthers with bows, arrows and spears. I went on some of these hunts, though with a rifle always slung over my shoulder. Those were the days when India's wild-life – despite depredations by shikaris of every hue: princelings, officials, businessmen and others – was still abundant. In Orissa's forests, and especially where I was, it was not unusual to see a Royal Bengal Tiger of rare beauty walking towards the car at night with its majestic stride. I have to confess with considerable mortification that I shot two or three myself, and I have been trying to get over my feeling of guilt ever since.

Equally engaging were the sexual mores of the aboriginals. Young men and women moved in and out of one another's huts without causing hurt or ill-will. This drove some of my North Indian carpenters and masons delirious with excitement, and several of them settled down to lives of conjugal bliss with the aboriginal girls. The men seemed to work much better as a result of these arrangements. Unfortunately the connubial joy of Balbir Singh, a burly carpenter, was rudely interrupted when his wife, with their two little children, travelled all the way from Jullundar to bring him to heel. It took her seven days to get there and she burst unexpectedly on the scene one evening after getting off the bus from Vizianagram. Not one to waste any time, she caught him by his shirt-front, dragged him out, and set about him in front of everyone. The poor man was totally demoralised and two days later was led off to the bus stand on the first leg of the long journey home.

Life in Koraput was a far cry from what I was used to in Poona and Delhi, or the years I had spent in Punjab during the war. It was a small district headquarters township, nestling in the hills, very beautiful and clean, with only the top officials and their families and staff resident there. There was nothing else – no cinema, club, or restaurant. The nearest little town was Jeypur, the domain of a former princeling, about 12 miles away. I led a quiet existence with an occasional dinner at the house of one of the officials, though such evenings were rather staid in contrast with the rollicking dinners I had with an English couple, Tom and Jean Atkins. Tom, who was responsible for recruiting labour for the tea gardens in Assam, had a beautiful house, where I spent many spirited (and spirituous) evenings which helped relieve the tedium of life.

The many solitary hours I spent on my own gave me plenty of time to read, as there was nothing else to do. I started writing, too, and in time encouraged myself into believing I owed it to India to get my pieces published. However, whatever I submitted seemed to come back with alarming predictability, until my first piece was accepted and published by *Shankar's Weekly*, India's answer to Punch.

An even more exhilarating break was on the way. One night, after an early dinner, I set out with my rifle and shotgun to look for the game that often appeared on the roads after dark. I asked the driver to drive towards Rayagada, a rail-head 70 miles away on the Raipur-Vizianagram line. There was little traffic that night and even after an hour's driving we didn't see any game. I decided to return home and, as we were looking for a place to turn around on the narrow hill road, I suddenly saw in the headlights of the car a beautiful blonde woman walking towards us. In pitch darkness, on a remote forest road, with the possibility of prowling tigers!

As I got out of the car she ran the few remaining steps and fell sobbing into my arms. She was a public health specialist working with a WHO anti-malaria team based in Rayagada. After she had driven alone to one of the villages where they were working – a few miles off the main road – her jeep had broken down on the way back. Her driver was on leave that evening. With no possibility of a passing car that she could flag down on the side road, and with the unnerving sounds of the jungle that pick up at night, she had panicked and rather unwisely walked the mile or so to the main road, where she saw the distant lights of my car coming down the hill.

Sitting on collapsible bucket chairs which I always carried in the boot of my old Hudson, we had a drink or two and a sandwich until she seemed restored. Her name was Ingeborg and she was Danish. She was on a two-year assignment in India with another eight months to go. The team leader was a Canadian, Dr Burford Weeks, who had been a Lieutenant Colonel in the medical corps during the war and knew India well. He and I became good friends; my relationship with Inge became much more than that.

I drove her to Rayagada, another thirty miles away. She had done a wonderful job with the few rooms in the Inspection Bungalow allotted to her, and we sat on her verandah drinking aquavit till the first light of day. She then made a superb breakfast before I returned to Koraput in a blissful state. We met often after that. The first time she came to spend a long weekend with me in Koraput its little official community was quite outraged, but they got used to my ways, and the rest of my stay in Koraput was an unforgettable interlude.

We took two weeks off to travel to Calcutta and on to Darjeeling and Kalimpong. Our huge room in the stately old Mount Everest Hotel in Darjeeling looked out on superb views of the Himalayas.

The drive from Darjeeling to Kalimpong, with the terraced tea gardens on either side of us and the Teesta River snaking its way through the foothills, was yet another revelation of India's beauty. Then, after another couple of months, we paid a quick visit to Delhi where Inge, understandably, stayed at the Imperial Hotel and I with my parents in our family home. A few months after returning to Orissa she completed her assignment and left for Denmark, from where she was to go to her new posting in Burma. I saw her off at Calcutta and came back to my corner of Orissa which suddenly seemed very empty.

But I would also be leaving Koraput soon, first for a brief spell at Poona and then to open an altogether new chapter of my life in Bombay. A friend and I had talked about starting a small publishing company – whose first periodical would be *The Indian Builder* – and the idea was finally taking shape. I had been drawn to writing during my years in Koraput, and could not think of a better way of combining this interest with my experience in construction. With a magazine of my own I would also bypass all those tedious editors who tended to bounce my articles back at me. The future seemed very promising.

Chapter 3

The Fifties: Challenge and Fulfilment

I don't think that it is on the threshold of life that one feels chaotic. It
is when one has crossed the threshold that one discovers that things
which looked simple and feelings that felt simple are infinitely tortu-
ous and complex.
Amrita Sher Gil, the painter, in a letter to Jawaharlal Nehru

BOMBAY at the beginning of the fifties was still one of the great
cities of the East, a town of immense physical charm with its hills,
harbour, beaches, palm trees and lush foliage, and the Arabian Sea.
No less appealing was its mix of cultures. India's many people and
their talents had continued to make Bombay an urbane, elegant,
civilised city whose vitality had still not metamorphosed into urban
insanity, while each of its human constituents had helped it develop
in specific ways.

Among the Indians who had long made Bombay their home, were
the Parsis, descendants of Zoroastrians in Persia who had come to
India in the seventh and eighth centuries to escape Muslim persecution. A story is told of how, when they landed in Gujarat on India's
west coast and requested permission to stay, they were handed a jug,
brimful of milk, by the local chieftain, indicating that his territory
was already full. One of the Parsis is said to have carefully slid a coin
in the jug – others contend it was a spoonful of sugar – without
spilling a drop of the milk, and the chieftain, convinced that these
people would not displace his own, consented to their stay. Quite a
few gravitated to Bombay and contributed much to its ambience. Its
art galleries, museums, a great hotel – the Taj Mahal – not only reflect
its civic standards and its way of life but also their pride in this city.

Others too had left their own distinctive imprint on Bombay: the
Khojas, Bohras, Gujaratis, Marathas, Goans, and Punjabis. The Punjabis cornered Bombay's burgeoning film industry which in turn
attracted talent – directors, producers, actors, actresses – from all
over India. Of the large number of Muslims who lived in Bombay,
two sects have always stood out: the Khojas and Bohras. After the
death of the prophet Muhammad in AD 632, Islam split into two

divergent groups, the Shias and Sunnis, with the Sunnis accepting the caliphate as the true successor of the prophet and the Shias questioning this line of succession. The majority of Indian and Pakistani Muslims are Sunnis, as indeed were the Mughal Emperors. The Khojas are Shias, and the bigger of the two subdivisions among them are the followers of the Aga Khan.

The Khojas are phenomenally wealthy, thanks to their trading activities which started several hundred years ago when sailing vessels from Arabia called at Bombay to buy, sell and barter goods. Many of these traders settled in Bombay, while continuing to maintain their trading links with distant countries. Their wealth multiplied, much of it in property – they built enormous housing estates in Bombay. Their life-style has changed, too, from the traditional and conservative, to contemporary, Western ways.

For the first few months after my arrival in Bombay in 1952, I lived as a paying guest on Napean Sea Road with one of the prominent Khoja families of Bombay, the Chinoys. They were young and forever on the go, whether to the races, to clubs or, on Sundays, to Juhu or one of the other beaches. I stayed with the Chinoys until I got my own apartment, and this was an encouraging beginning to my ten years in Bombay.

The reason I had chosen to move there was that it had become the country's communications capital with its major publishing activities, printing plants and other facilities. But it was tough getting started. Though knowing scarcely anyone, I had to form a company, find and furnish an office, get a telephone (not so easy in those days), recruit staff, put together a magazine, find a printer, and sell space to advertisers. Brashly (or confidently as I saw it) I announced my intention of starting a whole string of magazines. I found a fairly adequate office in a building called Janmabhoomi Chambers opposite the Alexandra Docks on Ballard Pier. Though Ballard Estate was a prestigious area in which to have an office, that particular stretch of it certainly was not. Sailors came pouring out of the docks from across the street to be offered every kind of comfort by touts and pimps and offering many smuggled wares in return. It was an animated scene, made livelier still by brawls.

I found an excellent printing press around the corner, on Frere Road. The Caxton Press was under British management, and it was with the help of Fred Borton, its English general manager, that I brought out the *The Indian Builder* on January 1, 1953. I shall never forget the triumph of holding the first copy of my own 56-page magazine.

Fred introduced me to many of the top men in Bombay's advertising agencies, the very first being Edward Fielden, the local head of the international agency J. Walter Thompson. Thanks to my innocence, my meeting with Fielden got off to a hilarious start when I asked him to sell advertising space in my magazine on whatever commission he felt was fair. Fielden delicately explained that it was not the job of advertising agencies to secure advertisements for publications; their clients were the advertisers, and agencies selected publications to place their advertisements in. Fielden was sporting enough to buy the magazine's back cover for a four-colour advertisement for his client Goodlass, Wall Ltd., the manufacturer of paints. My first leading article – introducing the magazine – had gone to press, secure in the knowledge that I was the editor and no one could alter a word of it:

> The idea of starting *The Indian Builder* took shape when it was realised that the colossal building industry of this country urgently needed a medium which would place in the limelight its activities, achievements, problems, hopes and aspirations, so that its vital role in the national development schemes could be fully appreciated. The awareness of this necessity was the driving force. It gave impetus to the idea of launching this publication, and it is our determination to ensure that it adequately fulfils the need.

It did fulfil it for the next thirty-five years, fourteen on its own and another twenty-one after it was merged with *Design*, which I started four years later.

The texture of my life was changing through the new friendships I made in a city which, while physically big and beautiful, could also be impersonal and insular. I did not have the advantages which I had enjoyed in Delhi, where I was accepted because of my family and its many connections. Bombay had its own social arrangements and establishment rules.

*

The two friends who helped me most in the early years in Bombay were Frank Moraes and Mulk Raj Anand. Frank, a Catholic from Goa, was editor of *The Times of India*. Mulk, who came from a goldsmiths' family in North India's holy city of Amritsar, was a novelist of repute and editor of the art magazine *Marg*. A great, almost non-stop talker, he dressed in Indian clothes most of the time (though he would often don startlingly brief shorts) and led a bohemian sort of existence in a section of an old mansion on Cuffe Parade, in the company of many genuine art aficionados as well as those with unrequited cultural aspirations. He also had a rambling house in Khandala, a hill resort about seventy miles from Bombay, to which he repaired to do his writing and where I often joined him for week-ends.

Frank Moraes, despite his stature as a powerful editor and author (and later Nehru's biographer), was cast in the Western mould – in his clothes, his establishment, his life-style – a seaside apartment in Mafatlal Park – and the daily routine around which he liked to arrange his day. This usually included a stopover at the bar of the Ritz Hotel, to which I was introduced by him. He also helped to get me a liquor permit, essential for survival during those prohibition years. His advice was invariably helpful in opening the right doors for me.

Another warm friendship I formed at the time, through Frank, was with C.R. (Shaun) Mandy, a tall, jovial, well-built Irishman who edited *The Illustrated Weekly of India*, which was owned by the *Times of India* group. He was a genial host and one of the regulars at the Ritz bar, to which we gravitated at the lunch hour and where Raju, the warm-hearted bartender, used to enter far fewer drinks on our liquor permits than we had actually imbibed.

Another habitué of the Ritz, and an admirer of Raju, was Olaf Hauge, the Bombay manager of Standard Vacuum Oil Co. An American of Norwegian descent, barrel-chested, with enormous biceps and given to ferocious arguments when in his cups, he was one of the very first friends I made on arriving in Bombay. Two years later, in August 1955, Olaf returned from leave with tall, beautiful and witty Veronica Nisbet as his bride. Her English parents had moved to Canada, where Veronica was born. She studied in Canada and the US and lived for a time in London where she took up journalism. She was an editor of *Queen* magazine when they married. Our friendship, like their marriage, has endured over the years and now, forty years after I met Olaf, the three of us still manage to get together frequently, either in India or in the US. I was deeply touched when in 1958 – they had moved to Calcutta by then – they asked me to be the godfather of their second daughter, Andrea. Sadly, Olaf died last month.

The company I had formed was doing well and in 1955 I started another monthly journal, *The Pharmaceutist*. Apart from aspirin and a couple of handy home remedies, I knew nothing about pharmaceuticals, but it was a major growth industry in India and I felt there was a need for a magazine to cover its activities. It got off to a splendid start under the editorship of Dr Alex Leiser, a German expatriate who had resided in Bombay for many years.

3. The Fifties: Challenge and Fulfilment

In January 1956 Bombay, for so long a stable and secular centre of trade, commerce and civilised co-existence, suddenly slid into a welter of bloody violence which left 80 killed and 450 wounded. Overnight the Maharashtrians turned against their Gujarati neighbours, though both were citizens of the cosmopolitan city. Bombay's January riots – following the Central Government's decision to reorganise the states of India on linguistic lines – were the result of the same short-sighted, unprincipled, power-obsessed politics that would lead the country to near-disintegration in the eighties and nineties.

The Congress party had first proposed the linguistic reorganisation of the provinces (later called States) in 1920, the year it established its own country-wide committees on those lines. Later, in 1929, the Nehru Report (prepared by Jawaharlal Nehru's father Motilal) committed the Congress to restructuring India on the basis of language. In 1949, just two years after independence, Dr Pattabahi Sitaramayya, the Congress president-elect, reiterated this in his inaugural address. Before the transfer of power, pledges could be made without the challenge of having to implement them, but now they had to be observed. Ironically Jawaharlal Nehru was himself opposed to the reorganisation his father had recommended twenty years earlier, but his belated resistance was unable to stop the language zealots.

Under the States Reorganisation Act, passed by Parliament in 1956, two linguistic states were to be formed out of the composite Bombay state – Maharashtra and Gujarat. Extremists mobilised Maharashtrian mobs in an effort to ensure, through arson, mayhem and murders, that the city of Bombay would go to Maharashtra and not to Gujarat. Mobs were to become the storm troopers of political parties across India in the decades ahead, kindling the prejudices and fears of the people at large in order to capture power at the polls. This came to be considered a legitimate tactic and part of the 'democratic' process.

Some Indian leaders were aware that the politics of language would place the political and social stability of India – and not just of Bombay – on the firing line. Yet linguistic chauvinism was unleashed on the fledgling republic despite India's history of internal wars and vendettas. Populism, which catered to the prejudices and linguistic passions of India's pressure groups, was allowed to prevail over principle. The States Reorganisation Act was also a reflection of Nehru's indecisiveness at a critical juncture. With his intellect and understanding of Indian history he should have foreseen it as a precursor of other agitations in the years ahead, each becoming

bloodier and more destructive, whether the provocation was religion, preferential treatment for sons-of-the-soil, the sharing of river
waters or any one of so many issues with populist appeal.

The damage might have been less had the reorganisation been
carried out within a year or two, but even in this the leadership failed.
The controversy dragged on for the thirteen years it took to form the
six new linguistic States. Meanwhile, mass protests and street violence cut a bloody swathe across the land, souring relations between
populations and neighbouring states, straining the loyalties of the
civil servants and police, and establishing a precedent of gory protests which continue to plague the country to this day.

There is no excuse for this disastrous time-table of the linguistic
states formed after reorganisation, whose inflammatory effect engulfed Bombay (which did finally go to Maharashtra) in 1956:

States formed	*On*
Andhra Pradesh	October 1, 1953
Kerala	November 1, 1956
Karnataka	November 1, 1956
Maharashtra	May 1, 1960
Gujarat	May 1, 1960
Punjab	November 1, 1966

One of the reasons why Punjab is still in flames over a quarter of
a century later is the delay in its formation and the way it was
handled. The Sikhs did not overlook the humiliating fact that sleight-
of-hand by New Delhi and political clout rather than principle were
what counted in post-Independence India.

An amusing incident, in those otherwise grim January days in
Bombay, involved an American evangelist – I think it was Billy
Graham – on a brief visit to the city. In a rush of evangelical fervour,
he announced his intention of cooling passions through the word of
God. When efforts to dissuade him failed, he was taken under police
escort to Shivaji Park where the rioting was reportedly bad. Frank
Moraes and Shaun Mandy were going along with some press people,
and Frank asked me if I would like to come. We drove off in several
cars and arrived close enough to the action to watch as the man
climbed on the roof of a car to talk to the crazed mob. He had scarcely
begun when stones started flying at him. All he managed to say was
'Let's get the hell out of here' before jumping into the car, and all of
us hurried back to the safety of South Bombay.

3. The Fifties: Challenge and Fulfilment

*

If neither Nehru nor his colleagues foresaw the price India would pay for its surrender to linguistic jingoism, perhaps I can be forgiven for failing to acknowledge the ominous portents. My own preoccupation in 1956 was not with politics but with my plans for publishing *Design*, a magazine of arts and ideas. I was determined to make it different from any other design magazine. Although in the broader sense it was to be a magazine of architecture, in acknowledgment of architecture's pre-eminence among the creative arts, its editorial coverage would express my conviction that no architect or designer – or any creative person – can work in isolation from practitioners of the other arts. So it would cover not only architecture and the visual arts, but would also carry articles on music, dance, drama and poetry. Just as the country's physical landscape was becoming an architectural wasteland, the performing arts were being cornered by newly-formed societies and coteries, founded by the *nouveaux*, and the not-so-*nouveaux, riches*. And they were less interested in a quest for new concepts and expressions, and more in satisfying their own longing for recognition as patrons of the arts.

The increasing number of buildings of hybrid design springing up everywhere, because of India's accelerating pace of development, often gave the impression that an architectural renaissance, a new flowering of creativity was under way. It was nothing of the sort. The architecture of these buildings was derivative and dishonest, with a few artful touches added to make it look 'modern'. Worse still were the dreary 'departmental' buildings turned out by the government's own architects: office buildings capped by massive domes which were fobbed off as respectful salutations to past forms. Tradition was fraudulently interpreted in those days, and architecture was not even discussed.

Design, aspiring towards heroic goals, would set things right. Its editorial objectives were, of course, over-ambitious. It could not possibly provide continuing and adequate comment on all the subjects I wanted it to cover; nor did the contributors exist for such specialised writing. There was also the question of costs. A well-produced, wide-ranging, adequately staffed magazine devoted to arts and ideas would be horrendously expensive, and I did not have that sort of money. But I had determination. I decided to restrict the first six issues of *Design* to sixteen pages each month, and to enlarge it gradually. Nor would we carry advertising during this period. The first issue of *Design* appeared on January 1, 1957, a significant date

43

since the magazine was to play a major part in my life. The hard work that went into it was rewarded by the contact it led to with architectural writers, architects, artists and designers not just in India but in other countries as well. Though I had not yet been abroad, I was in touch with many people whose work I admired, especially John Entenza, editor and publisher of America's west-coast magazine *Arts and Architecture*. This slim publication reflected his personality and beliefs, and that is how I wanted *Design* to be: not a fat, commercial magazine but a publication with individuality, which mirrored the convictions and concerns of the individuals behind it. It had to be the result of a distinctly personal vision, not a corporate effort. Though *Architectural Forum* was in fact corporate property, being yet another magazine in the *Time-Life* stable, I liked it because of the writings of Peter Blake, its Managing Editor. When we finally met in New York, during my first visit to the US in 1961, we started a friendship I have valued ever since.

Over the years, our office in Janmabhoomi Chambers was the setting for many unexpected visits and encounters. One of these was during the lunch hour in early 1953, when a man walked ito my room and announced, 'I am your sister's husband – you might want to punch me on the jaw or shake hands.' I took him to lunch. Rasil had joined the United Nations in New York as an intern for three months in 1948, and her future husband, Romen Basu, was already on its staff when they first met. They married three years later. When news of it reached Delhi my parents were terribly upset. They had wanted my sister to marry someone of the Sikh faith, according to Sikh marriage rites (most certainly not a civil ceremony in New York!) and from a family they knew and could relate to. Romen was a non-Sikh, a Bengali, and his family, with entirely different attitudes, customs and beliefs, lived a thousand miles away in Calcutta. Everything was contrary to what they had hoped for. My mother was particularly shaken. Neither she nor her older brother and sister ever quite got over the disappointment, though my father did. But they were enchanted when Rasil returned home to visit us after a couple of years with her first daughter, Amrita, and later with the second, Rekha. They were saddened yet again when it became increasingly clear that Rasil – who was starting on a permanent career in the UN – had opted to live abroad and they would not see their grandchildren grow up around them.

Another visitor to Janmabhoomi Chambers who was to have a profound influence on my attitude to twentieth-century art was Nobuya Abe, a Japanese painter. Nobuya was creative, well-read and compassionate. He dropped by unannounced one day with a letter from Gurcharan Singh, India's outstanding potter. We took to each other from the moment we met in 1953, which was long before I started *Design*, and Nobuya helped lay the groundwork for it.

I could not at first make head or tail of the two surrealistic paintings Nobuya did when he was in Bombay, and which he presented to me, but it was fascinating to watch as he explained, with sketches and splashes of paint, how artists of the surrealistic school had arrived at this particular style of painting. Under his tutelage I began to relate to the imagery emerging from the artist's subconscious, and to understand the idiom of disquieting symbols and forms. At about this time *Life* magazine published an article on contemporary Japanese painters and included one of Nobuya's paintings, the caption of which, in effect, said that his work symbolised a sense of Asian supplication. Nobuya was furious. He sent off a stinging letter to *Life* (I do not remember if it was ever published) accusing its editors of racial arrogance, unable to understand either his work or the Asian psyche.

Nobuya's sense of time was non-existent. He had planned to spend three days in Bombay, and stayed three months. He had already exceeded even his own standards in China where he had gone well before World War II. He saw the war coming but ignored it, and when he eventually returned to Japan after it was over, he found that his wife, thinking he was dead, had remarried. She passed out on finding him standing at her doorstep one day. Nobuya took it all in his stride and remarried as well.

He was one of the few people whose encouragement pointed me in the direction which finally led to *Design* and to my life-long involvement with the arts. The last time we met was towards the end of the sixties, in Rome. He had gone to Europe for a few weeks, and typically stayed several years. We saw a lot of each other before he died in Rome. He generously gave me two of the marvellous rubbings of tombstone art he had made, one of a headstone in Yugoslavia and the other from Japan. They hang in my study to this day.

The Indian painter whom Nobuya most admired was Narayan Shridhar Bendre, to whom he introduced me almost forty years ago. One of India's outstanding painters till his death in February, 1992, Bendre, unlike many others, ignored the superficial and concentrated on his own inner vision of people and events. During the years 1959-1966 when he was Dean of the Faculty of Fine Arts at the Maharaja Sayajirao University of Baroda, it ranked as India's finest art school, producing some of her best contemporary painters. After our first meeting Bendre and I were close friends till his sudden death.

Yet another visitor was the American novelist Christine Weston. She had met Rasil in 1947, in the north Indian hill station of Mussorie, through their mutual friend, Ann Johnson, who had helped Rasil get a scholarship to the Yale Law School. Christine was born in India of a French father, whose family were indigo planters, and an English mother. Her ties with India never weakened and two of her novels – *Indigo* and *The World is a Bridge* – are set there. She established long-lasting Indian friendships and dedicated her book *Afghanistan* to Radhi Uttamsingh, whose daughter Sheila describes in amusing detail their visit to Nirad Chaudhuri, the last of the great Anglophiles, soon after Independence. Overflowing with enthusiasm at the freedom which had finally dawned for India, Christine burst on Nirad with words of excitement and hope. Nirad was unimpressed. He had outdone even British writers in praising the British and now he voiced his pessimism about the future. If we could not even make a tonga (horse carriage) properly, he asked, what could we hope to make of our destiny as an independent nation. He outdid the British that evening by serving sausage sandwiches, something even they would have had qualms about.

A great admirer of Jawaharlal Nehru, Christine was keen to write a book about him and travelled with him on one of his tours across the country, but she failed to get the co-operation she needed from those around him. They wanted to keep their own options open.

*

Having outgrown the Janmabhoomi Chambers office, I moved to a somewhat bigger one in Colaba, not far from Bombay's harbour front and the magnificent Taj Mahal hotel. The appropriate name of the building, Ionic, was all too often misspelt, the most favoured variations being Ironic and Tonic. The building next door, called Corinthian, offered less room for improvisation.

The layouts and typography of *Design* during the first year owed much to Dolly Sahiar, *Marg*'s brilliant art director. In fact Mulk Raj Anand's magazine would never have created the visual impact it did, through the imaginative use of types, the unconventional make-up of its pages and the frequent use of textured paper inserts, but for her. Soon after we moved to Ionic, a graphic designer, Dilip Chowdhury, called one day to say he had just returned after several years in England, had seen *Design* and liked the concept. I was impressed by him the moment he walked in. His enthusiasm for his work was infectious and, as it turned out, his creative skills equalled his devotion to good design. His youthful idealism – he was twenty-two then – had brought him back to India at a time when many other designers and professionals, mesmerised by the attractions of the west, preferred to settle there. Perhaps his early schooling at Santiniketan had also had something to do with it, but he was mainly influenced by his two teachers, Hans Schleger and Tom Eckersley, at the London School of Printing. They were both convinced that Indian designers, sympathetic to India's own design traditions, should be in the vanguard of any contemporary design movement in India.

Dilip and I met several times after his first visit to our office. Over lunch one day at Gordons, an austere eating place with no frills but superb food near Churchgate station, we came to the conclusion that he should come and work at *Design* as its art director. Knowing that the magazine was losing money, he handsomely agreed on a salary far lower than the one he could have earned from any of several advertising agencies which were beginning to come into their own in Bombay.

Our memorable association, from 1958 to 1960, ended when Dilip went to work for *Asia* magazine in Hongkong. His contribution to *Design* was magnificent. Later, after I became great friends with Hans Schleger and his designer wife Pat, I realised what an impression Hans and his design philosophy had made on Dilip. Hans was born in 1900 in Germany, and like many of his contemporaries was inspired by the Bauhaus. This is how Walter Gropius, its director after World War I (he was on our editorial board until his death in 1966) had described Bauhaus ideals in 1918: 'The Bauhaus embraces the whole range of visual arts: architecture, planning, painting, sculpture, industrial design and stage work. The aim of the Bauhaus was to find a new and powerful working correlation of all the processes of artistic creation to culminate finally in a new equilibrium of our visual environment. This could not be achieved by individual withdrawal into an ivory tower.'

Hans's years at the art school in Berlin brought him under the influence of this movement, its emphasis on the development of people, not objects, and its rejection of the artificial distinction between 'fine' and 'applied' arts. In 1924 Hans took his ideas – and ideals – to New York and made a reputation there, but returned to Berlin – still an artists' Mecca – in 1929. Uneasy at the prospect of Nazism, he left for London in 1932. According to Pat 'he arrived on a foggy November afternoon, fell in love with it and stayed for the rest of his life'.

Dilip had imbibed many of Hans's ideals, and I believe that his urge to explore the 'untried world', as well as my enthusiasm for his explorations, helped cement our relationship. He certainly helped the magazine to win the first prize in the National Awards for Excellence in Printing and Publishing.

Soon after *Design* had established itself, I decided that some form of international collaboration was necessary and felt that an Editorial Board would be the most appropriate way of going about it. Aside from men and women of calibre in our country, I wrote with some trepidation to several abroad whose work I admired, among them Nobuya Abe, Marcel Breuer, Siegfried Giedion, Walter Gropius, Richard Neutra, Isamu Noguchi, Eero Saarinen, Philip Johnson and Peter Blake. They agreed without exception.

On a visit to Delhi in the mid-fifties I went to an exhibition of paintings by Satish Gujral. He and his wife Kiran invited me to their home in the Constitution House, where, thanks to Nehru's intercession, they occupied a few rooms. Apparently Nehru had seen Satish's powerful canvases, chronicling the grief, terror and bloodbath of India's ill-fated Partition, and when he met him at a reception and asked him where he lived Satish had replied 'on the roadside'. Even though this was not entirely true, he and several of his family, who were all refugees from West Pakistan, did live in cramped quarters, and his predicament had moved Nehru enough to provide official accommodation for him.

The first stirrings of the artist in Satish began when he became totally deaf at the age of eight. The overwhelming loneliness which followed, combined with the pain in his bed-ridden body which had come repeatedly under the surgeon's scalpel because of osteomyelitis, had found an outlet in artistic self-expression. His supportive father sent him to art school at first in Lahore, then Bombay. Back in West Punjab and with the horrors of Partition unfolding all around him, he witnessed a degrading and debased period of India's recent history at close range, as revealed in some extraordinary canvases. Satish avoided gory details. The victims in his paintings are not the dead, whose lives had ended senselessly and with apalling suddenness, but the survivors in whom the horrors would live on for the rest of their lives.

I saw his work in Delhi for the first time. By then he had already spent two years in Mexico on a scholarship. Mexico's teaching methods differed from the more aggressive approach of European and US schools. While the latter tended to superimpose their attitudes on aspiring artists from older civilisations, the Mexicans asked them to respect their heritage, just as they themselves revelled in their own traditions and reflected them through their art.

3. The Fifties: Challenge and Fulfilment

As well as admiring Satish as an artist, I was impressed by the tenacity with which he had overcome his afflictions. In the years ahead he would work on ceramic murals, terracottas, collages, metal sculptures and, eventually, architecture. His design for the Belgian Embassy in New Delhi would be a *tour de force* of contours and concavities, of voluptuous lines, textures and sculptured forms. It would win international awards and cause considerable discomfort to established architects unamused by the sudden success of this interloper. But all that was still in the future.

*

Soon after *Design* began publication, I went to a small dinner at the home of Rae and Valentine Britten. Rae was political counsellor at the UK Deputy High Commission. I first met Raj and Romesh Thapar at this dinner and what followed was a friendship that lasted thirty years – until their deaths within months of each other in 1987. I remember Raj remarking with great warmth how impressed they were with *Design* and how intrigued that such a magazine had been launched by a Sikh.

She confirmed what I already knew about the ambivalent feelings Indians have for one another, and when it comes to criticism Sikhs seem to attract more than others. This could be because of their self-confidence or swagger or rugged qualities or military traditions, or possibly all four. I was not only aware of the raised eyebrows at my emergence on the cultural scene, but quite enjoyed the discomfiture of some of the aspirants to Bombay's cultural leadership. In Bombay, as in other cities, people jealously guarded their own little enclaves, whether these had to do with painting, sculpture and graphic design, or the performing arts, or even political isms. Architecture, of course, was not then a conversational topic, since people did not quite know what to say about it. But although the cultural ghettos were well-fortified, Bombay's rich human mosaic had supportive people as well, many of whom admired my efforts to establish, with no previous experience, an unusual publishing enterprise in a city I had only recently arrived in. Thus the principle of natural justice prevailed, the resentful ones being balanced by those of a more generous outlook.

The Thapars were in the latter category. Romesh was the most unlikely Marxist I had ever met. Everything about him was cast in the Establishment mould. The Thapars had a beautiful apartment on Malabar Hill, were members of the exclusive Willingdon Club, and entertained graciously. Romesh's father was a General in the army.

His father's younger brother was to become the Indian army's Chief of Staff, and another brother was a member of the Indian Civil Service. Raj's father had also risen to a high position in the government. But Raj and Romesh had chosen an ideological route different from those of their families, though the family influence helped them in many ways.

Together they had produced the Communist Party's weekly newspaper, *Crossroads*, but they closed it down because of differences with the Party, with which Romesh became disenchanted. His spirits were low as a result, but Raj's cheerfulness managed to sustain them through their setbacks. Romesh was not always calm and rational in his assessments, but each disillusionment left him wiser.

I learnt a great deal about Marxist doctrine from both of them, especially about the contrast between the rhetoric and the reality. For my part, I informed them about the battles that lay ahead between the real-estate conquistadors and the defenders of urban sanity. Very few people could yet see the danger that mindless urbanisation would pose for our major cities. I did not foresee its scale myself, but I was beginning to sense the potential dangers. The politicisation of urban planning, and the manipulation of zoning laws, would generate enormous wealth for city politicians, political parties and developers.

I wanted Raj and Romesh to become involved in the battles that lay ahead because of their interest in causes which left others cold. They were responsive, even though their real love was politics, and we often talked of ways in which we could fight when the time came. But when it did come – a few years later – we were estranged. By the time we came together again, in a closeness greater than before, not only Bombay but Delhi also were on the way to complete destruction.

The fifties were still a decade of optimism and, for me, exciting encounters. In October, 1958 a young sculptor, Krishna Reddy, who would achieve international fame as a printmaker, arrived at our office on his first visit to India after eight years in Europe, most of them in Paris, where he had worked with the celebrated sculptor Ossip Zadkine, then in Milan with Marino Marini and in Britain with Henry Moore. In 1950 Zadkine had introduced Reddy to Stanley William Hayter, a pioneering figure in the world of modern printmaking and founder of the Paris print-studio, Atelier 17. Krishna was to become its co-director for over ten years before moving to New York in 1976.

His success was to be acknowledged in the seventies by the Nobel Prize Committee under its programme, *Homage au Prix Nobel*. He was invited, 'as one of the most distinguished artists of our time', to make an original graphic print for inclusion in a rare portfolio of prints.

Another friendship of lasting value was launched one morning in November 1958, when the Canadian Trade Commissioner in Bombay, who was a friend of mine, rang me up to say that he needed my help. A Canadian couple had arrived in his office with an imposing introduction from Ottawa, and wanted to know all about Indian dancers, musicians and artists. My friend, who was more versed in trade figures than the arts, begged me to take the responsibility off his shoulders. He would do anything for my assistance. In those days of prohibition, I suggested a case of Scotch, and we settled for half. That was the beginning of a warm and enduring friendship with Nicholas Goldschmidt and his wife Shelagh. Though a composer, Niki, as he is known to all his friends, also organised outstanding music festivals in Canada, including an annual festival of the Arts in Vancouver. He was in Bombay in his capacity as Managing Director of the Vancouver Art Festival to look for Indian talent he could invite there. Unfortunately, before his ideas could materialise he resigned over differences with the Festival Committee and moved to Toronto, but I stayed with them in Vancouver in 1963 and in Toronto after that.

*

With Morarji Desai, an ardent prohibitionist, as the state's Chief Minister, prohibition was seriously enforced in those days, to the extent at least that such laws can be. Permits to drink could be obtained, though not without some influence and only after producing a doctor's certificate, testifying that the applicant needed to imbibe alcohol regularly to avoid impairing his health. An astonishing number of Bombayites found their health threatened. Such was the demand for permits that an impressive directorate of prohibition was added to the other departments of the government. Drinking in homes and hotel rooms, far from decreasing, increased, because of the challenge involved. Unfortunately, prohibition led to a vicious cycle of crime centered in Bombay. Initially confined to boot-legging, it would in time diversify into other forms of smuggling, protection rackets, contract killings and the criminalisation of city and state politics.

My own brush with prohibition is amusing in retrospect but I could have done without it at the time. I had thrown a rather convivial dinner party at Ben Nevis, the apartment building I lived in on Warden Road, to which Bakul Khote, an Air India executive, and his Polish wife, Tina, had brought a friend. By the time they arrived, in the confusion of the party, I never quite got his name. It was only when the telephone never stopped ringing after the September 1958 issue of *Encounter*, published in London, appeared in Bombay that the perfidy of its editor, Melvin Lasky, who had put away so much of my gin that evening, was brought home to us. This is what he had written in his article, 'An Indian Notebook':

Bakul picks me up to take me to a 'typical party', typical that is for India's unique cosmopolitan centre. It is a 'chic' affair, and for a moment I felt myself in Paris or New York, except for the fact that the women were more beautiful, the men wittier, the whole atmosphere gayer and more informal. The host is a wealthy Sikh who publishes a new art magazine. Jim B. is a filmmaker who has just won a national prize for a Burmah-Shell documentary. K is a pilot with Air India. Mrs P. is a divorcée who now works in an advertising agency and dreams of going to America. Mulk Raj Anand is the distinguished novelist, wears achkans and jodhpurs, and longs for the youthful years when everybody ('even your European friends,' he says to me sharply) was loyal to pure revolutionary ideals. K.K.T. is a Parsi merchant who has just returned from North German ports where he has bought two freight ships. Good London gin (bought on the anti-prohibitionist black-market) flows too easily. I remember now only sitting in the corner with Moti Lal, my hastily appointed 'guru' for the evening, pressing for information and enlightenment. I look at Mrs P., so darkly beautiful in a charcoal-brown sari, who seems so flirtatious. 'To yield to spontaneous emotion,' I hear Moti Lal saying, 'or to sensual appetite is felt to be wrong.' Here too? I asked, here too? 'This is especially the case with sexual satisfaction. Somehow it is always felt to be illicit and somehow impious.' My confusion is only matched by my disappointment. But Moti Lal is relentless. 'And the most scandalous conduct of all would be for a man and a woman to exchange smiling glances in public.' I turn away from further enlightenment, avoid the path of the lovely Mrs P., and become very depressed when Patwant announces in a drunken drawl, that the black-market gin is all gone.

In those days the prohibition department would raid the homes they suspected of stashing liquor. Someone high-up in the directorate whom I knew rang to say he wanted to see me urgently. I said, 'Sure, let's have a drink.' This made matters worse. When I arrived at his office he flung a pile of papers across the table: they were all clippings of the *Encounter* article, sent to him anonymously, with the piece on me highlighted for his attention! He found it very unfunny and said I had to get rid of whatever I had by that evening.

'I have half a dozen bottles; what do I do with them?' I protested.

3. The Fifties: Challenge and Fulfilment

'Get rid of them. Give them to friends for safe-keeping.'

'But they'll never return them.'

'That's your problem,' he said unhelpfully, though he did keep his men away from me.

Fortunately, Lasky had got many of the names wrong, so some of my friends were more relaxed than the others, but Jim Beveridge, a Canadian, was easily identified as the film-maker and so was Naomi Punja, the 'darkly beautiful' and 'flirtatious' Mrs P. She was livid. Romesh Thapar escaped as Moti Lal.

There was a sequel to this episode. One day in Berlin in February 1960 Hellmut Jaesrich, editor of *Der Monat* magazine (*Encounter*'s stable-mate), asked me to lunch. He suggested I come to his office and we would go to his favourite restaurant nearby. As I entered his office he said, 'I have a great surprise for you', and shortly in walked Melvin Lasky. I refrained from strangling him though I did tell him he was a heel. He agreed. As penance for his past indiscretion, he offered to pay for the lunch. He also changed the names in his article when an anthology from the first ten years of *Encounter* was published in 1965.

*

Despite the fact that India's nationhood had already come under attack over the linguistic reorganisation of the states, my innate optimism sustained me through the fifties. Perhaps I should have seen through the speciousness of the arguments which were paraded in favour of the language formula. One was that reorganisation would help bring to the political forefront those who only knew their own language (the implication being that they were more 'Indian' than those who had the advantage of knowing English as well.) It was also claimed that greater opportunities would open up for more people in each state, and that reorganisation had averted what could have become a major crisis for the fledgling republic. With the passage of time it is easier to see that these were the arguments of provincial demagogues, and not of politicians with the larger national interest at heart. They were the forerunners of those narrow concerns which would increasingly influence India's politicians in the years ahead, and help religious, regional and caste bigots to enter parliament and state legislatures through prurient appeals to the sub-nationalism inherent in the Indian character.

But I have to admit that as the fifties came to a close my confidence in India was still intact. I did not view the few signs of social intolerance I had witnessed, or of political expediency overriding personal beliefs, as symptoms of a deeper malaise. On the contrary, I saw them as minor spin-offs of a major transformation that would take India from her degrading past to a proud republican future. All seemed well at the start of the sixties.

Chapter 4

The Sixties: The Pivotal Years

There are too many questions which fill the mind and for which there
appear to be no adequate answers, or if the answers are there, somehow they cannot be implemented because of the human beings that
should implement them.
                    Jawaharlal Nehru, in a letter to Bernard Shaw

THE 1960s provided us with a foretaste of the disgraceful decades
that lay ahead. Some of the hopes we had nurtured, our trust in
the future and our idyllic vision of independence would perish. Even
worse than the loss of face would be the emergence on India's
political stage of people lacking in character and integrity.

Just as the fundamental temper of the country was about to
change, so was the pattern of my life. On a visit to Delhi at the end
of 1959, I had met Karl Pfauter, the Cultural Counsellor at the
German Embassy, at a friend's house. I was impressed by his scholarship, we got on well together, and we planned another meeting. I
was hardly back in Bombay when I received a telegram from him
just after the New Year, saying, 'Kindly wire immediately whether
you can accept invitation to Germany middle February ...' That was
too soon, but I wired back that I would be happy to go in March. It
was an exciting prospect: my first journey abroad was to be as a guest
of the German government.

I took off from Bombay for Frankfurt on the morning of March 16.
There was a stop-over at Karachi for the better part of that day and
I was keen to see it again. Unfortunately this was against the Pakistani regulations. I had, however, spoken in advance to Sonny
Habibullah who lived in London with his wife Attia, the writer, but
had extensive business interests in Pakistan. This gave him considerable political influence, and he arranged for me to be whisked out
of the airport, given an extended tour of the city and reinstalled at
the airport after a fine dinner. My reception when I returned to the
airport was anything but cordial. Some sort of alert had been
sounded when I went missing and even the Indian ambassador,
Rajeshwar Dayal, had been informed. Sonny's friends, however,

kept me out of trouble and I was duly ensconced on the flight to Frankfurt.

*

Germany still bore some scars of wartime devastation, but massive reconstruction and industrial development had helped erase evidence of how much the country had haemorrhaged. Millions of tons of rubble had given way to gleaming new cities, broad autobahns, daringly designed bridges, industrial plants, housing, airports, museums and much else.

Utterly unlike India, it was a perfect introduction to the West for me. The Germans led disciplined lives, whether at home, in their workplaces or on the highways. We did not. They kept their neighbourhoods, cities and countryside clean. We could not be bothered. The Germans did not prostrate themselves before their postwar politicians, which we did in India, and would even more with time. I did my best to confront the culture shock at the very outset. (The confrontation was to become even more dramatic when I went to Switzerland after Germany.)

When Karl had asked me what I wanted to do, my reply was to see the distinctive arts and architecture of post-war Germany, and meet the artists and architects responsible for them. Bonn was a must, though the three days there were just about the dreariest of the entire visit. It had no art galleries, theatres or museums. Psychologically, the Germans considered it a temporary capital and gave no priority to a building programme for cultural activities. An argument often heard was that nearby Cologne offered all the cultural inspiration needed, but as I wrote at the time in *Design*: 'With so many major buildings being built there (Bonn) for every form of governmental activity it seemed the cultural field alone was being made to bear the burden of its temporary nature. As for the proximity of Cologne ... to be able to wander in and out of a musuem or art gallery is an altogether different experience for the people of a town than to have to drive out to another city to do it.'

The attitude of the Indian government towards projecting the cultural image of India abroad was equally abysmal. We had no Cultural Counsellor in our embassy.

After Bonn came Cologne, Essen, Duisburg, Hamburg, Berlin, Stuttgart, Ulm and Munich. Of all the cities I visited, Berlin stood out on every count: its character, the calibre of its creative people and the Berliners' sense of pride in their city. I was repeatedly told by Germans of all shades that their emotional association with Berlin –

4. The Sixties: The Pivotal Years

the historic, cultural, spiritual and political fountainhead of an undivided Germany – would never change. Proof of this was provided by the work of the artists and architects I met, the buildings I saw, the museums I visited. Of the creative men and women the most impressive were Bernhard Heiliger, the sculptor, the painters Alexander Camaro and Theodor Werner, architects Wassili Luckhardt and Paul Baumgarten and the Director-General of Museums in Berlin, Dr Reidemeister. I asked Luckhardt to tell me why pre-war undivided Germany, in spite of architects like Mies van der Rohe and Walter Gropius, had failed to come up with creative and original architectural statements. Why hadn't a Corbusier, Wright, or Aalto emerged in Germany?

Luckhardt blamed historic influences. One of the 'elders' of modern architecture and a contemporary of Mies and Gropius, he said Nazism's outlook on the arts had been revealed in the early thirties in its attitude to the Bauhaus. The Bauhaus symbolised democratic ideals, Nazism symbolised power. The Bauhaus was cosmopolitan, whereas Nazism was nationalistic. So the Bauhaus experiment had to end and, when it did, men of stature left Germany. There was a near total vacuum from then till the end of the war because the buildings which found favour with the Nazis had to be massive, with a militant quality symbolic of the might of the Third Reich. Therefore, while the ideas born in Germany flourished elsewhere, they were stifled in their own country. In the post-war years, architects, painters and sculptors struggled to search for a design philosophy to bridge the gap of twenty-five years, which started when Hitler came to power in 1933 and which had had such shattering human implications.

In Bernhard Heiliger's atelier in the Hochschule fur Bildende Kunste in Berlin, the biggest art academy in Germany where he taught, I found him at work on sculpture monumental in scale, powerful in form, and unique in its treatment of material. He himself conveyed a feeling of unlimited but controlled energy, and he was able to transfer some of it to his sculpture. In his view man and his environment were in a state of constant growth, and the basis of his sculpture was his belief in the organic growth of things. 'Sculpture is not just a play with aesthetic forms. Sculpture is restrained vitality and spatial reality.'

For Heiliger the commencement of a new work was 'always the most exciting moment – probably because of the reaching out for what is still unknown and still invisible. That moment is not without fear of the slowly developing forces and energies which on the one hand have to be freed from their shackles but on the other hand have

57

to be brought again into a discipline, into a harmony, into an orderly relationship of forms.' His sculpture, mostly in bronze, illustrates the fact that, though man's own form has remained unchanged, his mind has constantly opened up new horizons, unleashed new energies, and been poised to take new flights.

If I were to pick on one particular experience which made my visit to Germany unforgettable, I would say it was meeting Heiliger. We hit it off at our very first meeting, and the same evening he and his beautiful and tempestuous companion with flaming red hair, Rangwi Maeter, took me out to dinner. We met every day after that during my Berlin visit, and they joined me in Munich, where I finished my German tour. The three of us then drove to Lucerne and on to Zurich where we stayed in a villa a friend had lent them.

My introduction to Zurich by Bernhard was also an exhilarating experience. He knew it as well as his own Berlin. We met artists and collectors, went around the city's galleries and museums, and wined and dined with gusto. On one epicurean evening of charm, wit and animated conversation, when the photographer Rosselina Bischof came to dinner, I narrowly averted a spirited outburst by Rangwi who was unamused by the impression Rosselina was creating on Bernhard. She calmed down when I promised her my undivided attention for the rest of the evening.

*

After our farewells in Zurich and a few days in Geneva, it was Paris in April. I had heard of Paris's magical quality of making people incurably romantic within minutes of getting there, and I can testify to it! Tina Khote had written to alert her friend, Keeni Kessler, of my arrival and, when I called her from Germany, we made plans to dine together on my first day in Paris. Tina's delectable description of Keeni was, if anything, understated. She was tall, blonde and beautiful, perhaps a fraction taller than me, which was disconcerting. Her strikingly animated face was framed by her long hair, and her eyes sparkled. My first sight of her put me in a festive mood for the entire visit.

We dined in a little restaurant she had chosen with particular care, which she said was her favourite for special occasions. That 'special' held promise. I offered to make a deal with her: if she initiated me into the delights of French cuisine I would, when she came to India, place before her the mouthwatering dishes which had so distracted the Mughals from the business of governing their empire that they had lost it. She agreed. She ordered an irresistible meal, and it was a memorable evening. So were the days that followed.

Keeni took me around the different quarters and landmarks of Paris and introduced me to many of her friends. Her apartment on Rue La Fontaine in the sixteenth arrondissement was elegantly furnished. Keeni was Dutch and had been married to a Canadian, from whom she was divorced. Her son Adrian's schooling had brought her to Paris. When not in Paris she lived in Lausanne and, being a passionate skier, she had a ski lodge in Crans sur Sierre in the Swiss Alps. If it dawned on us during those few days in Paris that we were on the verge of falling in love, we did not put it into words. I was thirty-five and felt that if our relationship was to be serious, we needed time to assess whether the intensity of our feelings could bridge the cultural divide on the opposite sides of which we had grown up. At the end of what seemed an incredibly fleeting visit we vowed to meet again before the year was out, though we were not yet sure how.

My next stop was London and a very agreeable surprise awaited me at Heathrow. My old Bombay friends Ralph and Billie Benton (I had first met Ralph in Koraput) were now living in London where Ralph headed Ingersoll Rand. They had decided to give me a fitting welcome and had rented a vintage Rolls Royce to pick me up at the airport.

London seemed amazingly familiar considering I had never been there. This was not altogether surprising since Britain's history, London's landmarks, the glories of empire and the noble deeds and virtuous ways (!) of her people had been drilled into us in school. So the odd feeling I had throughout my stay there was that I had seen it before. The street-names, victory columns, statuary, parks, old buildings, double-decker buses and the Thames were all so familiar. As was the weather. The big disappointment was Buckingham Palace. It seemed rundown. After singing 'God save the King' for years in school, one had expected the King to be better housed. The palaces of most of India's major princely families quite outclassed it!

After a week in London and two days in Rome, I arrived in Cairo, my last stop on the way home. I was looking forward to visiting Egypt, as ancient as my own country, and spending a week with Olaf and Veronica Hauge who had moved there in 1959. Cairo's crowded bazaars and the medley of sounds, smells, shapes, colours, languages, urban insanity, densely populated lanes, squares and neighbourhoods provided a welcome whiff of home. With its zestful and chaotic mix of moods and activities, it was a change from the bleached-out look and orderliness of European cities.

Interspersed with the milling crowds were the structures of ancient lineage, some going back to the Pharaohs. The timeless Nile flowed serenely through this mingling of the old and the new, the river which had seen it all, like the Ganges or the Indus or its other historic counterparts in India.

I was puzzled by the intensity of my involvement with Egypt. Could it be because of our similar historical experiences? Of being savaged, conquered and colonialised at various periods in our history? Or was it because our present concerns too had much in common, with the western powers intent on manipulating our destinies? Not that we lacked our share of lamentable fellow-countrymen adept at creating strife. Egypt and India shared this dubious distinction too. Egypt has always seemed to me to belong more to Asia than to Africa and, though I was to visit many Asian countries (Japan, Taiwan, Vietnam, Thailand, Indonesia, Singapore, Malaysia) before sitting down to write *India and the Future of Asia*, the idea for this book came to me in Cairo.

A fact which always came up in conversations with thoughtful Egyptians during this and a subsequent visit, and which strengthened my resolve to write the book, was our utter dependence on western media for news of one another – the same media which Norman Mailer said 'would not be media if they did not have the instincts of a lynch mob'. Events in Asia were interpreted for just about all Asians by the West's newspapers, magazines, books, wire services, documentaries, movies, radio and television, since Asian leaders ignored the fact that, in the armoury of a modern state, these are the sinews of power. The perceived wisdom of the analysts, academics and correspondents of the West shaped Asian attitudes and our perceptions of each other, not to mention the attitudes of intelligent Westerners, of whom my friend, Olaf Hauge, was one. Even now, after forty years, he still accepts the American media's interpretation of Asian events, and is unwilling to acknowledge the existence of any distortions in its coverage. No matter how well-reasoned an Asian viewpoint – in, say, an Indian newspaper – on an immoral and unprincipled move by the US administration against an Asian nation, Olaf would uphold the messianic view of events as interpreted by the US media.

*

I returned to Bombay on May 3, 1960. So much had happened in the first four months of the year, it seemed unreal. I was full of ideas about the future, but I was even more excited by the direction my life would take with Keeni. Within days of coming home, however, it became clear that the fabric of India's public life was fraying. Betrayals of political trust were gradually corrupting high public office, with some politicians beginning to look on it merely as a source of gainful employment. This trend would in time attain epidemic proportions, starting with Kashmir. According to P.A. Rosha, Kashmir's former Director General of Police, Bakshi Ghulam Mohammed of the Congress Party, who headed the state administration as its Prime Minister (this designation was later changed to Chief Minister) from 1953 to 1962, 'was the most consistently corrupting influence Kashmir has seen'.

Why was his corruption condoned in that sensitive state by Prime Minister Jawaharlal Nehru, especially as the political and territorial integrity of this earthly paradise was already under threat? The answer is that political expediency was in the ascendant. The Congress, obsessed with staying in power in that state, saw in Bakshi the right man to help it, and so his corruption was overlooked. This cynical disregard for proprieties in public office – along with other self-serving acts of the Congress – would gradually push the people of Kashmir towards a fratricidal war and finally into demanding independence from India.

An equally cynical game – no less damaging to the polity of the fledgling republic – was being played in another state, Punjab, by another Congress Chief Minister, Partap Singh Kairon. The damage he did to his state was of a different nature. Though he made no money himself – which some members of his family certainly did – Kairon subverted the structure of government. Convinced that no politician can succeed unless he can bend the system to his will, he started the process – to be increasingly emulated by central and state ministers – of making the civil, judicial and police services subservient to the ruling party. He was in office from 1956 to 1964, but it was only during the latter half of his administration that Kairon determined to undermine the morale of the services. Interestingly enough, he had been committed to the idea of rooting out corruption among his officials and political colleagues in the early years of his administration, but he believed that the only way he could achieve this was by instilling a sense of fear in them. To this end he weakened the organisational independence of key institutions, such as the police, and he used the police to coerce his colleagues and opponents alike.

E.N. Mangat Rai, who was Chief Secretary of the state administration for almost five years during Kairon's Chief Ministership and admired his extraordinary drive and initiative, later observed that

'Kairon was, I believe, the first top-level politician in India system-atically to use the knowledge of the police and their rights of investigation to build information for the influence and control of (fellow) politicians'. He later used the police for the control of admin-istrative officials as well.

Kairon was a dynamic Chief Minister. Unlike Bakshi in Kashmir, he did much for the development of the state of Punjab, especially its water resources and agricultural infrastructure, including the establishment of one of the finest agricultural universities in Asia. He helped to place Punjab on course for the green revolution which in turn enabled India to become self-sufficient in food, and his agenda for the services too would have been widely accepted had he not deviated from his original aim of infusing a greater sense of purpose in them. But, like all driven men, he was impatient of the checks and balances which are built into a democratic administrative system to keep political adventurism in check, and he weakened them beyond repair.

Bakshi Ghulam Mohammed, on the other hand, did nothing for Kashmir's development, but he left the bureaucracy alone. He con-centrated on building a personal fortune.

In the final reckoning both set dangerous precedents for India's political governance, as they became role models for the next crop of politicians. If the linguistic reorganisation of the states in the fifties was the first sad step towards the erosion of India's cohesiveness, money-grabbing by men in high public office and disregard for the established systems of government were two more steps on the road to infamy and shame. The odds against an orderly, well-governed and just Indian state were mounting. Its inner weaknesses were beginning to surface and it was about to face a great blow to its self-esteem at the hands of the Chinese, notwithstanding the fact that India had forcefully advocated China's admission to the United Nations.

*

Despite the severity of Washington's assault on Nehru's policy of non-alignment, he had a better sense of world history than most of his critics. As early as 1950 he had observed in a letter to Sir B.N. Rau, India's delegate to the UN, that 'it is a complete misunderstanding of the China situation to imagine that they function like a satellite state of Russia ...'. He was also astute enough to know that India could only contain the assertive, battle-tested Chinese through direct diplomacy. Unlike the United States and Soviet Russia, India had not emerged strong and powerful from her recent experiences. Partition had left her weakened. Though she had won the 1947 war with Pakistan over Kashmir, it had taken its toll of her resources. The millions of refugees who had still to be settled were an additional burden. Yet another factor was her economy which had to be transformed from its subservient colonial status to that of a power-in-the-making.

Nehru's non-alignment coupled with his China policy were therefore designed to keep India out of big-power rivalries, and to give her time to develop her economic and defence capabilities. Unfortunately, he picked a very unsuitable person to head the Defence Ministry. His friend, Krishna Menon, a man of mercurial and satiric temperament, irascible, brilliant in debate but compulsively rude, was asked to oversee the shoring up of India's disputed borders with China. He was the wrong man for the job at this crucial time. By playing favourites in the higher commands of the armed forces, and by his crude and irresponsible comments, Menon alienated many experienced and seasoned commanders, while showing no special skill at organising India's defence. He once told a meeting of middle-ranking officers: 'Seventy-five per cent of our difficulties come from the Chiefs of Staff. I am not saying they have not made up their minds, because they haven't got minds to make up.' Quite astonishingly, Menon still believed that if it came to the crunch, Russia would restrain China from a showdown with India. In giving Menon his way in the critical area of defence, Nehru allowed friendship to cloud his better judgment, which was especially strange as he himself had accurately assessed much earlier the real nature of the Sino-Soviet relationship. Moreover, events had since shown that these two were on a collision course themselves, and that Russia could no longer influence or restrain China.

These conflicting signals were eroding India's image abroad and the final blow would be dealt by the Sino-Indian war in October 1962. Was the war inevitable? Or did Nehru falter in the field of diplomacy because he relied on the erroneous impression of India's military preparedness which Menon gave him? Though there is enough evidence to prove that humiliating India and establishing herself as the paramount Asian power was one of China's foreign policy goals, there are also indications which suggest that China may not have been totally inflexible about negotiating her border dispute with India.

In a letter to Nehru of November 7, 1959 Chou En-lai proposed that despite the steadily worsening situation the door should still be kept open and 'a favourable atmosphere for a friendly settlement of the boundary question' created. He also made several suggestions in a persuasive appeal for a statesmanlike solution to the contentious issues facing their countries. It could, admittedly, have been another ploy. Nevertheless, it was an opportunity for gaining more time to prepare militarily, should diplomacy fail. Perhaps because Nehru felt confident of India's strength – mistakenly as it turned out – his reply, though prompt, did not give much hope.

Later, when Chou En-lai suggested personal diplomacy through a meeting between Nehru and himself on April 20, 1960, it was Nehru who queered the pitch. Just one week *before* the Chinese premier's arrival in Delhi for the talks, Nehru wrote to the Prime Minister of Nepal to say he saw 'no reason why we should weaken it (India's strong case) at any point'. Chou was expected in Nepal immediately after his Delhi visit, and this was Nehru's way of conveying to him India's lack of interest in continuing the negotiations. It was to be the last time the two Prime Ministers ever met.

A last-ditch effort was, however, made once again at Geneva in July 1962 when the Chinese foreign minister, Marshal Chen-Yi, met Krishna Menon, who was accompanied by a seasoned Indian diplomat, Arthur Lall. Quite a few details of the border problems were discussed, and though nothing specific emerged – it was not expected to – room was left for further negotiations, as the joint communiqué suggested. But the furore in the Indian Parliament – which was in a truculent mood, having been repeatedly and wrongly told how strong India was militarily – put paid to this initiative. As Lall later mentioned in his book, *The Emergence of Modern India*, and in a conversation with me, 'there was an outcry in the Indian Parliament against his (Menon's) negotiations with Chen-Yi ... At that point Nehru, already a sick man, denied that there had been any negotiations at all, which was far from the truth.'

*

The countdown to the 1962 war with China emphasised, so far as I was concerned, the distance between Bombay and New Delhi. The case for a move to Delhi was becoming stronger. But this is running slightly ahead of my own story because, at the end of 1960, TWA rang me to ask if I would accept an invitation on their inaugural Boeing service to Rome. With Keeni very much on my mind, I said I would, if they would take me on to Paris – which they did.

Keeni met me at the airport with a bottle of champagne on ice. Paris was beautiful in December – cold, crisp, only at times overcast: perfect weather for an aperitif or two before lunch, followed by a superb bottle of wine with the meal. We walked a lot and went to many museums and galleries. The evenings were spent at the theatre or movies or dinners with friends. I remember a lively evening with Man Ray and his wife, Juliette, at the Brasserie Lippe. The printmaker Krishna Reddy, who had visited me in Bombay, and his attractive American wife Shirley, took us to visit Georges Braque, Ossip Zadkine and Stanley William Hayter. During those two weeks in Paris our romance took on a new colour and excitement and we felt we had to be with each other all the time.

Shortly after my return to Bombay, I was told by Daniel Oleksiw, head of the Bombay office of the United States Information Service, and Tim Efimenco, its Cultural Affairs Officer, that the US government had invited me to visit America. I was happy to accept and we settled on April 1961. Among the people I would like to meet I mentioned especially architects like Mies van der Rohe, Philip Johnson, Walter Gropius, Louis Kahn, Richard Neutra and Paul Rudolph and the painters Mark Rothko, Joseph Albers, William de Kooning and the man who had started the 'happenings' movement, Alan Kaprow. Among the writers on architecture, I mentioned Peter Blake and John Entenza, as well as others whose work I also admired. When I suggested going to New York via Paris, TWA promptly arranged it. I was becoming very fond of TWA! This time it was April in Paris and I arrived on the 13th – a day enormously auspicious in the Sikh calendar because on this day the Sikhs were formally baptised (as the Khalsa) in 1699. After a blissful week I was on my way to New York and to a warm welcome by Rasil and Romen and their two little daughters, Amrita and Rekha.

Our flight arrived in New York late in the evening and my first impression – as we banked over the city to land – was that it had rivers of light flowing through it. The effect created by the headlights of thousands of cars, and the sculptural quality of light in motion, struck me as almost a new art form, spread literally over hundreds of square miles, with no artist to take credit for it. This first visual impression of America has never left me, nor is the excitement any less each time I see it.

The drive to the Basus Fifth Avenue apartment in Manhattan was less inspiring, and so were some other aspects of the city I saw in the following days. This is what I wrote of that experience, in *Design*:

What is coming up – and this is particularly true of New York – are buildings which are no more than towering hulks of expensive materials lacking qualities which move or excite or which say something above and beyond the provision of living and working areas ... One wonders why it is that there are only two or three really outstanding buildings in New York and the rest are of no consequence.

The two that impressed me most were the Seagram building and the Guggenheim Museum. As for the rest of Manhattan and the other boroughs, most of what I saw was mediocre, often tawdry, and bereft of character. A copy of *Harper's* magazine which I picked up when I was there had an article by a man who with disarming frankness confessed that he had till recently been a member of the real-estate tribe but had now reformed. 'They (the builders-cum-developers) are businessmen concerned not with aesthetics but getting the most rent per square foot out of their investment. However, when the public allows the quest for profit to dominate architectural values and the municipal interest almost *completely*, as it has done, it is accepting a monetary perversion which seems beyond that of any known previous civilisation ...'

Speculators and real-estate operators had the same vicious grip on other American cities. Clearly, the desire to make them more livable, appealing and free of the neurosis and tensions generated by crowding, could not prevail in the face of these vested interests. How could our planners benefit from the experience of American cities? I wrote in *Design*:

What is important at this stage is a wide-awake awareness in our planners of the dimensions city-planning problems eventually acquire. At the moment that awareness in our city authorities is lacking. If it is a question of housing, our present approach is to build houses if they have to be built. And planning, zoning and designing can wait till later. But in a country the size of ours, with a population such as we have, what does later mean? Can we afford to rebuild so soon? Others can, but can we?

A tragically short-sighted view also seems to prevail that the day is still far off when the volume of traffic in our cities will reach the proportions to which it exists in America, and that when the time comes the problem will be faced. But problems of this nature were faced by men of vision in preceding generations and if the vision is a trifle blurred, as unfortunately is the case at times, the experience of others can be profitably studied to see what lessons can be learnt from it. And what mistakes avoided.

Lastly, what is most important for our planners is to see how real-estate operators take over cities, so that similar take-overs can be prevented here, even though Bombay is already half way ground under their heel.

The greed of our real-estate operators too was going to unleash urban chaos on Bombay, Delhi, Madras, Pune and other once-graceful cities of India, littering them with crass commercial constructions – symbols of our rapaciousness and indifference to India's great building traditions.

To compensate for the uninspiring physical form of the major cities, America's creative men and women can be credited with the concept of building vertically. New York's Seagram building is still, in my view, the finest skyscraper ever built.

Phyllis Lambert, the daughter of the president of the Seagram Company, Sam Bronfman, was an art student in Paris in 1954, when she learnt from a *Time* magazine clipping sent by her father that a new Seagram building was to be built on Park Avenue. She caught the next plane to New York, determined to talk to him about its architecture. She must have been a tough young lady (though I did not get that impression when we had lunch together in Chicago), because her father took the work away from the original architects and put her in charge of the entire project.

After an exhaustive search during which many architects were carefully considered, the choice finally fell on Mies van der Rohe. At Mies's request, Philip Johnson, Head of the Department of Architecture at the Museum of Modern Art, agreed to collaborate with him on the design of the building. Now, seven years later, Johnson arranged with Phyllis Lambert that she would take me to meet Mies. In a wheel-chair by then, he was disinclined to entertain visitors, though he still came to his Chicago office every morning, but, because of Phyllis, he greeted me warmly and was very generous with his time.

He explained his philosophy to me in some detail when I asked him about his design values. He felt that 'values' was too abstract a term. It meant nothing. What one *did* must be valuable. His own approach to his work summed it up. 'I don't want to be interesting,' he said. 'I want to be good.'

Philip Johnson on the other hand wanted 'to *be* the new elegance'. To that end he has introduced elegance and sophistication to the American scene – qualities generally attributed to the older cultures of Europe. Philip's own glass house in New Canaan, Connecticut, is a *tour de force*. It is one large area of rectangular space enclosed in glass. Steel columns support the roof and the four walls are of glass from floor to ceiling. There are no partitions and division of space is achieved by two low cabinets, one of them serving as the kitchen. This cabinet has all the kitchen equipment installed in it. The bathroom is a brick cylinder, a section of which has a fireplace.

Around the glass house are thirty acres of woods, rolling lawns and a lake. There were only two structures then on Philip's property – the glass house and a brick house for guests where I have often spent weekends – but over the years other remarkable buildings were built: a sculpture gallery, a gallery to house his collection of paintings and a library.

Frank Lloyd Wright's Guggenheim Museum on New York's Fifth Avenue was one of the most remarkable buildings I saw throughout my stay in the US, both in terms of form and the dynamics of the space within it. As is usually the case when someone wants to shake people out of their torpor, the building came in for severe criticism. It was called anti-painting, anti-museum and a threat to the works of art within it. This is nonsense. If anything, viewing paintings hung on the continuous ramp that circles around and creates viewing areas as it rises ever higher, was a more rewarding experience than being in a series of rooms or halls crowded with people, as invariably happens in most museums. I believe the sheer audacity of its design was why Guggenheim attracted so much criticism.

I first met Peter Blake, the editor of *Architectural Forum*, at a lunch given by Andrew Heiskell of *Time* magazine. We were to become great friends, though we started off with sharply divergent views on the Guggenheim. He had called it 'Wright's last slap at the city. No building could be designed to fit less well into the established urban pattern ... .' I felt established urban patterns were what accounted for the dreariness of most cities. Peter and I agreed to disagree on this.

Of the painters I met on that first visit – in addition to other significant American architects like Louis Kahn, Paul Rudolph, Charles Moore, Edward Barnes, I.M. Pei – the two whose work, and conversation, have stayed with me over the years, were Mark Rothko and Joseph Albers. I was impressed by the nature of their personal search which had influenced the evolution of their work. Albers's white-on-white prints and Rothko's three or four horizontal bands of paint were important milestones in a lifetime's striving to reach the goals which all serious painters set themselves.

Apropos of Rothko, I remember going to lunch with Kenneth Galbraith (then American ambassador to India), soon after my return from the US and getting involved in an argument with him over the Rothko painting in his living room. Works by outstanding American painters in those days, I was told, were loaned by US museums to the State Department which then sent them out to some of the US embassies. Galbraith made a waggish remark about modern art in general while pointing at the Rothko on the wall, and it vastly intrigued the other guests to see an Indian defending an American painter from the gibes of the US ambassador.

Before leaving New York in May 1961, I arrived at an important milestone in my own life. My sister and her family, who were unamused at being kept in the dark about my growing involvement with Keeni, suggested I invite her to New York. She was delighted to come. Not only was her visit a family success, but we both decided we had waited long enough to start our life together. Rasil immediately threw an engagement party and it took me the better part of next day to recover from it. For a terrifying moment I couldn't even recollect what the party had been about!

Fortunately, I had succeeded in bringing my parents around to the idea of accepting my marriage to a non-Sikh mainly because they felt they had waited long enough to see me married. So the engagement was celebrated with a clear conscience and we arranged to be married in the winter of that year in New Delhi. Keeni sportingly accepted the idea of a traditional Sikh wedding in deference to my parents' wishes. It was just a simple service at home with only immediate family, in quite a contrast to the often bizarre extent to which weddings in India are celebrated. My parents had invited some of their friends for breakfast after the ceremony and Keeni was touched by the warmth of their welcome. For our honeymoon we motored to Simla and then beyond it, into the environs of the beautiful Himalayas.

A dinner had been planned on the lawn of my parental home on our return, and Ratna Fabri, a friend and superb designer, had converted it into a magical setting with candles, hangings, lanterns, *objets d'art* and masses of flowers. Brian Brake, the New Zealander, whose photographs of the monsoons in India would be published in book form and in magazines around the world, took photographs of the festivities. It was an unforgettable farewell to my bachelorhood.

Despite the good life in Bombay, where Keeni and I set up home, there was no escaping the fact that New Delhi was the centre of political decision-making. Since I had decided to try my hand at political writing as well, it made sense to live close to the capital's subterranean politics. It had become obvious to me that no amount of critical writing on urban mismanagement, high-rise buildings and dishonest land-use policies would help India's urban development, so long as criticism was levelled only at architects and planners. The real culprits were the politicians, backed by corrupt officials and real-estate developers, and since politicians only responded to criticism which threatened their political existence, the general press – not a design magazine – was the place for it.

So after a few months in Bombay, we moved ourselves and the magazines to Delhi. I had decided to build a floor on top of the family home in New Delhi and had picked a very innovative and angry young French-Canadian architect, Luc Durand – he had come to work in India for a couple of years – to design it. He found it an exciting challenge since the original house – somewhat in the art nouveau style – had been built in the thirties. It had curvilinear lines and forms which, while appropriate for the time it was built, could hardly be replicated twenty-five years later, and certainly not by the editor of *Design*!

Luc and I had endless sessions. The design we eventually agreed upon, startling in its simplicity and clarity, related satisfactorily not only to the existing ground floor, but also to the house's beautiful environs of fifteenth-century monuments surrounded by a park. Luc succeeded in giving the new addition a distinct personality while respecting the existing building's right to its identity. He refused to plaster the inside walls, or use paint on them. All the untouched, unplastered brick surfaces were to be lime-washed, as well as the ceilings. Since the floors would also be in white terrazo the eventual contrast of the white with the greenery all around was striking, especially as Luc had provided large windows throughout and placed them just inches off the floor. The natural waxed finish of the woodwork next to the white of the walls and floors made another arresting design statement.

Just as we were about to start construction in April 1962, my world seemed to disintegrate around me. Keeni and I, in Delhi for a few days, were sitting on the lawn with friends when I saw my mother walk across the verandah and into the living room to listen to the evening news on the radio as she always did. A few minutes later we heard a shout and saw considerable commotion. As I ran into the room I saw my mother lying on the floor, felled by a massive heart attack. Even though our family doctor was almost next door and arrived within minutes, there was nothing he could do. She had died instantaneously.

I struggled to come to terms with her death. She had been an understanding, loving and caring mother who had done much to instil confidence in me, making me feel that there were no limits to what I could achieve. She had been supportive and present throughout my life, and had now gone out of it forever. Only years later would I fully understand the extent to which her faith and beliefs had influenced my own convictions and shaped my responses to the critical encounters ahead. The source of her strength was not blind religious faith but a sensible understanding of the balanced outlook and rational thought which she found in the Granth Sahib – the repository of her faith. Like countless other Sikhs, she turned to it for the insights and philosophical reassurances of men of wisdom, whether at a time of rejoicing or of grief, and the scriptures – with a directness and simplicity rare in sacred writings – had helped her retain her poise and balance. While many people, as I had observed, read the holy book by rote, as a routine to be got over with, she reflected on what she read and then applied it to her own experiences. This helped to give her strength.

Though my own inclination was not towards religion, despite the environment in which I had grown up, I had absorbed more from her than I realised then. Years later, when the politics of Indira Gandhi, Jawaharlal Nehru's daughter and India's third Prime Minister, polarised the Hindus and Sikhs, I found myself turning to the same repository of rational thought which had given my mother strength. And since there was no room in it for despair, I found myself constantly renewed by it.

It took me time to resume life which had come to a standstill that evening in 1962. I cancelled plans to go abroad that year, though Keeni went to Europe to see her son Adrian and spend the summer holidays with him. My mother's older sister, despite the loss of a sister she had loved deeply, was an abiding source of strength in those difficult days.

*

In October of that same year, India found herself at war with China. It was a war which would debilitate her and from which Nehru would never quite recover. India was outwitted by the Chinese both in diplomacy and on the battlefield. No matter how events are recast, India's devastating defeat in October 1962 was the result of her political leadership's gross mismanagement of the first major crisis since Independence in 1947. China's actual encroachments into Indian territory, which are extensively documented, generally date from July, 1954. This gave India eight years to prepare for the eventual denouement in 1962. But a fact which has scarcely been written about is that, even earlier, New Delhi had word of the presence of Chinese troops in the Subansiri Valley of India's North East Frontier Agency (now known as Arunachal Pradesh).

In November, 1953, the 17th Squadron of the Indian Air Force, comprising six Harvard 2-B aircraft, had been moved to Jorhat in

Northern Assam in response to an incident in which an Indian political officer and his party had been ambushed and killed by Dafla tribesmen of the Subansiri Valley. The task of this detachment was to reconnoitre the valley and, by flying close to the villages of the hostile tribesmen, impress on them that they should be less aggressive. During several of these flying missions not only Dafla tribesmen but what appeared to be regular troops were also observed. Since they were not Indian they could only be Chinese. The information was doubtless passed on to the Air Force's high command and from there to the Cabinet. What did the Cabinet do about this proof of the presence of Chinese troops in Indian territory?

The Indian leadership failed to put the valuable information it was getting to good use and lulled itself into believing its own rhetoric. Nehru and his cabinet colleagues were inexperienced in the conduct of wars and unaccustomed to handling the military, none more so than the Defence Minister, Krishna Menon, who had had no experience of ever commanding anything. He now compounded this deficiency by ignoring the Army Chief's repeated warnings about the unpreparedness of the armed forces and their need for more budgetary allocations. This was an indefensible attitude in view of India's deteriorating relations with China.

India's policy so far had been one of not provoking the Chinese, even when they had intruded into Indian territory. A change in this policy was suddenly sprung on the army command by the Defence Minister at a meeting on September 10, although neither he nor Nehru had consulted the Army Chief beforehand. The first General Thapar knew of the government's decision to order Indian border forces to fire on armed Chinese intruders was at this meeting. As in the past, Thapar protested, but he was ignored. He should have resigned, but did not do so. Indeed the Prime Minister never personally discussed this sensitive matter with the Chief of the Indian Army. He had left the country on September 7 and was out of India when the meeting of September 10 took place. Written orders were only sent to the army command on September 22 and even Krishna Menon was away from September 18. It was an odd time for both to be absent, given the very real danger of a war with China.

But worse was to follow. As the two countries drifted closer to war, Nehru made what was perhaps his gravest mistake. He master-minded the appointment of his favourite general and fellow-Kashmiri, Lt. Gen. B.M. Kaul, who had no war-time command experience, to head a hastily assembled army corps against the Chinese in the North East Frontier Agency. It was an unbelievable appointment in what could become a critical theatre of war. To

Kaul's credit it must be said that he was energetic, hard-driving and dedicated, and not lacking in personal courage either. But he was weak in the two areas crucial to every commander – he was neither a tactician nor had he commanded troops in battle.

Kaul, recalled from leave on October 2, met Nehru, Krishna Menon and other officials the same afternoon and was given command of IV Corps – *formed the previous day* – on October 4. He left for NEFA on October 5. This was strange enough, considering that the army command had been pressing for resources and clear directives for over a year, but another blunder followed. On October 11, Kaul returned from the forward areas to report to Nehru. At a long meeting in the Prime Minister's house he explained with maps, sketches and photographs why the army would not be able to evict the Chinese from the areas they had invaded. Nehru listened patiently, then spoke for two hours on Sino-Indian relations. Finally, he said, 'We don't want our army to commit suicide', and he agreed to hold back on the earlier decision to evict the Chinese. Yet, astoundingly, at a press conference the next morning, before leaving for Sri Lanka, he said the army had been ordered to 'throw out the Chinese as soon as possible'. Many in the army believed that this statement to the press was Nehru's way of putting the army under pressure and getting it to agree to an unequal fight.

Kaul flew back to his headquarters but, stricken with high-altitude pulmonary oedema, had to be flown back to Delhi on October 18. His attending physician, Brigadier (later General) Inder Singh, a world authority on high-altitude illness, diagnosed his condition as very serious. Despite the imminence of war, no one was sent to replace him.

On October 20, the Chinese struck. A thoroughly shaken political leadership now gave the army a free hand, *after* the enemy had gone on the offensive. On October 24, Lt. Gen. Harbaksh Singh, one of the finest fighting generals in the army who was to play a key role in Pakistan's defeat in the 1965 war, was ordered to take over Kaul's corps. Within hours of his appointment, I was subsequently told by several army officers, the spirits of the troops in NEFA had soared.

The new Corps Commander quickly assessed the weakness of India's forward positions and prepared a battle-plan in which Indian troops would fight on ground more favourable to them. He was confident of drawing the Chinese into a situation in which the factors of ground, relative strength and time would favour India. China would have the added disadvantage of finding her extended supply lines cut off with the imminent onset of winter. Harbaksh's commanders and troops were inspired by his leadership and felt that the

Chinese could be taught a lesson at Sela and Bomdila. However, on October 29, only five days after his appointment, Harbaksh Singh was withdrawn and replaced by Kaul, who was still a very sick man. He had insisted on being sent back and Nehru, despite the Army Chief's protests, had agreed. The short war that followed shattered the nation's self-esteem as news of India's humiliating defeat was flashed around the world. A certain victory had been turned into defeat by the interference of India's politicians, bemused by a sense of their own self-importance.

At such times it is the real or imaginary sins of those who fight a nation's wars on the battlefields that are unfairly highlighted. India's rout was mainly due to political gamesmanship at a time when military preparedness should have been the prime concern. It was certainly not due to the poor fighting quality of her troops though the weakness of several senior commanders contributed to the defeat. Nor was there any lack of logistical support, shortage of supplies or insufficient cooperation by agencies like the railways and others. The Air Force's airlift operations too were superb, as was the staff work at army headquarters.

As for the dramatis personae, Krishna Menon was the first to go. At a meeting in his house late on the night of October 31, at which the army and air chiefs were present along with the Cabinet Secretary, the Foreign Secretary, the head of the Intelligence Bureau and some others, Menon, as was his wont, suddenly turned on the Army Chief and asked with vicious sarcasm: 'Where will the army stop – in Bangalore?' (Bangalore is over 1,200 miles away in Southern India). For once his goading went too far for General Thapar, who told him, literally, to shut up. The thoroughly rattled Defence Minister was not allowed to finish a single sentence.

'I'm conducting a conference ...' he began, to be told, 'You don't know how to conduct one.'

When Krishna Menon tried again, 'I am the Minister of ...', Thapar interrupted, 'You don't deserve to be a Minister.'

Krishna Menon's last conference was over. He was removed from office the next morning and Nehru took over the Defence portfolio. Thapar's outburst was provoked by a vicious and arrogant Defence Minister who had been needling him for over a year, and could, perhaps, also have been triggered by a sense of self-reproach at staying on in office when he should have resigned on principle months earlier.

On the evening of November 19, having landed in Delhi after a visit to the forward areas, where the Indian forces were now in full retreat, Thapar went to the Prime Minister's house and offered to resign. Nehru refused to accept his resignation, but next morning changed his mind. The Cabinet Secretary, S.S. Khera, called at Thapar's residence and conveyed to him Nehru's wish that he should resign after all. Kaul resigned a few days after Thapar, went into obscurity and died in the early seventies. Nehru, a broken man, was to die within eighteen months of India's defeat.

The year 1962 ended on a very sad note.

*

Each of my three magazines started publishing from Delhi in 1963 and, despite the travelling I had to do between Delhi and Bombay, it was good to be back in the city I loved and had grown up in. Although it was changing, it was not yet the wasteland it would become. The vandals – in the form of real-estate developers – and their political partners-in-crime, were still to appear on the scene. Nor had the city fathers as yet given way to the disgraceful breed of political godfathers who, to keep themselves in power, would create more constituencies by cramming the poor and underprivileged in 'planned' shanties in large parts of Delhi. Instead of building satellite towns and providing people with decent, civilised living and working conditions, they would lure them to Delhi, where each of the new and deliberately populated areas would be legitimised as a parliamentary constituency to satisfy the ambitions of the corrupt, latter-day political dons. In time, Delhi's parliamentary seats would increase from four to seven.

*

But all this was still in the future. The high walls of greed were still to be built by private developers. The mess that the Delhi Development Authority would make of this city of proud lineage was still some years away. So was my own disillusionment, when wealthy owners of spacious residential properties used their influence to get them cleared for commercial development.

Peter Blake, in his book *God's Own Junkyard: The Planned Deterioration of America's Landscape*, tells a story of an American senator who saw in the vandalising of the American landscape a reiteration of the spirit of free enterprise. 'In the name of culture, in the name of aesthetics whatever that is,' said the late Robert S. Kerr of Oklahoma on the floor of the Senate in March 1958 (only he pronounced it *ass-thetics*), 'it will be a grave day in this country when we reach so high an *ass-thetic* pinnacle that men are willing and able ... to deprive

75

citizens of their vested rights .... What kind of culture (is this?) .... It is a kind of culture one can find in Russia. It is a kind of culture Hitler went down the drain trying to implement in Germany ... .'

Many such crass arguments would be made to justify Delhi's degradation also.

In the spring of 1963, I accepted an invitation from Peter Blake to attend the International Design Conference in Aspen, Colorado, of which he was Programme Chairman. The theme of the Conference was *Design and the American Image Abroad*. One of the features of the programme was a series of panels of six speakers for whom six tables, each with ten places, would be booked at one of Aspen's restaurants. The idea was that each panellist would preside at a table hoping that ten people attending the Conference would join him for lunch (for which they had to pay) and discussion (which was free).

My panel devised a strategy. Each would sit for fifteen minutes at his table, but if there was no sign of a crowd making its way in his direction he would quietly leave for a reassuring rendezvous with the others. Happily all the six tables did well that day, but my friends felt I had an unfair headstart over them (literally) because of my colourful turban.

Aspen provided me with a clearer picture of the phenomenal growth of ideas, techniques and of ways for communicating with people globally.

*

Jawaharlal Nehru's death on May 27, 1964, was to have a profound effect on India's outlook, on its political progress and on morality in public life. Nehru, an idealist and humanist, had a profoundly liberal outlook, but visionaries have often found it difficult to give practical form to their vision. His vision of India clearly necessitated an overhaul of the entire administrative system of governance starting from the village panchayats (council of five elders elected by a village to conduct its day-to-day business). Over eighty per cent of the population lived in nearly 600,000 villages and they needed to be involved in the politics of an independent India, but Nehru did little to make this possible. The old colonial apparatus, in which the district official was the fountainhead of power, remained unchanged. Rulers continued to rule from the top and decide what was right and what was wrong for the people, whose participatory role was ignored. To an already entrenched bureaucracy were added legislators of increasingly dubious character and qualifications.

Nehru, because of the immense authority he enjoyed, could have changed all this. Few would have opposed his reforms, just as few questioned his foreign policy. Unfortunately, he was not a practical reformer. His economic formulations, too, with their emphasis on excessive state control of industry, were ill-judged. His strength lay in his secularism. Though a consummate Brahmin, with all the canniness which has helped the Brahmins (who form a mere three and a half per cent of India's population) to control the levers of power for centuries, he did not stoop to playing India's religious communities against each other. Nor was he corrupt, as many of his successors would prove to be.

He was succeeded by a very unlikely man. People found it difficult to believe that Lal Bahadur Shastri – short, gentle and unassuming – could ever replace his charismatic predecessor but, in the brief span of nineteen months of his Prime Ministership, he rose magnificently to the occasion. A man of impeccable integrity and self-confidence, he drew his strength from the traditions of the land in which he was born and educated. He had never been abroad and was not burdened by *isms*. India had shaped his outlook and his ethics.

At first people tittered when they saw him in the newsreels. They found him an unconvincing helmsman of an unmanageable land, but gradually he was accepted as that rare person who seemed more interested in coming to grips with India's problems than trying to solve the world's. His conduct both before and during the second Indo-Pakistan war, in September 1965, elevated him to the pantheon of India's greats in people's hearts and minds.

*

There were personal tragedies in store for me before the end of 1964. I lost, within weeks of each other, my father, who died of a heart attack; my warm and loving aunt, who had been almost a mother to Rasil and me; and then her brother. These three deaths ended a chapter in our close family history. The India we had known was being edged out to make way for a very different country.

Meanwhile, I had started work on my book *India and the Future of Asia*. In the course of my research I visited Japan twice, as well as Thailand, and I made a second visit to Cairo. In 1965 I went to South Vietnam, the Philippines and Australia. Landing in Saigon was quite an adventure. It was a city under siege and the Viet Minh in the surrounding countryside made it dangerous for incoming aircraft. There was every chance of being hit by the Viet Cong's ground fire, and as our plane came steeply towards the runaway, it almost seemed as if we were going to crash. With death all around it, Saigon was intensely alive. It was an amazing mosaic of pushing and jostling people crowding the cafés, hotels, nightclubs and massage parlours, with an endless movement of American and South Vietnamese military, police and civilians driving every kind of vehicle. I managed to get a good room at the Continental Palace Hotel, an old colonial structure with impressive columns, generous spaces, high ceilings and an open-air terrace restaurant. It faced an old church, and beyond it, on the other side of the square, was the Caravelle Hotel, on the top floor of which was the Press Club, the watering hole to which all the media repaired. There were hundreds of them in Vietnam.

With the help of several friends, I met a number of influential people, who tried to brief me on the incoherent and impossible situation in Vietnam. Barry Zorthian, the US government's chief information officer, who had formerly been posted in Delhi, arranged to have me put on a flight to one of the fighting zones and as we drove to an Australian unit for briefing after landing on a military strip, we passed a jeep which had blown up a short while before. Bodies and limbs were still scattered everywhere.

After Vietnam and a brief stay in Hongkong I arrived in the Philippines. Manila's lifestyle was lavish, and its alliance with the US appeared to guarantee its stability, although such an alliance did not seem to be working for the Vietnamese. But the Philippines and Vietnam were similar in the schism that existed between the shanty-dwellers and the privileged rich of both countries, and in the remoteness of the leaders from those they professed to lead.

The Philippine leadership was somewhat similar in this respect to the elite emerging in India. In my country, too, a deep divide was developing between those making their way to the top at any cost – the political, corporate and professional elite – and the underprivileged majority. Visually the capitals provided the most obvious comparison – each with its islands of affluence surrounded by sprawling slums.

*

After further travels in Australia, the US, Canada and Europe, I returned home in August 1965 to find India on a collision course with Pakistan. In a little over three weeks the two would be at war, and once again it would be over Kashmir.

The bloodshed which had attended the unnatural birth of India and Pakistan in 1947 had spread within two months to the beautiful border state of Jammu and Kashmir. This magnificent stretch of land,

4. The Sixties: The Pivotal Years

the size of Britain, or what was once West Germany, has the majestic snow-covered Himalayas as a backdrop and boasts breathtaking lakes, valleys, rivers and pine forests. Rich in culture, the three regions of Jammu, Kashmir Valley and Ladakh are home, respectively, to Hinduism, Islam and Buddhism. With their creative skills the people of the valley produce wonderful crafts such as hand-woven carpets, shawls, silks and woolen fabrics, walnut-wood furniture, papier mâché and metal work. They grow the finest saffron, apples, pears, almonds and walnuts. The incredible beauty of the land draws tourists from the world over.

Once the playground of the Mughal Emperors who had been drawn by its sheer physical beauty and bracing mountain air, this entire region fell to the victorious Sikh Emperor, Ranjit Singh, at the beginning of the nineteenth century. It became a part of the Sikh empire carved by his military victories out of the territories, states and strongholds of the Afghans, Mughals and others who had ruled India for more than 700 years. He established his capital at Lahore from where the Mughals and Afghans had for many years exercised their sway over India.

His death in 1839, however, put paid to his vision of a prosperous and redoubtable Sikh state dominating the northern reaches of the Indian subcontinent, and keeping at bay the invaders who came from beyond the Hindu Kush mountains. His successors with their vicious infighting weakened the Sikh kingdom and it became a part of British India in 1849. Before that, in a complicated round of treaties, indemnities, concessions and much else, the British had detached several territories from the Sikh empire, including Jammu and Kashmir. The wily Gulab Singh, a Dogra, not a Sikh, had been the ruler of Jammu and a vassal of the Sikh king. Now he was named the independent Maharajah of Jammu. When, with remarkable foresight, he offered to pay ten million rupees out of the indemnity levied on the Sikhs, the British threw in Kashmir as well. This more than doubled his territories, which had now become another dependable sphere of imperial influence in the sprawling Indian subcontinent.

This is the Jammu and Kashmir over which India and Pakistan were to fight three wars (1947, 1965 and 1971). Kashmir was the direct cause of the first two, and it has been at the core of the bitter and unresolved dispute between the two countries.

After Independence, when the subcontinent's former princes merged their states with either India or Pakistan, Kashmir's Maharaja chose neither. He harboured hopes of a sovereign independent Kashmir. As a Hindu ruler of a predominantly Muslim populated state, with two antagonistic powers poised on either side of him, he

79

was sitting on dynamite, though he seemed unaware of it. When Pakistan lit the fuse in October 1947 by sending thousands of tribesmen across the border into Kashmir, a thoroughly shaken Maharaja ceded his state to India and departed from the capital, Srinagar, on October 26. By then the tribesmen had reached the outskirts of Srinagar which had just one squadron of cavalry. India responded swiftly. She flew in more troops and equipment in a massive airlift and pushed back the Pakistanis after bloody fighting. Though they still control some of the territory today, Pakistan had suffered a humiliating defeat. Jammu and Kashmir had been saved.

That humiliation has rankled, and the 1965 war was the second attempt to resolve the contentious issue of Kashmir through force of arms. Emboldened by the massive military aid she had received from the US between 1956 and 1962 which had changed the balance of military strength in her favour, Pakistan again opted for aggressive action. Two other factors influenced Pakistan: India's defeat by China in 1962 and Pakistan's assiduous wooing of the victor. Her improved relations with China encouraged her into believing that Beijing would collude with her in an Indo-Pakistan conflict. She also assumed that India's best formations would be facing the Chinese on her eastern borders and not in the west where Pakistan was planning to surprise her. Both assumptions proved wrong.

As in 1947, so also in 1965, Pakistani irregulars, guerillas, trained saboteurs and agents infiltrated into the Kashmir Valley, starting in January. By July there had been 1,800 violations of the cease-fire line, and in August it became obvious that Pakistan's clandestine activities were aimed at creating a major insurrection in Srinagar, severing access to the state capital. The plan was for a Revolutionary Council (ostensibly of Kashmiri people) to proclaim the state's independence from India. The Council's 'Proclamation of the War of Liberation', to be broadcast over Radio Kashmir on August 9, 1965, would be the signal for Pakistani forces to move into Kashmir in strength.

The Western Command of the Indian Army, who so far had confined their operations to mopping up the infiltrators, now decided to launch an offensive against some of Pakistan's bases and supply lines. On September 1 Pakistan launched a major counter-offensive with the aim of cutting off Kashmir from the rest of India. This was the start of the twenty-two-day war.

Fortunately India's Prime Minister, Lal Bahadur Shastri, was a man of determination and courage. He had spelt out India's policy in straightforward terms: any aggression against Kashmir would be seen as an attack on India. In the event of such an aggression the Indian Army would cross the international border. So when Pakistani forces and armour launched their counter-offensive in Kashmir, two Indian Army Corps crossed into Pakistan and moved menacingly towards the cities of Lahore and Sialkot. When the cease-fire was declared on the night of September 22-23, after three weeks of bitter fighting, Pakistan had been decisively defeated.

Militarily, this short war proved once again that it is not armour or weapons so much as leadership, from the highest command to the officers in the field, that counts. Pakistan's superiority in armour – she had sophisticated Patton tanks while India still relied on ancient Centurions and Shermans – failed to win the day. The pivotal role in the war was played by Lt. Gen. Harbaksh Singh, GOC-in-Chief, Western Command, who showed superb military judgment and leadership, visiting his Corps commanders, divisions, brigades, regiments, battalions and companies, often in the thick of battle, at all hours of the day or night. His excellent relationship with the equally outstanding Lt. Gen. Jogindar (Jogi) Singh Dhillon, General Officer Commanding the XI Corps, was probably due to the fact that the decisive battles were fought in Punjab, the land they had both grown up in and whose fighting traditions and lore were deeply rooted in both of them.

With this background, it was inevitable that Harbaksh would turn down the advice of the Army Commander, General J.N.Chaudhari, that the XI Corps, which faced the Pakistanis in Punjab, should fall back behind the Beas River after some initial reverses in early September. This move would have meant abandoning to the enemy Punjab's territories west of the Beas River, including the holy city of Amritsar. To Harbaksh this was unthinkable.

At a reception in Rashtrapati Bhavan (the President's House) in New Delhi, which followed the presentation of awards for the 1965 operations, President Radhakrishnan, with Harbaksh and Jogi sitting on either side of him, said in a voice loud enough for Chaudhari to hear: 'We were told to expect bad tidings, but both of you saved the country.' It became common knowledge later that Chaudhari had prepared Shastri and Radhakrishnan to expect a military reverse in the Punjab.

The important question today is: did India's political leadership learn lessons from this war? Looking back on events since then, the answer is, no. The same errors of judgment continue to be made, and the blinkered outlook of politicians and civil servants still influences military affairs. The military establishment has still not been restructured along lines that other major democracies have chosen for their armed forces. The concept of Joint Chiefs of Staff, responsible for the administration of the armed services and under the overall control of a Minister, with no civil servants in-between, is a logical step the Indian government should have taken as far back as the fifties. But instead of experienced professionals dealing with the affairs of the armed forces, the civil service continue to do so.

In strategic matters and planning for contingencies the Chiefs of Staff would serve national security needs better, and in times of war they would jointly conduct operations, with a Supreme Commander in overall command of all the services. In the 1965 operations the Air Chief unilaterally withdrew the air force and severely handicapped operations on the ground in the Western Sector, whereas if there had been a unified command under Harbaksh, with the Air Force functioning under him, it would have helped to shorten the war and lower the casualty rate. The Indian leadership still ignores these considerations. Successive governments, lacking the will and a larger vision, continue to mistrust the nation's military and gravely endanger India's security.

Another lesson of the 1965 war concerns the wartime role of civilian populations. General Dhillon praises the part played by them. 'It was a valiant role. When we had to give ground to the enemy in Khem Karan there was no panic or criticism – only a stoic acceptance of the situation and an orderly, disciplined, deliberate evacuation which did not create any administrative or other problem for us. None of the other towns and villages were evacuated. There was no fear. The shortage of transport had forced us to take on hire hundreds of civilian trucks to augment the army's own resources. The drivers came with their trucks and moved and behaved in an exemplary manner; they obeyed orders like soldiers in uniform and showed complete unconcern about exposing themselves to risks against which there was no cover.'

Harbaksh has stories to tell with the same message. The first news of the infiltration campaign launched by Pakistan in Kashmir had come from a young herdsman, Mohammed Din. While tending his cattle on August 5, 1965, he had been approached by two armed strangers who wanted information. They offered him money for it. 'The lad grew suspicious and under the ostensible excuse of complying with their request rushed off to the nearest police station at Tangmarg. Within a short space of time the army was alerted and a strong patrol was on its way. In the ensuing action the group of infiltrators disintegrated.' Another villager, Wazir Mohammad, came across armed men who looked unfamiliar and alerted a nearby army unit which promptly launched mopping-up operations. There were many instances of this nature.

If notice had been taken in New Delhi of the wartime role of civilian populations, the situation in the crucial border states of Punjab and Kashmir would not have deteriorated to its present crisis. Punjab alone has well over half a million armed forces (including paramilitary forces and armed police) to keep insurgency under control. There are as many in Kashmir. Successive central governments, by using force to deal with dissent in these two states, have created a dangerous and unmanageable problem for the future. With their anger on the boil, the civilian populations cannot be expected to help the military in the future. Will the Indian Army have to fight the next war on two fronts – one against the country's own discontented populations and the other against the enemy? This was not a concern in 1965. It is now.

But though many of the inherent weaknesses of India's political class had begun to surface in the sixties, it was a peaceful decade compared to what was in store in the seventies and eighties.

*

Earlier that year, while still in New York, I was lunching one day with Philip Johnson in June, at his favourite corner table in the Grill Room of the 'Four Seasons' restaurant which he had designed in the Seagram building. I told him it was odd that he had never been to India – a country with some of the world's greatest architectural masterpieces. his reply was, 'Why don't I do it over Christmas?'

'Why don't you?' I said.

He arrived on December 21 to spend two weeks with me. I had arranged a hectic schedule for him – including visits to Agra, Fatehpur Sikri, Khajuraho, Jaipur and Chandigarh – and the impressions of his visit he sent me on returning to his own familiar world made fascinating reading, especially his comments on Le Corbusier's buildings in Chandigarh.

Chandigarh is the city Corbusier designed for the capital of the portion of Punjab which came to India after Partition in 1947, when Lahore, which had been the capital of the undivided state, went to Pakistan. My friends and I took Lahore's loss as a personal affront. When we were in college, we had spent our Christmas holidays there each year, and spent the rest of the year planning our next visit. Lahore was magical: its women were vivacious and seductive, its Mughlai and north-Indian food mouth-watering, its boulevards, restaurants and bazaars vigorous and zestful.

Chandigarh is unique architecturally, but lacks the colour, texture and soul of a traditional Indian city. I am sure it will acquire these qualities one day. Credit for its existence goes to Nehru who decided to send emissaries around the world to find the finest designer for the new capital, and that is how Corbusier came to be chosen.

Before his visit to India, Johnson, in a review of Corbusier's *Complete Works, Vol. V* had written: 'It is a real proof of our greatness as a cultural period that such an architect as Le Corbusier was given the job of building on such a scale. (Should the Western world get the credit since the city is in the Orient?)' An excellent observation. But he could have added that, although Corbusier had been denied the opportunity to design even a single building in the US till then, India had given him an entire city to design!

After his visit, Philip Johnson wrote to me:

The clearest thing that comes to mind, of course, is confusion. A talk with you and your extremely brilliant friends and associates is as exhilarating as an Oxford parliamentary discussion would be in England. And yet, there seems to be an entirely separate and different world that is apart: old Delhi, the villages, and the slums. A Westerner like myself can have no contact with that other world. It is so different from ours that it is somehow frightening ...

... More new things (were) thrown at me, more visual novelties than my eyes have ever come across before in such a short time. Indeed, that is the sharpest of my impressions – the totally new visual world that I was plunged in without preparation. My schoolbooks taught Greek and Roman and Gothic architecture, not Hindu or Moslem. It is quite a wrench to the mind, and I am still sorting out the impressions ...

The easiest thing for me to grasp are the city plans, but that may be only because my eyes are peeled at the present time for aspects of cities rather than buildings. The top of the list is, of course, Fatehpur Sikri, with Tughlaqabad second ...

... The disappointment (of Chandigarh) was in no way the architecture. Corbusier remains the great master of interlocking space modulators. The ramps behind the vaults of the High Court, the entrance spaces of the Assembly building; experiences like these will be important throughout architecture. But the *city* of Chandigarh as a place for humans to congregate, strikes me as a total disaster. Even if he did want to create monuments out in the open countryside, even granting that this might be a viable approach to a city, there is no possible relation physically among the three buildings that are there, nor any possible relation of the government center to the city they are in. Even L'Enfants' Washington was a better idea. It seems to me that Corbusier must have taken his idea for a government center from Louis XIV's Versailles.

Unlike Philip Johnson, who only admired Corbusier and not Chandigarh, I have always admired both. Earlier Peter Blake had written to suggest I should not 'let those sons of Allah drop any firecrackers on the place'. This was in 1965 when India and Pakistan were fighting each other. He said he was 'putting together a whole issue on Le Corbusier ... What would you think if, as a memorial to Le Corbusier, we collected enough cash, worldwide, to finish, completely, his center for Chandigarh?'

Philip's impression that there was 'no possible relation physically among the three buildings there' was the result of this incomplete centre.

Peter attended an architectural seminar in Delhi that year, and wrote of the vivid impressions he formed of India and her people.

First, there was New Delhi, Lutyens's incredible, vast, overwhelming, mindboggling statement about who was who and what was what – a staggering demonstration of British imperial power.

The Raj Path – so vast that you could hardly see the buildings at the Viceroy's end from the arch in the middle – was virtually empty: now and then a car; now and then a bicycle; now and then an Indian jogger or other athlete (I remember a rather fat and surprising lady in shorts and T-shirt doing pushups on the lawn, in the shade, of course!).

And then there was Chandni Chowk, in old Delhi – so chaotic, so crowded, so colorful, so demented, so full of life and excitement and so noisy, so marvellously cacophonous – the very antithesis of the Raj Path. Nobody had designed it, and yet it was the only place really worth being in, in Delhi. It was what urban life was all about.

I went to Chandigarh, of course, and admired Corbu's unbelievable buildings, and the setting of this town against the foothills of the Himalayas; but I couldn't help thinking of Chandni Chowk and noticing how little Chandigarh seemed to reflect the life of India's people.

Joe Passonneau, who used to be the Dean at Washington University's School of Architecture in St. Louis, once told me that you go to India (if you are American or European) and you either hate it, or you never want to leave. I think I never wanted to leave.

1965 was the year of my architectural enlightenment. Basil and Joan Spence had also come to stay with me in April and we had – along with some other friends – spent two weeks on houseboats at Srinagar in Kashmir. Basil and I talked for hours as we were rowed in a *shikara* (a colourfully cushioned, flat-bottomed boat) through the lotus leaves of the idyllic Dal Lake. Though he, Philip and Peter came from entirely different backgrounds, they all had in common a profound understanding of architecture. Each responded differently to the stimulus of India. While Philip Johnson found the 'other world' (Old Delhi, the villages and the slums) frightening, to Peter Blake it was seductive. Basil Spence was comfortable with both the old and the new, as he had convincingly proved in his design for rebuilding Coventry Cathedral, which German bomber raids had destroyed during World War II.

When Basil had taken me to see Coventry, I was struck by his bold attempt at turning Britain towards an acceptance of the new without subverting the principle of co-existence with the old. He gave his ideas practical form by including bombed-out remains of the old Cathedral in his design for the new one: a superb integration of the architecture of another age with contemporary design.

Largely as a result of these extended conversations in 1965, it was becoming clear to me that the principles which influence the approach to architectural and urban problems, can extend beyond the design of buildings and cities: they can be equally appropriate to the shaping of political, economic and social attitudes. Existing traditional patterns of life cannot be ignored in order to make way for what is perceived as 'modern' design – especially when it is not in conformity with a country's resources and climate and the needs and customs of the population. In the same way, economic and social policies are not valid either if they ignore the legacy of history. That is what happened when the colonial administrative apparatus which India had inherited – complete with the imperial preference for rule from the top – was unquestioningly adopted by the newly independent India. Moreover, Western models of economy and technology were accepted wholesale without any attempt to integrate the special traditional skills of millions of Indians.

My involvement with design and urbanisation was thus opening up new possibilities of political commentary and analysis.

The generally accepted rules of democracy were about to be flouted as 1966 dawned on an unsuspecting country. On January 10 Lal Bahadur Shastri died of a heart attack – tragically, at a moment of great personal triumph, after signing a peace agreement with Pakistan's President Ayub. Within hours of the news of his death men of political power swung into action in New Delhi. They ranged from the Chief Ministers of the Union's sixteen states to legislators, party workers and lobbyists, and the outcome of the eight days of feverish and furtive parleying, horse-trading, arm-twisting and brow-beating which followed was the choice of Indira Gandhi as the leader in Parliament of the party in power and the future Prime Minister of India.

She had been eighteen when her mother, Kamala, died and Nehru, despite his preoccupations with the Independence movement, had tried to fill the void in many ways. With his intellect, vision, and wide-ranging view of history, he shared his perceptions, concerns and assessment of people with his only child, writing her some of the most moving and memorable letters from jail, where he frequently found himself during the freedom struggle. Later, when he became Prime Minister and after her marriage to Feroz Gandhi had foundered, she was his constant companion and confidante, with an insider's view of the complex play on India's political chessboard. Then, in 1959, she was elected President of the Indian National Congress, the country's dominant political party. As Nehru aptly put it: 'At first Indira Gandhi had been my friend and adviser, then she became my companion and now she is my leader.'

But her election to the Prime Ministership was not without its share of ironies, because the factor which finally influenced the Congress Party's kingmakers to chose her was that in their view she was a person who could be manipulated – made to carry out their policies and political directives. It was a fatal miscalculation, an astonishing misreading of her character. While those who brought her to power would soon be consigned to history's dustbins, Indira Gandhi would go from strength to strength for sixteen years, as we shall see in the next chapter.

*

As if to compensate for the new and suspect political class which was beginning to spread through the capital, Delhi provided pleasant diversions as well. Its geographical location and its capital status meant that it had its fair share of visitors. An amusing interlude at about that time was provided by two of them, David Holden and Anthony Armstrong-Jones (Lord Snowdon). David, an old friend and a correspondent of the London *Sunday Times*, telephoned me one evening. They were doing a cover story on India for the paper, with David writing the text and Snowdon taking the pictures.

The evening turned into a party. Vasant Sheth, who was visiting Delhi for a couple of days, also dropped by, to be joined a little later by Atma and Sushi Jayaram through whom I had first met David Holden. After several rounds of the good stuff, it was generally agreed that we should go to the Moti Mahal, an eating place located in a downmarket setting in Old Delhi known for its great Mughlai dishes. It consisted of countless tables and chairs in a sprawling courtyard with a troop of *Qawwali* singers seated on a raised platform. (The words of the *Qawwali* – a form of singing that flourished during the Muslim period and is as popular today – are mostly devotional, though some are quite *risqué*.)

Even though the place was packed on this particular evening, Kundan Lal, the owner of Moti Mahal, found us a table near the singers. The leader of the *Qawwali* group, a brilliant performer but ugly as sin, was in full tilt, prompting his singers to outdo him if they could. To add weight to his emotional outpourings he kept pitching garlands of marigolds at us from the flowers his admirers had heaped before him. It wasn't long before Snowdon was recognised and we promptly had a crush of curious people ringing us. For a while it seemed we would have a small riot on our hands – always possible in India at short notice – which the Government of India and the British High Commission would have found both embarrassing and unamusing, since Snowdon had arrived a day before he was officially expected in order to spend it incognito in Delhi.

*

A visit to Scandinavia in August that year saw the start of an enduring friendship with a remarkable Finnish woman, Armi Ratia. It lasted till her death in October 1979. Armi became a legend in her own lifetime. Her Marimekko range of fabrics, and later dresses, which she started producing on a modest scale in 1951 and which at the time of her death were known worldwide, had put some of the great *haute couture* houses to shame – a spectacular achievement for a woman who was born seven years before the Finnish Republic, in the province of Karelia, later a part of the Soviet Union. As a child, Armi saw her homeland and everything her family owned destroyed in the devastating Winter War with Russia in 1939. She had escaped with a raincoat and a gas mask. Confiding that she had nothing else to wear under the raincoat, she said, 'my family burnt their houses and escaped so that the Russians wouldn't find anything when they came. All three of my brothers were killed in the fighting and so was my sister's husband.' These experiences not only instilled the survivor's instinct in her but proved enriching too – because from her tragedies came an enduring warmth and respect for others with promise: for all those artists and designers who produced the bold, colourful, fun-filled and startling designs with which Marimekko exploded on the staid Western scene.

I met Armi through Rebecka Tarschys, the art critic of Sweden's *Dagens Nyheter*, who invited me to fly from Stockholm to Helsinki with her, for a visit with her friend, Armi Ratia. After a couple of days in Helsinki, we drove out to Bokars, Armi's retreat on the Baltic, 75 kilometres east of Helsinki. She was in the process of entertaining over seventy people to lunch – half of them houseguests – on the rolling lawns of Bokars, which reached out to the sea. She entertained with flair and made me feel that the party was just for me, which was far from being the case. Her looks and personality helped, but what set her apart was the aura she created around her. This communicated the presence of a person with will-power, energy and a limitless zest for life.

If inviting friends to feast at a lavish spread to the acompaniment of a prodigious amount of drinking is in the very nature of the Finns, Armi, by general acclaim, was a pace-setter in the field. I can vouch for it, since I very nearly drowned myself in the aftermath of an evening at which, as usual, she had about fifty people to dinner. It was held in what was formerly a cow-shed but which with considerable imagination she had converted into a setting for her parties. The cattle-trough which ran through the centre of this long building had been made into a receptacle for hundreds of candles. And on either side of this pool of shimmering light, tables and chairs were laid out for dinner with the buffet and drinks at one end, and the orchestra at the other.

We got off to a good start at around seven that evening and after generous rounds of vodka, schnapps and wine, accompanied by a great deal of food and much dancing – during which one of the more inebriated and enthusiastic dancers nearly cremated himself on the candles – we were on our brandies when, around eleven, Armi announced that it was time for the sauna. I had never heard of this before and, in the benign frame of mind I was in, assumed that it was yet another drink, or an exotic Finnish dance we were about to get into, or, when people started to get up, that it might be an anthem. With most guests already headed for the mysterious sauna, the four of us left behind finally caught up with them in a building by the edge of the sea. People had already shed their clothes in a large covered area – open to the water – and had disappeared through a door. As the other three started to undress, I fell into the mood and stripping with equal alacrity was soon in the buff. But at the mention of steam, I said I couldn't go in: it would make the starch in my turban run, and a limp and starchless turban just wouldn't do. Whereupon one of the comely members of our group took off her pink frilled shower cap and perched it on my turban.

Our entrance created quite a stir, but things soon settled down, and after we had sweated profusely for twenty minutes or so there was a general livening up as everyone swatted themselves with twigs of birch leaves and then headed out of the door and on to a long, narrow jetty which projected out into the sea. Running single-file on it and jumping into the cold sea water where it ended, was an integral part of what the sauna was about, which I of course didn't know. I was so caught up with enthusiasm for the sport and, having earlier matched the Finns drink for drink, I clean forgot that I couldn't swim. Only after taking a flying leap into the Gulf of Finland did I realise what I was in for. Fortunately the SOS I managed to bellow out before going under was heard by Armi who quickly sent a strapping Finn diving after me. She sent another one after the pink frilled cap with my turban in it which was lazily drifting away towards Leningrad. We were both rescued, but with the quantities of Baltic seaweed and water I had swallowed some pumping out was needed to restore me to my former combative condition.

Bokars reflected Armi's personality. Its generous sweep of lawns and meadows embraced the sea. It also captured the wildness of the offshore islands and beyond them the Gulf, on the other side of which lay Russia. There were many houses, cottages and barns, and a windmill, on the grounds. *The pièce de résistance* was Siikavaara, the 120-year old family house she had transferred piece by piece from Karelia, to be built in a meadow at Bokars. Because of the many houseguests, Armi had for a while given me her bedroom and this in itself was a memorable experience. Not only because of the art works, memoirs and manuscripts with which it was filled but more so because of the huge window through which she could always see Siikavaara. It reminded her, she told me, of her childhood; of the distant past with her parents, brothers and sisters, when she had spent the few happy years she was to know for a long time.

Armi had insisted that Marimekko should produce fabrics which brought brilliant splashes of colour to a people just emerging from the grey and wasting years of a long war. The designs of Marimekko dresses – authentic and not imported from London or Paris – represented an imaginative break with tired and repetitive clichés.

A few years after my visit to her, Armi came to spend some days with me in Delhi and she was staggered by the range of skills and talents of India's craftsmen, and the limitless scope they offered. Armi showed us how much we could do in India, given our great traditional skills in producing cottons, silks, handprinted and woven fabrics and much else. We lacked just one thing: the adventurous spirit; the confidence to cast off the old forms and the nagging doubts which inhibit inventiveness and innovation. When I contrasted the originality and distinctive nature of Marimekko's creations with our own imitative 'fashion industry', it was obvious that we needed to imbibe some of the Finns' fierce sense of freedom and uninhibitedness; so we could approach with more confidence the opportunities that lay before us.

4. The Sixties: The Pivotal Years

I was not to see Armi again until May 1979 when I spent a few days with her in Helsinki and Bokars. Sadly, in October of that year she died.

*

As 1966 neared its end, there also ended with it a phase in my life which had started on a celebratory note. The shared, durable and continuing richness which Keeni and I had looked forward to would not, it was becoming obvious, be ours; the many expectations we had in our marriage would remain unfulfilled. Our drifting apart was uncontrived, though several things contributed to it. The most significant was our travels – in opposite directions – with mine largely focussed on Asia to collect material for my first book – which was due in October – and Keeni's visits to Switzerland to be with her son, Adrian. These kept us physically apart for extended periods of time. It was not easy for her to be thousands of miles away from Adrian, whom she adored, and though he visited us during some of his school holidays it did not make up for the absences in-between. The influence on Keeni of her formidable mother, who had never been reconciled to our marriage, did not help either.

Another factor was the vacuum of political perceptions that had grown between us and which we were unable to remove through more meaningful efforts to see one another's viewpoint. To Keeni, Communism was an indecent imposition on a free and just world. She felt that state terror and intimidation alone were keeping the populations of the Communist nations quiet. I saw it differently. While the ruthless aspects of Communist rule were reprehensible, there were hundreds of millions of people in Communist countries who were better-off than they had ever been under the feudal rulers of, say, Russia. This was unacceptable to Keeni.

Nor could we agree on colonialism. Keeni, with her Dutch upbringing, and coming from a family which had considerable economic stakes in the old Indonesia, felt that the immense contribution her people had made to Indonesia had been trashed by post-independence leaders, principally President Sukarno. I was unable to subscribe to the morality, methods or goals of colonial rulers. Their cost to those colonised was enormous, destroying their spirit and self-esteem and substituting in their place a clammy sense of inadequacy and self-hatred. If some of the men and women who came to power in the newly-independent nations could not lay claim to the stature or moral authority which their new responsibilities required of them, it scarcely justified colonial rule.

The effort to tread warily on subjects which led to acrimonious arguments was proving exhausting, as we were clearly unprepared for this sort of emotional anarchism and unaware of the danger it was posing to our marriage. There was no conscious or cruel attempt to reject the relationship, but the effervescence and excitement was going out of it. Our marriage, willed by our romantic ambitions, was no longer working. And though we were not formally divorced for several years, our life together had ended.

*

On the last day of September the postman delivered two advance copies of *India and the Future of Asia*, the official publication date of which had been set at November 14 by Knopf, my publisher. It was a very vitalising experience: this actual feel of a copy of my book in my hands – a culmination of years spent in pursuit of an idea which, though beguiling, had at times seemed elusive and chimerical. A few days later another copy arrived, this time from Faber and Faber who were publishing the book simultaneously in Britain. And then, some weeks later, came advance copies of *Life International* which had given several pages to excerpts from it in its October 31 edition.

*

1967 entailed more travelling than any other year, and began with a trip to Australia in February as a guest of the Australian Government. It was the most carefully planned visit to any country I had been to and took me to Sydney, Adelaide, Melbourne, Canberra and Brisbane. As an Indian, and an Asian, I was particularly keen to get a sense of the 'White Australia Policy' I had read about for years. And I certainly was not helped to form a balanced view when, quite early on in my visit, someone showed me a headline in the December 1960 edition of *The Bulletin*, 'Australia for the White Man'! But the problem of racial prejudice was more serious than these crude manifestations. For many Australian politicians, the latent racial bias of their white constituents meant votes, especially if Asian migration – woefully limited at best – could be played up as a major threat to White Australia. Politicians as a rule are never averse to cashing in on racial bigotry when elections are in the offing, or at times of economic recession, and Australian politicians were no exception. Since elections and recessions seem to recur with monotonous frequency, racial prejudice is kept alive by one or the other.

I was told that, after World War II, it was government policy to provide return fares to possible migrant couples from Northern countries, so that they could see the attractions of Australia for themselves before migrating. Asians, on the other hand, were barred from immigration; they were allowed in limited numbers only towards the end of the sixties and seventies. Not surprising, considering that the Australian immigration minister, Arthur Calwell, had in 1947 spelt out his government's concerns in perfectly unambiguous terms: 'We have twenty-five years at most to populate this country before the yellow races are down upon us.' For reasons of brevity, perhaps, he left the brown races out of his call to the barricades.

For the record, the Asian component of the Australian population is barely 3.5 per cent even now. And yet, as late as 1988, the Fitzgerald report on Immigration suggested invidious restrictions on immigrant family reunion rules – rules which would scale down immigration from Asia. Hardly a sensible suggestion, since several parts of Asia beyond Australia are developing, not only economic, industrial and military muscle which could outpace Australia, but, more important, a resurgent sense of Asian self-esteem and pride which will soon come to expect more mannerly policies from her.

Yet, the positive easily outweighed the negative in the character of the Australian individual. I could see a sustained opposition to political shortsightedness and chicanery on the part of intellectual and liberal Australians. There was also an extraordinary frankness and warmth among men and women at every level which transcended any latent racial streak they might have. This, combined with the unique Australian characteristic of cutting through social humbug with an easy informality, is a most appealing quality and one which was reflected in the political leaders I met on a personal level. Each of them – starting with Harold Holt, the Prime Minister, Paul Haasluck, the Foreign Minister, and the leader of the Opposition, Gough Whitlam – were less guarded and more forthcoming than most of their counterparts I had encountered in other countries. During the long interviews with them in Canberra, in which the racial question was adroitly side-stepped, or the racialists were roundly renounced in colourful language, what did become clear was that the impediment of the British connection in framing Australia's external policies was becoming less of a factor. Indeed twenty-five years later this feeling has grown and Paul Keating, the Prime Minister, has now advocated an end even to the purely symbolic ties with Britain.

But more impressive than anything else I experienced was the calibre of their painters, sculptors, ceramicists, architects and weavers. I do believe that the reason why Australia, given its limited population, has produced such gifted artists is its isolation. The incredible distances that need to be covered to reach it have, I believe, in part provided the impetus to Australians to prove that their country can produce persons of outstanding creative flair equal to the best anywhere. Unlike older countries, with their long artistic traditions, contemporary Australia, with no such history to fall back upon, is establishing its own standards of creative excellence.

*

On October 17, 1967 I landed at Tel Aviv's Lod Airport, on my way to spend the first night of my stay in Israel in Haifa's Dan Carmel Hotel. I had arrived just four and a half months after the Six-Day War.

Over the years I have carried a picture in my mind of two men contentedly passing the time of day on a bench outside Haifa. That picture symbolises many things for me: the end of a search spread over centuries; the rewards of perseverance and faith; the security of a cherished homeland; the right to spend life's last years in peace and dignity. Those two men represent in microcosm the story of a dispersal which began after the Babylonian captivity two and a half millennia ago. And during my week in Israel, as a guest of the government, the existential feeling of living in the past and the present at the same time never once left me.

The Biblical associations of the places I visited – Nazareth, Tiberias, Beersheba, Jerusalem – and the rugged landscape seemed so familiar because the rocky hills and ravines were the setting for all the legends we had been taught in the Convent School. These elements combined to create powerful feelings, as if I had a personal involvement with this land and its people. The timing of my visit, too, contributed to the feeling. As I walked the streets of Tel Aviv and other cities and mingled with the Israelis, I found myself deeply affected by the upbeat mood of these recently-victorious people. In a strange way it took me back twenty years when, after moving to Poona, I had been troubled by the indifference of the people there to the bloody post-Partition massacres that were at that very time rocking Punjab and the neighbouring territories in North India. Part of me had attributed their insensitivity to the tyranny of size: to the fact that geography can militate against the cohesiveness of a nation, prevent its constituents from identifying with tragedies taking place at another end of a large country. Nor does multiplicity of religions and languages help the cause of cohesiveness. My visit to Israel confirmed my thesis. Because of the country's small size, no Israeli – this is in no way meant to overlook the contributory factors of religion and Jewish history – would survive a national disaster, which, by its very definition would endanger the life of every single individual. This greatly helps the collective Israeli determination to fight and survive. Not so in India. Our tragedies, throughout our history, though they bloodied the land and took a terrible toll, never affected all of India at any given time. They could not, because India was too large. And finally, when the entire land came under the sway of a single power, it was too late and we gave in to whatever fate had in store for us. We adjusted to it and learnt to live under the new dispensation.

The difference between our history of compromise, adjustment, acquiescence and surrender, and the Jewish experience is that, though the Jews also acquiesced and compromised in the past, now having achieved their Promised Land they are not about to sit back and relax; to endanger the prize they have won – the vision of which had helped them survive their tragedies. The lessons learnt from their past weaknesses, the success of the Zionist revolution and the inspiration Israelis derive from their return to their historic homeland have all helped to create a new generation of assertive and confident Jews. The young have turned their backs on the ghetto mentality. Here again the difference between our two countries stood out.

We have been able neither to nurture and harness the emotional resurgence which attended Independence nor to convert it into a new dynamic which can help us shed the shackles of our slavish past and move us towards the promised future. Our politics and administrative system, though participatory in theory, are feudal in practice. For the common man, more accurately for hundreds of millions of Indians, the only difference between the old and the new is that the old rulers have been replaced by those of a different complexion. The Promised Land in India is opening up only for a small percentage of the political, bureaucratic, industrial, business and professional elites. Not for the masses of Indians.

*

Israel, by contrast, is the Promised Land for all Jews. Or almost all, since the racial arrogance of European Jewry is beginning to discriminate against Jews of a darker hue. And so are the opportunities offered, sacrifices demanded and dangers faced. It is a wholly participatory state. Not that religion is such a cementing factor as appears from the outside. There are so many interpretations of Judaic thought – some barely tolerant of each other – that the idea of a

religiously cohesive state deriving its strength from its shared Jewishness is far from being the case. The different forms of Judaism
practised in today's Israel could almost be as many religions. The
secular, liberal Zionists make up half the population, and the modern
Orthodox Jews – who favour a secular state but are more religious
than the secularists – constitute about 30 per cent of the population.
The remaining 20 per cent consist of more determined religious
groups of which the majority are implacably Orthodox. Israel's
strength really comes from a sense of shared nationhood. And from
an ever-present awareness of the dangers posed by the adversaries
who surround her.

'Far from having built a "new Jewish identity", or a "new Jew",'
observes Thomas Friedman in his outstanding book *Beirut to Jerusalem*, 'Israel seems to have brought out of the basement of Jewish
history every Jewish spiritual option from the past 3,000 years; the
country has become a living museum of Jewish history ... .' The
number of political parties in a nation of less than five million – there
were over twenty parties when I was there – is also a pointer to the
polarisation taking place over the definition and direction of Israel's
Jewishness.

But I doubt if these divisions are ever allowed to weaken national
security, or the will to fight for Israel's survival, such as divisions in
India do.

Among the striking achievements of the new state were the steps
it had taken to green the deserts, harness scarce water resources and
establish a formidable scientific and technological base. I remember
seeing a narrow water channel taking water all the way from the
fertile North to the southern desert and convert it into a rich agricultural resource. Even though the thrust of Israeli technology was
towards meeting the country's military needs and making it a nuclear power, it was helping hone skills which would place the nation
in the league of major industrial producers.

I was dismayed by reports of Israel's savage response to the
Palestinian protests within her borders. My admiration for the
courage and endurance of the Israelis was tinged with disappointment as I found it difficult to accept that a people who had faced
great persecutions themselves could so savagely repress the un-
armed protests of those under their rule. And if the militant
Zionists of Irgun and other underground groups during Britain's
control of Palestine, had killed, dynamited and destroyed in pursuit of their goals, then the overkill of stone-throwing Palestinians
by the Israeli military was without any justification. Since political
protest is often shaped by circumstances, and the suppressed rage

of the Israeli Arabs eventually took the form of *intifada*, the accumulated wisdom of an ancient people could have devised a more humane strategy to deal with what was essentially a civil disobedience movement.

As a modern state which has much to export – produce, technology, industrial products and impressive agricultural know-how – there is no justification either for Israel's covert help to repressive governments for putting down protest movements by their own people. Sadly, she has shown no aversion to exporting such skills, even to countries of no direct interest to her existence. While there was an understandable need for the priority given to developing one of the world's finest intelligence services, in view of the many West Asian nations committed to Israel's destruction, the marketing of Mossad's skills to distant and corrupt leaderships in exchange for diplomatic recognition or trade preferences is morally indefensible.

Yet it is difficult, despite such instances of political cynicism, to forget the many-faceted appeal of the Israeli personality. Whether as writers, playwrights, artists, architects, craftsmen, scientists, surgeons, businessmen or academics, their pursuit of excellence has taken them to the very top. I was particularly struck by their obsession with archaeology. It seemed as if no one was unaffected by it and the most rewarding way of spending a few days of a holiday would be to go on a 'dig' and perhaps come up with a relic from the soil of their ancient land. I sensed in this an inner need to reach out for contact with the past. To look on the evidence uncovered – of generations which had lived and flourished millennia ago – as a life-line which offered sustenance, pride and proof of their own hopes and beliefs that had sustained the Jewish determination to return to the Promised Land.

If I had to single out one person I enjoyed talking to most, I would say it was Yigal Allon, the Minister of Labour, a highly decorated General and a key figure in the ruling Labour Party. I called on him at his home early one Sunday morning. He proceeded to make breakfast: slicing the bread, frying the eggs, making tea and very considerately heating the milk too, because I said I had never enjoyed hot tea with cold milk. We settled down to a fascinating discussion. He said he understood the compulsions India faced in not recognising Israel, but he could not understand why a sovereign country like India did not set them aside to acknowledge the undeniable fact of Israel's existence. Or why Mrs Gandhi in June that year had held Israel responsible for the conflict in West Asia. I told him I also found our stand on Israel's recognition indefensible. The manner in which he expressed his views was neither offensive nor reproachful. And that was my experience everywhere in Israel throughout my visit there. (India and Israel have now finally established full diplomatic relations.)

Chapter 5

The Seventies: A Declining Morality

I sometimes wonder whether I am licking the right boots.

Malcolm Muggeridge, *Hero of our Time*

This was the decade of Indira Gandhi. The two lead players on the stage of the Indian subcontinent at the start of the seventies could not have been more different. She was cultivated and aloof, autocratic and imperious, and yet shrewdly disarming and deceptively shy, a poor speaker but one with an intuitive feel for the right phrase. He was big, bluff and impolitic, immoderate in speech, often profane, with Bacchanalian appetites, a twisted sense of history and a misplaced confidence in his military abilities.

Fate in its own way had assigned them historic roles, and while Indira Gandhi played hers to perfection Yahya Khan faced the humiliation of overseeing the destruction of his own country. While Gandhi's star would rise, Khan's would make an ignominious exit from Pakistan's Presidency.

Their dissimilarities were also reflected in the conditions within their countries at the start of the seventies when epic tensions were again building up between India and Pakistan. Indira Gandhi's party had won a landslide victory in the general elections in February 1971, while Yahya Khan, countermanding the results of the elections held in Pakistan after years of military rule, had in March handed East Pakistan to the army. This move would precipitate another war between the two traditional adversaries, giving Indira Gandhi the opportunity to prove herself, not only to the Indian people, but to the world at large.

She had already emerged as a surprisingly astute practitioner of political gamesmanship. Since coming to power in 1966, she had carefully observed the Congress Party's performance in the 1967 elections, which had reduced its majority in Parliament and lost it half the states. Even though she was the Prime Minister, it was clear that the traditional leadership of the Congress was to blame for this debacle. She saw in this an opportunity to go over the heads of the established leadership and develop a personal rapport with the

Of Dreams and Demons

people and perpetuate her own power. But people had to be convinced of her credentials. And she set about this task zestfully, nationalising the major banks and abolishing the Privy Purses of the former Princely rulers which the Constitution had guaranteed as compensation for acceding to India after Independence. She went still further in August of that very same year by getting her candidate, V.V. Giri, elected as India's President, in open defiance of the man whom the 'kingmakers' of the Congress party had chosen and whose candidature she herself had initially agreed to. By using a senior member of her Cabinet against the Party President during this period, she also changed the time-honoured Congress culture of pluralist politics.

On December 1, 1969 she split the Congress in two, bringing to an ignoble end an organisation which for almost a hundred years had symbolised the struggle for India's freedom. The rump organisation inherited by the men who had brought her to power was effectively sidelined, setting a precedent for disgruntled elements in political parties to break away and form their own. The divisive game of party-splitting would be played with much enthusiasm in the years ahead.

So by the time the rundown began for the February 1971 elections, this quiet and cultivated inheritor of the Nehru legacy had emerged as the only person on the political scene who cared about the poor and the dispossessed – who had by a few courageous moves cut the privileged people down to size so she could invest the vast resources now at her command in schemes to uplift the poor. She had crisscrossed the country to bring this message home to the masses, and they trustingly now looked on her as their new messiah. To further drive home the point, she chose a telling slogan for her 1971 campaign: *garibi hatao* ('Remove poverty'). The poor loved it. And when the results came in, she had won with a massive margin.

This, then, was the Indira Gandhi, fresh from her victories and the undisputed darling of the Indian masses, who now faced Yahya Khan. But what caused the tensions between the two nations to increase? The March 25, 1971 crackdown in East Pakistan and the subsequent savagery of the military against the restive Bengali population had led to a growing number of East Bengal refugees moving across the Indian border into West Bengal. A trickle soon became a mass exodus and, by April, three million had reached India's refugee camps. By June the figure stood at five million. At the rate they were moving it was estimated that India would have ten million refugees on her hands by October-November – which she did. They were, moreover, arriving in a volatile and disturbed region of India and

100

creating law-and-order problems. Staggering sums of money were required to feed them and safely contain the epidemics that were breaking out in the camps.

In step with the escalating crisis, domestic pressures were mounting on the Indian Prime Minister to intervene militarily in East Pakistan. And with the formation of a provisional government of Bangladesh on a few acres of no-man's land on India's border – in fact it was housed all along in a building on Calcutta's Theatre Road – there was also a growing demand for its recognition.

The major powers, with the exception of Soviet Russia, applied no political or diplomatic pressure on Pakistan to take the refugees back. Instead, by a masterly sleight-of-hand, they, and the United Nations, in order to get a handle on the deteriorating situation, insisted on treating it as an international crisis, while letting India foot the bill for the millions seeking sanctuary on her soil, although some food for the refugees was received from abroad. The exodus was seen as India's problem, but not if she showed signs of dealing more firmly with Pakistan.

In the face of these conflicting pulls and pressures, Indira Gandhi kept her balance. She refused to opt for a military solution until she had prepared public opinion for it and established before the world the legitimacy of India's efforts to avoid it. She travelled extensively, addressing public meetings: explaining, exhorting, analysing the problem, exuding optimism, involving people and, of course, projecting herself as a leader who could be cool in the face of a looming crisis. Which she was. She also made certain that the USSR would stand by India in the event of a military showdown, especially in view of the Nixon Administration's refusal to differentiate between the Indian and Pakistani roles in the developing crisis. On August 9 India signed a 20-year peace treaty with the Soviet Union, establishing an alliance which would prove of enormous significance in the months ahead.

Indira Gandhi put personal diplomacy on the line as well, by visiting seven Western capitals in October and November to put India's views before those who were complacent. Throughout those months she was amusing yet earnest with her audiences. 'We cannot shake hands with a clenched fist,' she replied once when asked why India had not been able to come to terms with Pakistan. At another time she said, 'Everybody admires our restraint. We get verbal praise, but the others are not restrained and they get arms as well.' But her best remarks were reserved for a letter she wrote to President Nixon after India's victory over Pakistan: 'We are deeply hurt by the innuendos and insinuations that it was we who have precipitated the crisis and have in a way thwarted the emergence of solutions ... Be that as it may, it is my earnest and sincere hope that with all the knowledge and deep understanding of human affairs you, as President of the United States and reflecting the will, the aspirations and idealism of the great American people, will at least let me know where precisely we have gone wrong before your representatives or spokesmen deal with us with such harshness of language.'

Interestingly enough, it was Pakistan who struck the first blow on the evening of December 3 by launching bomber raids over Indian airfields at Amritsar, Pathankot, Srinagar, Avantipur, Uttarlai, Jodhpur, Ambala and Agra. Just after midnight, Indira Gandhi came on the air to announce that India was at war and that same night the Indian armed forces, under the command of Lt. Gen. J.S. Aurora, struck on the eastern front. Simultaneously an offensive was also launched on the western front.

The 14-day war which followed saw the end of Pakistan's control of its eastern territories, the emergence of Bangladesh as an independent republic, and the capture of over 90,000 Pakistani troops by the Indian army. Not surprisingly, the Nixon Administration had ordered a taskforce of the US 7th Fleet in the Pacific – led by the nuclear-powered aircraft carrier *Enterprise* – to head for the Bay of Bengal. Unimpressed by this show of force, Moscow ordered the Soviet Fleet in the Indian Ocean to sail for the East Bengal coast. Fortunately for everyone concerned, Pakistan conceded defeat when the fleets were still some distance from the war zone.

The dark side of the events which changed the balance of power in the subcontinent was India's role in training, arming and encouraging the activities of the Mukti Bahini (an underground movement) within East Pakistan. Its task was to mobilise the population against the largely West Pakistani administration. This it succeeded in doing. Estimates vary as to the number trained by India in camps on the Indian side of the border, since elements of the East Bengal Regiment and East Bengal Rifles who had defected were also inducted into the Mukti Bahini. However, its total peak strength is generally placed at 100,000, out of which there is little doubt that India trained the largest number while supplying them with most of the military hardware.

Against this background India's outraged reaction several years later to Pakistan's covert support of dissident elements in Punjab and Kashmir is somewhat unconvincing, taken at face value. If her own self-interest had necessitated support to a sizeable subversive force in East Pakistan, it was clearly in Pakistan's interest to exploit the subsequent discontent in Punjab and Kashmir, and in India's interest to defuse that discontent politically. This New Delhi did not do.

5. The Seventies: A Declining Morality

Having helped to dismember Pakistan, it failed to provide honest and efficient administrations in Punjab and Kashmir, thus exposing them to the designs of a recently humiliated neighbour. Although Indira Gandhi's successors – from her own party – are to be blamed for the continuing deterioration of the Centre's relations with these two states through the eighties and nineties, the initial mishandling of the situation was her doing.

She was at her best in dealing with a national crisis, but too autocratic in her handling of political dissent. This prevented her from recognising the obvious truism that India's own states could resent New Delhi's arrogance just as much as East Pakistan had resented Islamabad's overbearing ways. Despite the obvious danger of allowing such discontent to grow, her dealings with the states of Punjab and Kashmir became increasingly manipulative and authoritarian and when their people balked at accepting their subservient status in a republican system, the security forces were sent to deal with them: with a situation which required honest governance, more autonomy and greater respect for the states. Because it was *not* a security problem.

The years following India's victory over Pakistan were to reveal another very disagreeable side of Indira Gandhi. Riding a wave of popularity, she was well-placed to pursue a constructive agenda for India. Instead, she proceeded to usher in a period of increasing authoritarianism, debased morality, spreading corruption, political betrayal, dynastic aspiration and divisive policy. All of which was aimed at perpetuating her power. But if she degraded the Indian polity, she did, during her years in office, inject a new dynamic into several sectors, like oil exploration and refining, fertilizer production and scientific research. She insisted on a lesser dependence on foreign aid. But as the new industrial projects were in the public (or state) sector, corruption too escalated. The massive capital investments for new plant and equipment opened opportunities for major bribes which often became the criteria for the orders placed – not the quality of the product but the extent to which the competing manufacturers could be milked. And those who shared in the loot included ministers, legislators, officials, freebooters and fixers. Corruption became an integral part of India's public life, flourishing in the congenial conditions created for it.

*

My second book, *The Struggle for Power in Asia*, was published around this time in 1971. In it I pointed out that India was one of the four nations in the world which was generating true power since she had

103

size, manpower, natural resources and political unity. A nation that had these could resist all forces inimical to her. She also had a 'rule of law, good administration, adult franchise, increasing agricultural prosperity, a broad industrial base, and constitutional safeguards against arbitrary suppression of individual rights'. Our institutions still inspired hope, then.

While the aim of my first book had been to place India's pivotal role in Asia in perspective, in the second I had covered the changes taking place in Asia that Western writers were prone to play down. 'The struggle which is centred in Asia today is destined to shape the world of tomorrow, for the ferment of ideas, aspirations and actions, which has gripped so great a part of the human race, will inevitably leave its imprint on the rest of it. Yet the tragedy of our time is that instead of turning to the Asians, to find out what they think of this struggle on their continent, Western opinion on Asia continues to be shaped by Western minds, catering to Western needs.' I knew this would lead to charges of chauvinism, but that was a minor hazard, and in any event chauvinism was a human, not an exclusively Asian, condition.

What I had found particularly irksome were views such as that of the Swedish economist, Gunnar Myrdal, who had pronounced in his three-volume *Asian Drama*, that 'from a practical standpoint Asian nationalism is hardly more than a phantom', and to support his argument had approvingly quoted Louis Fischer, who saw the unity of Asia as 'a myth, and those who speak in its name are spinning fantasies. The desire to unify Asia politically is an abstraction.' For added effect he said it was 'a type of endeavour in which, alas, quite a few Indians gladly indulge'. Since I disagreed with such rootless and alien preconceptions which did not accurately depict Asian attitudes, I had decided to deal with them in my second book.

No one had the desire – or the ability – to unify Asia politically, and it was incorrect to equate Asian nationalism with a political unification of Asia. Whether it is called nationalism, or any other name, there is a sense of shared concerns in Asia; of common goals; of what constitutes the rightful interests of Asians – in keeping with their self-esteem, as defined by them.

The influencing of many Asian governments by the major powers was an unfortunate fact of Asian political life. And one of the aspirations that many Asians – though not always their leaders – shared was the urge to free themselves from such unsubtle domination. To assess the extent and intensity of such feelings, I had travelled through Asia and seen a live and coherent 'Asianess' striving to assert itself there. I had met many of those who helped shape and influence their countries' policies – often in the wrong direction. Amongst those who gave me time and talked to me at some length were President Ferdinand Marcos of the Philippines; Prime Minister Harold Holt of Australia; Takeo Miki, Foreign Minister of Japan; and Takeo Fukuda, Secretary General of Japan's ruling Liberal Democratic Party.

More than three years later, in 1974, I had a letter from the publishers André Gérard Marabout in Paris offering a contract for a French edition since what I had written still had validity. It appeared as *Le Jeu des Puissances en Asie*. Equally gratifying was the call I had from my friend Jean-Daniel Jurgensen, the French ambassador in India, asking me if I would include their houseguests Edgar Faure and his wife in the dinner I had asked them to, that week. He said that Faure, a former Prime Minister who was at that time the President of the French National Assembly, had read my book before his current visit to India and was keen to talk to me. It felt good to know that an independent Asian view was finally getting across!

*

My first meeting with Indira Gandhi was in the Prime Minister's room in Parliament House, in 1972. I had written her a letter seeking her personal intervention in saving the historic city of Delhi, because 'a new breed of developers and hopeful landlords was on its way to amassing fortunes out of the high property and land values in the Capital', and because 'this combination of unprincipled promoters and ineffective or corrupt officials and politicians, will succeed in destroying Delhi unless steps of far-reaching importance are taken now'. I had suggested the setting up of a Commission through Act of Parliament for overseeing proposals for all major buildings, parks, street furniture and structures which had a bearing on the Capital's historic character. Her sympathetic response came in the form of a phone call from her secretary, Mohni Malhoutra. The Prime Minister, he said, was planning to call a high-powered meeting to discuss the ideas I had outlined in my letter and would like me to participate.

The meeting was held in August. She had asked everyone concerned to attend, including three Cabinet Ministers, chairing it herself for almost two hours. I was astonished by the sensitivity of her remarks on the aesthetics of the physical environment throughout its duration, especially since I was only familiar with her not very reassuring avatar as a politician. I was the only outsider present – all the others represented the government – and since my letter to her was the *raison d'être* for the meeting, she turned to me soon after it began and suggested I explain my concerns on the conservation of Delhi's historicity and form. She brooked no interference – nor showed any impatience herself – even though I insisted on stating my case in some detail.

After I had finished, and the discussion began, her observations proved superior to any of the others. She agreed that a physical heritage of monuments and old structures was a very fragile thing, which could not stand before those more inspired by the idea of making money in the present than preserving the past, unless government intervened. Typical of the bureaucratic mindset was the view advanced by one of her colleagues – obviously averse to yielding any power to an autonomous body – that the Commission should be established by an executive order, and not an Act of Parliament. I disagreed, pointing out that the Commission could just as easily be struck off by another executive order if it became too independent for the vested interests and their sympathisers within the government. As a statutory body it would have both autonomy and longevity. She upheld my view.

Within a year and a half of the meeting, she had ensured the setting up of an Urban Art Commission for Delhi, by an Act of Parliament. My comment on it then, in the January 1974 issue of *Design*, was that: 'Credit for this goes to the Prime Minister, Mrs Indira Gandhi, at whose insistence this concept was given concrete shape, and who found time – despite the pressures on it – to ensure that the proposal was neither shelved, nor diluted along the way. Mrs Gandhi has shown a sympathy and concern for the physical environment which is in marked contrast – but for one or two fine exceptions – to the apathy with which the rest of her colleagues look at the whole range of aesthetics and the arts.'

She asked two of her aides to enquire if I would be willing to head, or serve on, the Commission, but I declined, preferring to stay on the outside and contributing whatever I could through *Design*.

My impression of her sensibilities after this meeting was very different from my assessment of her as a political person, which only accentuated still further the enigma of Indira Gandhi. A cold and unsentimental politician one minute, a sensitive aesthete the next, she could erase in a moment the promise of a winning smile with an icy demeanour. Refined and cultivated, she gathered several advisers around her who were coarse and uncouth. To some extent this was understandable, given the political needs of her office. But their inclusion in her inner councils was puzzling, as was their presence in the Prime Minister's household. This was yet another side of the riddle of Indira Gandhi.

5. The Seventies: A Declining Morality

A group of better-educated political hopefuls had gathered around her too. She was the rising star and they were there to play any role she had in mind for them: as strategists, plotters, conspirators or purveyors of gossip; anything to inveigle themselves into her favour – getting her to accept their indispensability. Some of them had helped her marginally, during the frenetic days before her elevation to the Prime Ministership in 1966. Most of them were of no political consequence. Or standing. Men and women of character and substance seldom make conscientious courtiers. Indira Gandhi, in a spirit of *noblesse oblige*, had been charitable towards them; had rewarded them with Ministries in her Cabinet, party tickets to Parliament and such dispensations, in return for their absolute loyalty. Which is what she was looking for – not merit, experience, maturity and independence but commitment.

The one exception in this 'kitchen cabinet' was my old friend Romesh Thapar, who was not cut out to be a courtier or sycophant by intellect, inclination or temperament. When he did realise, after some years, how political power was changing Indira Gandhi, they parted ways. But the others stayed on – because they loved the trappings of power. Because, given their ambitions and insecurities, they could not conceive of an existence outside the corridors of power.

*

I found myself frequently drawn into passionate and acrimonious debates with the new class of political pretenders, power-brokers and opinionated insiders. Most of these parvenus thrived on political gossip and their real or imaginary proximity to politicians, thereby ensuring for themselves a circle of wide-eyed listeners wherever they arrived to socialise. The social norms had also changed to include these upstarts and confer instant status on them. Even though I was allergic to politicians myself, there was an intriguing – almost hypnotic – quality about the concoctions, disclaimers and fervid political discussions which raged everywhere.

It was this tedious atmosphere in Delhi that set me thinking about buying land – not too far away – for building a farm house, growing fruit trees and getting away from the Capital's asphyxiating atmosphere as frequently as I could. The site I liked best was along the Aravalli hills, beyond the Union Territory of Delhi and on the road to the desert state of Rajasthan. I would occasionally drive out to that stretch of the stark but beautiful Gurgaon-Sohna Road which had the Aravallis on the right and farmlands on either side of it: not very productive farmlands but with a rugged, determined character of their own, as if they refused to give in to the brackish water, the inhospitable soil, the blazing summers of that region.

I succeeded in buying eight acres in May 1973. It was thick with thorn trees which grow wild in India, on usually poor soil. At places the thickets were impenetrable and there was no well or water supply on the site. I was advised against the purchase and told that any well I bored would only produce brackish water, entirely unfit for farming or drinking. But I was adamant, determined to succeed no matter what it took. My three friends, who were to buy adjacent properties, withdrew, after failing to dissuade me.

Inevitably, though we tried boring in half-a-dozen places, we failed to tap fresh water. The soil test reports were equally dismal – the land was very alkaline and fit only for the wild scrub that grew on it. In the absence of earth-moving machinery clearing the thorn trees was also a problem, and they had to be removed manually – a slow and painful process given the vicious thorns which covered the trees and the ground.

The land was finally cleared. And I was confident of improving the soil through leaching and mixing various nutrients in it. But leaching required good water and plenty of it, which was not available. Good water resources of that region – in the form of underground fresh-water springs or channels – were erratically located. According to the villagers, if you stood a cow on any part of the land, you could find brackish water under three of her legs but fresh water under the fourth. It was as unpredictable.

The inspiration for solving the problem came from my earlier visit to Israel: from the narrow water channels I had seen which the Israelis had built for bringing water from their fertile north to the southern desert, converting it into rich agricultural land. So I finally bought a tenth of an acre of land a kilometre away which had clear water below it. I sank a tube-well, laid a four-inch underground pipeline between this water source and my farm, built an elevated water storage tank and another below the ground, and was finally ready to start my farming career.

During the time I was looking for land for my farm, I had experienced something which was to have a profound effect on me and make me face an altogether new challenge in my life. I was driving on the Sohna road on a particularly hot day when I saw a small group on the side of the road trying vainly to flag a bus. As I stopped the car, I saw a young woman in labour who was obviously in need of urgent medical attention which no village *dai* (midwife) could offer. There was a tragic desperation in her family's efforts to get her to a

108

hospital in a nearby town in time. We succeeded in doing that but the images stayed: the dusty landscape, the desperate look on the father's face, the unconcern of those who drove past with unseeing eyes, the fragility of human life.

These impressions lasted long enough for me to resolve to build a hospital there; to prove that private initiative can help in filling the unconscionable gap between the facilities that are accessible, though not necessarily available, to the twenty per cent of our urban people and yet are denied to the other eighty in rural India.

I persuaded my fellow-trustees in a small trust we manage to agree to the idea of a rural hospital. I then asked the State government of Haryana to donate us land, which it did. But the project remained on the back-burner because it needed major funding which our trust's resources were not up to providing.

With the farmhouse completed in 1975 and some of the trees beginning to take root, a new chapter had opened up in my life. I looked forward to my weekends: to escaping from Delhi and laying out a garden, planting an orchard, sowing the wheat and barley fields and furnishing the house I had built with local materials. Using stone from the nearby hills and lime and slate which were available from quarries in that region, I wanted to show that much could be built without cement and steel, the widespread use of which was adding to India's oil bills and foreign exchange indebtedness. After all, India had built some of the world's most exciting buildings long before cement and steel were heard of. My passionate involvement with the project persuaded several friends, including Romesh Thapar, Ebrahim Alkazi (India's foremost theatre director) and Rasil to buy land near me. Each of us could now escape for a while from Delhi into this wholesome environment we were creating for ourselves. But there was no escaping the destructive forces that were about to overtake India.

*

What happened was a climax to a judicial process that had started four years earlier. After the 1971 general elections, Raj Narain, whom Indira Gandhi had defeated in the Allahabad constituency, filed a petition in the High Court accusing her of corrupt campaign practices. Judgments in such cases take years to be delivered due to the work-load on the Courts, so it was not till June 12, 1975 that Justice Jag Mohan Lal Sinha, a reticent, upright man of undeviating commitment to the principles of law, upheld the petition, unseated Mrs Gandhi from Parliament, and debarred her from any elective office for the next six years. This, in spite of the fact that the days and weeks prior to the judgment had not been easy for him. A Member of Parliament had tried to bribe him; he had been shadowed by the central intelligence agencies and his house kept under surveillance in a desperate effort to discover the nature of the judgment he would deliver.

The news of Mrs Gandhi's unseating hit the entrenched politicians, officials and hangers-on with the force of a hurricane. They found it inconceivable that their present positions, privileges and power would have to be given up because of a mere judgment! As the faithful, driven by the apocalyptic vision of a future in a political wasteland, converged on her house urging her to disregard the judgment, Indira Gandhi wavered. She was not unversed in the ways of courtiers and their carnivorous self-concerns. But it was a heady experience to be told by them – and the crowds they kept bringing to her house in government buses and transport – that she was indispensable; that it was her destiny to lead the nation. There was no doubt she was popular with the people, but these crowds were part of a command performance. And she knew it. She was not a naive person.

Indira Gandhi was again on trial. Should she honour the ruling of the Court and resign? Or ignore it? It was a moral trial which she also lost. A few sane voices advised her to resign, appoint a caretaker Prime Minister from her own party, and appeal to the Supreme Court. They were confident that the decision would be in her favour, since the improprieties she had been held guilty of were of a marginal nature. But her finely-honed instinct for survival would not allow it. What if the Supreme Court gave an adverse judgment? Or if the caretaker Prime Minister refused to quit and assembled enough evidence to discredit her still further? There were enough skeletons in the cupboard which could come falling out if she wasn't around to prevent it.

In the end her 28-year-old son Sanjay Gandhi – who had helped stack most of the skeletons there – persuaded her against resigning. Sanjay's emergence on the national scene was the apogee of a phenomenon which has bedevilled Indian politics since Independence. All too frequently, the sons of Cabinet Ministers – even Chief Ministers of some of the states – have lorded it over official establishments, with disregard for constitutional proprieties and simple decencies. But it was the first time that a son, with no political experience or official position whatever, was allowed to take Prime Ministerial decisions. Why did Indira Gandhi, a well-read woman, who had come in contact with some of the finest ethical minds of our times –

in her grandfather's and father's households and as Prime Minister herself – allow this grave transgression?

The answer lies in the conditions which had shaped her contradictory character. As an only child whose beloved mother had died when she was eighteen, her early years had been lonely and frustrating, especially with her father often away either travelling or in jail. Further aggravation was provided by her two strong-willed aunts, Nehru's younger sisters. Indira Gandhi, unable to relate to them, had become even more introspective and withdrawn. The final blow came when her husband Feroze Gandhi died in 1960. Even though it was not a happy marriage and they had lived apart for several years, his death had left her deeply shaken. Their sons, Rajiv and Sanjay, were sixteen and fourteen at the time.

With Nehru's death in 1964, she closed the circle of her emotions around her. The only persons within that circle were Rajiv and Sanjay. Not that she had no friends. But the definition of friendship in her case was different. The few she had flattered themselves into believing they were close to her. Whether they were or not is open to question. She was not a very trusting person, and friendship – of a giving, caring kind – needs to be based on trust.

Even as others professed their absolute loyalty to her, she trusted only her sons and saw nothing wrong in Sanjay opting for the part of Prime Minister by proxy. She had indulged his fanciful dream of building a people's car but had very reluctantly and only after he had thrown tantrums, agreed to his acquisition of a vast acreage of land, capital, government sanctions, manufacturing facilities and dealerships for it, by the most dubious means. But he had stayed outside the corridors of power till his decisive stand against her resignation earned him both his spurs and her admiration.

Events now moved towards their dénouement. Having decided not to resign, she gave top priority to a plan of staggering audacity, contemptuous of the rule of law and disregarding elementary decencies. It revolved around the declaration of an Emergency by Presidential decree, in the event that her appeal to the Supreme Court should be turned down. It would vest the government with extraordinary powers to arrest political opponents, journalists, academics, students and others critical of her. Also on the agenda were stringent controls on the press, tax raids on those who failed to fall in line, constitutional amendments to consolidate her rule, postponement of Parliamentary elections, abolition of the Question Hour in Parliament and unlimited powers to the police to arrest, torture and jail persons without trial.

On June 24 the vacation bench of the Supreme Court, while

granting a stay on the operation of the High Court's judgment and allowing her to continue as Prime Minister pending the final decision of the full bench of the Court, denied her the right to vote in Parliamentary proceedings. The die was cast. A pliant President signed the Emergency Proclamation at 11.45 p.m. on June 25, 1975, and the police and security forces across the country swung into action within hours, arresting over a thousand persons that night. Among them were former colleagues of Indira Gandhi like Morarji Desai, who had earlier been her Deputy Prime Minister (and who would become the Prime Minister in a few years), Jayaprakash Narayan (JP), a man cast in the same mould as Mahatma Gandhi and widely respected for his ideals and integrity, almost all leaders of the Opposition parties, and many more. In the succeeding days and weeks the arrests totalled an astonishing 100,000.

The Cabinet, summoned to meet at 6 o'clock the next morning, was asked to give its approval to the Emergency, *after the event*. The appearance of collective Cabinet responsibility was considered unnecessary. That same day stringent censorship laws on all newspapers, magazines, wire services and other form of reportage came into effect. Hardly any papers had appeared in Delhi that morning anyway, since the power supply to the printing plants had been cut off before midnight! Despite the censorship, the press continued its dissent in many different ways: through inserts, blank spaces and quotes from Gandhi and Nehru. But it was a losing battle.

The more odious aspects of the crack-down soon followed. These included the manacling of political prisoners, their detention with criminals and cut-throats, inhuman jail conditions, torture and deaths in police custody, the terrorising of persons refusing to obey the directives emanating from the Prime Minister's residence, whose presiding deity was Sanjay Gandhi. Not surprisingly, his importance in the new scheme of things had drawn a squalid bunch of neighbourhood bullies, political upstarts, old school friends and small-time racketeers around him. The traits they had in common were sycophancy and soaring ambition. They moved in and out of the Prime Minister's house with ease. Existing administrative checks and balances to ensure an orderly and accountable system of governance were brushed aside, with Sanjay's hatchet-men and informers ready to inform on officials unwilling to do his bidding. It was not long before government machinery was working for the party in power, but, more ominously it had also become an instrument of terror.

I saw an example of this in the treatment meted out to Inder Mohan, a gentle, dedicated social activist who, although a Hindu, had worked for years among the Muslims around Delhi's Jama Masjid. When Sanjay's yes-men in the Delhi Administration had, in the name of 'beautification', savagely demolished Muslim shops around the mosque, Inder Mohan had gone to him to protest. That same evening a police team arrived at his house and beat him up. The next day they took him through the streets, barefoot and hand-cuffed, to a magistrate's court. He was thrown into a stinking rat-infested corner of a filthy room in a police station, where I visited him. When I contacted his two old friends – both Ministers in Indira Gandhi's Cabinet – neither raised a finger to help him. They were in no doubt of what was required of those she had placed in high positions: an abject acceptance of her – and now her son's – dictates.

There were numerous other cases. When the lawyers of Delhi's High Court Bar Association crossed Sanjay's path during the Emergency, over a thousand lawyers' chambers were demolished by bulldozers. When they protested, he had them arrested under the Maintenance of Internal Security Act. An institution founded by Mahatma Gandhi was not spared either. The Navjivan Trust Press, which once published the Mahatma's papers, *Young India* and *Harijan*, was closed down because it published a booklet containing a judgment on the closing down of a weekly, which in turn had published a speech by a former Chief Justice of Bombay criticising the Emergency! Even the publication of Court judgments was unacceptable. The central judiciary too had knuckled under during the Emergency, though some of the State High Courts refused to do so. But the ultimate irony lay in Indira and Sanjay Gandhi's rejection of their father's legacies.

After India's reverses in 1962 Krishna Menon had suggested that an internal emergency should be declared to deal with public criticism, but Nehru had turned it down as undemocratic. Thirteen years later Sanjay, by withdrawing the impunity with which journalists had reported Parliamentary proceedings, overturned the provisions of a Bill which his father, Feroze Gandhi, had introduced in Parliament several years earlier.

One of the most bizarre excesses of the Emergency was the forced and indiscriminate sterilisation of tens of thousands of people across the country. Vasectomy was the latest obsession to seize Sanjay's fevered mind. While there was a pressing need to control India's expanding population, Sanjay threw himself into the sterilisation drive with the same mindless frenzy he had brought to his other half-baked schemes. No sane criterion was laid down for deciding who would be vasectomised: neither age, whether married or single, nor the number of children already in the family. What mattered were the quotas which minor and major functionaries had to meet. And which – out of the need for bureaucratic self-preservation – they did. In keeping with the depravity of this drive, were the inhuman conditions under which sterilisations were carried out. The instruments used, the incisions made, the surgeons' unconcern and the physical conditions under which the 'surgery' was carried out all reflected the perverseness of that period.

Eventually, it was this insolent disregard for the sensibilities and concerns of people, which led to Indira Gandhi's stunning defeat in the March 1977 elections which were called after twenty-one months of the Emergency. Why did she hold the elections? Her son and advisers, perfectly at ease with their limitless powers and the amassing of wealth, were against them. But Indira Gandhi had her way, perhaps because she felt confident of winning. And also because intelligence reports misled her about her chances of victory. The other factor which influenced her decision was that international opinion was becoming more critical of the Emergency and she wanted to legitimise her rule through the elections. In the end the gamble failed and her party was routed, while she and her son were humiliatingly defeated in their constituencies. Something which had never happened to the Nehrus before.

Her government's efforts to smother India's soul were certainly affecting me and several of my close friends as well. Slowly and imperceptibly, we were moving away from the carefree days of unswerving optimism and laughter, and even my allegiances came into question. It seemed pointless to be crusading for architectural integrity, civic grace and urban sanity, when an insane few were holding the country to ransom. And craven officials were helping to subvert the rule of law. Even Delhi's Urban Art Commission, which Indira Gandhi had helped establish, was treated by Sanjay with the same disdain as other government institutions. That it was established by Act of Parliament was of little consequence since Parliament itself was irrelevant in the new order. Against the backdrop of the Emergency, what could one do which would be both effective and inspiring?

It was a trying time for people all over India, and while it took its toll of our hopes and optimism it went much beyond that. It also blunted our unending enthusiasm for the future and affected our pride and self-esteem. I am convinced that the cynicism and immorality which Indira Gandhi and her *enfant terrible* bequeathed to India during the Emergency are now permanent features of our political life. Eight years after her death duplicity and deceit in public affairs are as evident as they were in her time.

5. The Seventies: A Declining Morality

Morarji Desai, India's fourth Prime Minister, was sworn in on March 24, 1977. An experienced administrator with Gandhian principles – which were, however, stretched to protect a corrupt son – he restored press freedom and the independence of the judiciary, removed the bans on political parties, withdrew hundreds of false cases, cut the intelligence agencies to size and did much to restore the country's confidence in itself. The people helped too. Despite Indira Gandhi's efforts to project herself as a socialist Prime Minister, citing bank nationalisation and the abolition of Privy Purses as proof, she could not erase memories in the public mind of the disgraceful days of the Emergency.

*

My own life was brought to a standstill by a massive heart attack in January 1977. It was a traumatic experience, made doubly difficult by my having to face the fact of my own mortality. My premonitions of the future did not help either. The robust, vigorous and passionate life I had lived till then seemed a thing of the past and I saw myself as a physical wreck in the years ahead. As I luxuriated in a welter of self-pity and allowed the shock of my illness to wash over me, the images of the group by the side of the dusty road kept recurring. And I could slowly feel a growing determination to put my despondency aside and battle for the resources needed to build the rural hospital which I had vowed to realise. If I was fortunate to get admitted into the intensive care of a good hospital in time, I would prove that something worthwhile could be done for those not so fortunate – in areas neglected by our society's unconcerns.

After a month of hospitalisation I came home to new beginnings, in anticipation of a new promise, both for India and myself. Giving a physical form to my dream hospital became an obsession, despite the heavy flak it drew from some of my friends who found it difficult to see me as a medical missionary. I had succeeded in getting the state government to donate us a water-logged, snake-infested, unused and overgrown stretch of twenty-six acres of land. The quality of the soil was extremely poor – there were no canal or river irrigation facilities and the sub-soil water was unusable. But it was a challenge I was determined to meet and through it to prove several things which needed to be proved through actual demonstration. That building plants and factories on productive farmlands – as was done by Sanjay Gandhi for his car project – was wrong, as there was enough unproductive land which could be reclaimed for that. I also wanted to demonstrate my belief, by building a hospital, that our

115

concentration of medical facilities in the cities was generating resentment in rural areas which private initiative could and should resolve. I knew that our hospital could make an important point: that urban elites can and must take on larger social responsibilities than they do at present; that rural India is not 'another country'. It is very much a part of India: in fact her very heart.

As our work began to be noticed by the newspapers, this line from Shanta Serbjeet Singh's weekly column in the *Tribune* became my favourite: 'The hospital is now building a bridge between the city of Lutyens and the "other country" where 82 out of every 100 Indians live.'

The problem our Trust had was cash. Though it owned prime properties, they could not be sold for more than a fraction of their value because the tenancy rights of old occupants precluded higher rents and evictions. At this point Richard Manoff, a friend from New York who had done brilliantly in the advertising field, hit on the idea of establishing an American Friends of Kabliji Hospital and getting it tax-exempt status from the Internal Revenue Service, so that we could launch a fund-raising drive for it. With Dick as its Chairman and old friends like Philip Johnson and Irwin Shaw on the board, donations soon started coming in, largely due to Manoff's winning ways with people.

But our real breakthrough came in Canada. Among others who were willing to share in the excitement of what we were trying to achieve were close friends like Barbara Chilcott, Canada's foremost actress, her husband, the brilliant composer Harry Somers, and George Woodcock, one of the country's most distinguished writers whose studies on anarchism and George Orwell had won him international fame. They were of the view that individual human concerns should have little to do with discontents between nations. George Woodcock summed up their feelings for India and the Kabliji Hospital in a perceptive article in the *Vancouver Sun*:

> Regularly, a distinguished writer from some outside country visits India, is appalled by the inhuman chaos of the cities, the poverty of the *bustees* or makeshift slums, the decline of Indira Gandhi's great Congress party movement into a splintered congregation of corrupt and foolish politicians, and comes home to write a book that offers little hope for the world's largest democracy and its second most populous country.
>
> And when, like V.S. Naipaul, the writer is a citizen of a Third World country – Trinidad – whose ancestors came from the valley of the Ganges, we think he speaks with authority and accept as entire truth the gloomy version that Naipaul summarised in the title of his famous

5. The Seventies: A Declining Morality

book on India, *An Area of Darkness* .... Though I have never been in doubt about the extent of its problems and the difficulty of solving them, I have never shared the unrelieved pessimism of writers like Naipaul ...

My experience of India and other Asian countries over the past 20 years has taught me that, far from being areas of total darkness, although darkness does exist ... many small efforts are slowly changing life for the better. These efforts are carried on by voluntary groups, by the remnants of Gandhi's movement to regenerate rural India, and even by individuals ...

One of the Indians who has shown 'an affirming flame' with considerable brilliance is Patwant Singh, who recently visited Canada seeking support for his Kabliji Hospital and Rural Health Centre, in the village of Ghamroj about 50 miles from Delhi .... He decided to found an experimental rural hospital that would also be a public health centre, aimed at raising the quality of life as well as the expectancy of life ...

He designed his hospital on conservationist lines, choosing a patch of infertile marshy ground donated by the state government of Haryana (the only official gift he has received in India). He drained the ground and erected on it handsome low-profile buildings made cheaply from local field stone with lime mortar. He established two wards, totalling 40 beds, two operating theatres, one for eye ailments and one for general purposes, an out-patient department, and a dispensary ...

Already 42,000 patients have been treated promptly in its wards and out-patient department. But this is only a part – Patwant Singh might even say a minor part – of what the hospital is doing. There are immunisation programmes, educational programmes in personal hygiene, a family planning service ...

We were also supported by the Canadian government who, through the Canadian International Development Agency (CIDA), a division of the External Affairs Ministry, matched private donations dollar for dollar.

*

Some of us wrongly believed that the Emergency had taught India's political leadership a lesson. And it would avoid the mistakes which had already pushed the country to the edge of the abyss, once. Sadly the men who came to power in the wake of Indira Gandhi's unprincipled Prime Ministership were again at each other's throats, acting out their historic inadequacies and setting the stage for their own downfall and her return. They had learnt nothing, either from India's remote or more immediate past. The Janata party's three years in office (1977-80), while significant in the manner in which the repressive apparatus of the Emergency was dismantled, would be remembered more for the bitter in-fighting which made efficient governance impossible.

Very little of this was lost on Indira Gandhi: the in-fighting of the coalition in power, the people's disenchantment at the sorry spectacle the men in power were making of themselves, the opportunities which were opening for her. She observed the developing situation from the right distance and – shrewdly, intuitively, with an instinctive genius for political intrigue – was preparing the ground for the government's fall. Less than two-and-a-half years after leaving office she encouraged a revolt within the coalition, which led to the exit of Morarji Desai and the installation of Charan Singh as the Prime Minister. Within weeks a situation was created for his resignation and the dissolution of Parliament. In the general elections which followed in January 1980 she and her party won hands down.

In her second incarnation as Prime Minister, and her death less than five years later, Indira Gandhi would bequeath yet another legacy to India – even more violent and destructive than the Emergency. And this was her decision to woo the Hindu vote by making the Sikhs appear as a threat to India's unity. It would create still more divisions in a bitterly divided land.

Chapter 6

The Eighties: The Bloodied Landscape

Many of them, so as to curry favour with tyrants, for a fistful of coins, or through bribery, or corruption, are shedding the blood of their brothers.

Emiliano Zapata, *Plan de Ayala*

AT A PACKED meeting of India's foreign service officials in the conference room of the External Affairs Ministry in 1963 Jawaharlal Nehru was asked: 'What happens to the services if the communists are elected to power tomorrow at the Centre, here in New Delhi?'

His reply was: 'Why are all of you so obsessed with communists and communism? ... The danger to India is not communism. It is Hindu right-wing communalism.'

A little over twenty years later – for the very reasons which Nehru had feared – the eighties became the bloodiest decade since Independence, whose tragic symbols would be smouldering ruins, political assassinations, genocidal killings, military intervention abroad and religious intolerance. What Nehru could not have foreseen was that his own daughter would provide the *raison d'être* for the ever increasing communal bitterness.

Indira Gandhi's byzantine intrigues had started even before she took the oath of office on January 14, 1980. Routed in the 1977 elections in Punjab, its dispirited Congress party was given new hope by her plan to split the state's ruling Hindu-Sikh coalition (of the Jan Sangh and Akalis respectively) along communal lines. The Akalis had been anathema to the ruling party ever since their unrelenting opposition to the Emergency. And the time had come to settle scores with them. That the stoking of communal fires lies outside the democratic process was too fine a point for the political hit-men of the Congress party. Their strategy required a Sikh with a magnetic and mesmerising personality whose extravagant utterances could rally his co-religionists around him. The more he exaggerated the Hindu threat to the Sikh faith the better, since its appeal would wean the Sikhs away from the moderate Akalis and would put them in a

119

cleft stick. If they arrested him, they would be damned by their followers; if they did not, the coalition would be doomed, since their Hindu partners would demand his punishment.

Zail Singh, the man assigned the task of finding such a person, was adept at the game. He had risen from total obscurity to the Chief Ministership of Punjab, and it had been a heady experience. He wanted more of it, as most men do, once they have tasted power. Sensing great potential for the future in his assignment, he set about it with zeal. The criterion in the prevailing political culture was the promise of rewards, not the odiousness of the task. And he knew that if he could successfully handle this delicate mission – delicate, because the person chosen had to play a role unbeknown to him – nothing would be beyond his reach. As indeed it was not, because Zail Singh was eventually made President of India. His recompense was of a piece: another facet of the trade in the buying and selling of political support which was legitimised when the Congress split in 1969.

The man chosen was Jarnail Singh Bhindranwale. A preacher – from a seminary near Amritsar, with an impressive knowledge of the Sikh scriptures – Bhindranwale soon became a turbulent presence in Punjab. The press and government-controlled radio and television, with some canny manipulation by the Congress, gave his fiery utterances extensive coverage. No attempt was made to prevent him from polarising the Hindus and Sikhs. Nor was he arrested under the Indian Penal Code, which takes a serious view of persons inciting religious passions. Clearly he had yet to create further divisions in an already divided land. With a misplaced faith in her own ability to control the damage, Indira Gandhi continued through him to promote a policy which would unleash the communal forces that Nehru had feared.

Commenting on Nehru's remarks at the meeting in 1963, Y.D. Gundevia, India's former Foreign Secretary, wrote in his book, *Outside the Archives*: 'Call it famous last words. I have always looked upon what Jawaharlal said at this officers' meeting that day as not only his famous last words, but one of the most prophetic announcements that he ever made.'

Nehru himself had had an extended correspondence on this theme, almost thirty years earlier, with Lord Lothian, the British Liberal politician. On December 31, 1935, in a letter to Nehru he had observed:

If the constitutional road is rejected in India it seems to me almost inevitable that India will follow the example of Europe and start with religious wars, for the mass of the people will still, I think, respond to religious feelings once they are stimulated for political purposes, out of which she will emerge not as a unity but, like Europe, divided into a number of dictatorial states separated by race and language and armed to the teeth against one another both militarily and economically with their internal development consequently paralysed ....

Nehru, in his reply, had disagreed with several points, including the phrase 'constitutional road', which he felt was inapplicable since the people of India 'have no constitutional way open to them'. But the fact remains that Lothian's reading of the potential danger to India from religious wars showed a better understanding of the Indian reality than was shown by Nehru's daughter. Or, as later events would demonstrate, by most Indian politicians.

The communal divide in Punjab, further aggravated by the Congress party's return to power in 1980, was pushing the country towards the scenario Lothian had foreseen. Slowly, invidiously, the media had started projecting Bhindranwale as a prototype of the beliefs and aspirations of *all Sikhs* with less and less distinction made between him, the Akalis and millions of other Sikhs who had nothing to do with either of them. This blurring was not an oversight: the far from unbiased and unfettered press was prepared to hold all Sikhs accountable for the excesses of a few, so that in time this community could be targeted as the biggest danger to India's unity and sovereignty. Girilal Jain, editor of the widely-read *Times of India* and one of the most strident Sikh-baiters had, for instance, this to say of the unfolding events:

> It is 11 pm in the history of the Sikh community. It must reverse the clock. It is still possible to do so. But time is running out. The community must demand that the agitation be called off. The Sikhs must heed the warning before it strikes midnight. (*The Sikhs are in Danger*, March 7, 1984.)

There was no explanation of how the community should 'demand that the agitation be called off'. As if the Sikhs are a compact, tightly-knit, homogeneous little group – like, say, the Amish of Pennsylvania – rather than 15 million vigorous, individualistic and combative people who do not easily accept the dictat of others, whether of their own or another community. More serious was the invidious way in which all Sikhs were being made to appear hostile to a Hindu India. Since it is difficult suddenly to fault the Sikhs – who for generations have grown up with the Hindus, married their sons and daughters, shared their joys and sorrows, been acknowledged

121

as the defenders of the land and Hindu honour, and whose camaraderie, goodwill and fun-loving friendship was always welcome – a solid case had to be prepared against them. What had to be proved was that deep inside there was something wrong with the strain. The honour of the (Hindu) majority would be vindicated if the (Sikh) minority could be shown to have developed serious symptoms on breaking off from the parent (Hindu) stock.

Impartial writing suffered grievously in its efforts to prove Sikh 'perfidy', from the Sikh soldiers' refusal to mutiny against the British in 1857; to their 'gullibility' in the face of British machinations, their 'divisive politics', their sense of separateness and much else. If this whipped up Hindu resentment, that was just what the Congress wanted. It wanted to cash in on the Hindu votes by humbling the Sikhs, whose votes were too few to count for much anyway. If, in pursuit of this aim, tanks and artillery had to be brought in to destroy a sacred heritage – in the name of saving the republic – well, so be it! The worsening communal divide could be contained later.

Events were now moving towards a point of no return. Bemused by a sense of his own growing importance, Bhindranwale failed to perceive that once he had served the purpose of fanning religious fires his usefulness would be lost to the Congress whose mandarins, in a complete turnabout, would order his destruction and the destruction of the Golden Temple in which he had sought sanctuary. A carefully orchestrated propaganda blitz would provide justification for the final, physical assault on this exalted emblem of Sikh self-esteem and faith.

*

I was abroad when Sanjay died in a plane crash in June 1980. On my return I wrote to Indira Gandhi expressing my sympathy, and complimenting her on her poise and inner fortitude in the face of the tragedy. I did not extol his virtues, since I had agreed neither with his politics nor with his political conduct. She said in reply that 'Sanjay was much maligned, but, it is interesting to note, by people who did not know him nor made any effort to do so. That he bore the calumny and falsehood with dignity and even good cheer is to his credit and bears witness to his quality.' She also added that she had asked the office to fix an appointment for me to meet her.

At our meeting a few days later, I suggested that she should make an effort to talk to thoughtful men and women who, even though they were critical of her, could offer useful perceptions about the country's problems and their solutions. She was interested, and wanted me to arrange the first such meeting. Taking this as a gesture of courtesy and nothing more, I forgot about it until her secretary, Usha Bhagat, telephoned to enquire about the get-together.

'What get-together?' I asked.

'Of people you wanted the Prime Minister to meet.'

'I don't think they will be enthused by the prospect of going to the Prime Minister's office or residence for such a meeting.'

She called back the next day: 'Mrs Gandhi suggests you hold the meeting in your house.'

'That is difficult,' I told her, 'because it means buying new curtains for the study and so on.'

She rang the same evening. 'The Prime Minister wouldn't mind if you don't get the curtains changed.'

The informal meeting in September went off extremely well. I had talked beforehand to the six or seven persons on my list about this opportunity for making constructive suggestions to the Prime Minister and conveying our concerns for the future. I was keen to avoid awkward moments during the meeting because, if she was genuinely interested in hearing views which differed from her own, it was important to put them across in a manner which wouldn't throw her off the idea of other such encounters. I was also keen that our meeting should not be publicised – which it wasn't – as there were too many hangers-on who would derail initiatives they perceived as threatening their own interests.

About ten days later she thanked me for the 'delightfully restful' evening and went on to write that, since 'so much is happening or not happening which our committees cannot possibly keep track of', it was necessary to 'try to evoke greater public concern and involvement' in what was going on. She ended by asking the question: 'How can we go about this on a massive country-wide scale?'

It was not an easy one to answer. But I did identify a few areas in which efforts could be made to involve the people. 'Since public morale is a key factor in any scenario conceived on a country-wide scale, the first priority is to restore it,' I replied, pointing out that 'it is difficult to do that so long as an impression exists in people's minds that the state is helpless in meeting their most basic needs. Can this impression be removed? It certainly can.'

As rising food prices at the time were 'driving people out of their minds, affecting their sanity and morale', I suggested that government should come down heavily on the hoarders of huge stocks of grain, sugar and other commodities, which they were able to hoard under 'the protection and patronage of shady political elements and petty officials'. I felt that this drive against illegal hoarding could, within weeks, create a profound impact on the minds of people, help them regain their confidence in the government and make them more receptive to larger national objectives.

The next step would be to stop the erosion of institutions, especially the civil service and the police, as the 'unending inroads into their functioning have had a corrosive effect on them ... If the representatives of the government are themselves dispirited and weary of being pushed around by anyone with political connections, the quality of government inevitably suffers which, in turn, increases the suffering of those governed.'

I also suggested the induction of technocrats at ministerial level in the interests of 'efficiency in production, competitive industrial output, adoption of technology appropriate to our needs, a more pragmatic concern with the ratio between inputs and outputs and more coherent communication between ministries and the institutions they control ...'. I recalled the observations of one of the persons I had invited to our meeting, Fali Nariman, who ranked among the top two or three most brilliant lawyers in India and who had resigned in protest as the Solicitor-General when the Emergency was declared. He had explained with considerable clarity how it was possible to appoint non-elected technocrats as ministers of state, through a simple constitutional amendment. Her frank but shrewd reply had been: 'The politicians will not accept it.'

I then confessed to being 'baffled by the manner in which the country is being pushed ... into a dangerous quagmire of our own making', through the reckless pace with which we were building 'energy-intensive skyscrapers, vast airconditioned auditoriums, stadiums ... which presume on the unending supply of petroleum products ... as if the energy crisis was a well-kept secret our key functionaries had not been informed about'. I suggested severe curbs on building norms, as also on the use of materials produced by oil-based industries.

I admitted to 'not touching on health, family planning, minorities, students and several other areas of concern, but to touch on all would be unrealistic. The panorama is too vast.' I did, however, briefly mention the work we were doing in our rural hospital and said that 'if sixty such Centres are started each year around the country, 300 in five years, all of them funded privately but with the State's active encouragement, a staggering number of people will get health cover. (With each facility the same size as ours, providing medical cover to 200,000 persons; in five years 300 Centres would cover a population of 60,000,000.)'

I do not know what impact was created by any of these suggestions. Very little, judging by the fact that things continued on their benumbing and discouraging course. But one thing which I did suggest in that letter and which was to become official policy ten years later had to do with encouraging Indian talent abroad to invest and become involved with the country of its birth:

> In any strategy evolved to revitalise the country's critical segments, the potential of highly qualified and skilled Indians settled abroad cannot be overlooked. They are a national resource which, sadly, is not at the nation's disposal at this time. Many of them have outstanding achievements to their credit, while most others have mastered the methodology, skills and rational thinking which have helped the West score its economic and technological victories. There are numerous instances of those who, enthused by the challenge of doing something for their own country, returned here only to go back embittered because there was no reciprocity to their excitement and enthusiasm. These people are a resource we must draw upon; not all of them are bemused by the West's flashier life-styles. The Chinese, even under an extremely radical regime, have been successful in repatriating overseas Chinese talent.

Three months later, in December, she came to meet another small group. For a part of the evening, I had also invited several outstanding painters and sculptors who had each donated a work to help raise money for our hospital. I wanted her to see a preview of this collection because of her interest in the arts: a charming side of her many-faceted personality, because none of India's other Prime Ministers ever showed such a continuing interest in the contemporary arts as she did. Nehru, who had the vision to commission Le Corbusier to design Chandigarh, was an exception. But he was more animated by the excitement of intellectual challenge, whilst she was drawn to the visual arts. On her official visits to the US, some of America's distinguished avant garde artists would be invited to her suite in New York's Carlyle Hotel so that she could hear them speak on the changing social, political and art scenes.

*

At about this time powerful private and official lobbies were getting ready to turn Delhi upside down for the 1982 Ninth Asian Games (Asiad 82). I was emphatically opposed to the idea and spelt out the reasons in *Design*: 'Would Delhi, with its urban fabric already stretched beyond advised limits, be able to take the Asian Olympics with events held at thirteen major sites all over the city, the 12-day extravaganza to be preceded by a massive construction programme of 2-year duration?' The other question concerned the human element. 'Would it be fair to the harried, harassed and despairing citizens of Delhi – who have daily to go through ... Delhi's careering traffic; who stand in long queues for a single bucket of water from a public tap; who wait resignedly for hours at peak periods to board a bus; who breathe the polluted, poisonous air of Delhi; who live in foul slums – to be made to witness colossal sums of money and material invested in stadiums and Olympic housing complexes?'

I raised a hornet's nest – even more by the suggestion that the entire venue be shifted to Rai, about 50 miles from Delhi, which already had an excellent public school and sports facilities. With the building of the Olympic facilities there, it could become the first sports university of its kind in the world. The press and Delhi's politicians were outraged. They found the idea 'preposterous'. The capital's Chief Executive Councillor saw it as a move aimed at 'spiting Delhi's citizens'. Mrs Gandhi, however, reacted more soberly. She flew into Rai on a helicopter one morning, sized up the place, and decided that it should be the site of Asiad 82. In his cover story 'Indira's Power Politics' in the *New York Times Magazine* of March 23, 1980, Michael T. Kaufman, the *Times* Delhi bureau chief, wrote:

Just how wide the Gandhi personal touch reaches can be seen in a small incident that has not yet been reported in India. It took place during her second week in office, a time of dizzying activity. Her attention was drawn to an article in a small-circulation magazine called *Design* in which Patwant Singh, a distinguished architect, deplored certain building plans. Specifically, he charged that the Government committee appointed to organise the Asian Games to be held in India in 1982 was planning to build stadiums near some of the capital city's best-known archeological sites. Singh contended that, along with cultural treasures, the proposal would destroy the city's skyscape as well. Mrs Gandhi read the article, agreed with Singh and, with a single phone call, put a stop to the plans.

Sadly, she changed her mind under political pressure and the Games were held in Delhi, though she ordered some of the plans changed as reported by Kaufman.

*

Interestingly, the question of Punjab never came up during any of these meetings, because the situation had not deteriorated to the extent it would after 1982. Nor was the diabolical nature of the

Congress's plan quite clear then. But what did gradually become obvious was that reconciliation in Punjab was not on the agenda of the ruling party. Each initiative was allowed to stay on course for a while and then stonewalled just as hopes for a breakthrough were rising. Each failure, with remarkable finesse, was attributed to the Akalis – and in time to all Sikhs. In the public's mind their image as unreasonable, obdurate men bent upon keeping things at the boil, was being strengthened. And the traditionally moderate, though now frustrated, Akalis were being edged towards militancy.

Which was what Indira Gandhi wanted. Militancy in Punjab – and later Kashmir – had a crucial role to play in her new electoral strategy for replacing the votes of her former 'winning coalition' of the Muslims, other religious minorities and the rural poor. They had, in varying degrees, seen through the rhetoric of her concerns, and proof of this was provided by her party's defeat in the Andhra Pradesh and Karnataka assembly elections in 1983. The poor too had come to terms with the hollowness of the *garibi hatao* slogan, as had the Muslims with the slogan of secularism. So a profound shift had been decided upon behind the scenes: from secular, modern and progressive ideals, the Congress would now compete for the Hindu vote. Not openly, of course, but obliquely; by making it appear that the future of the unified, republican Indian state was endangered by the actions of the Sikhs and the Muslims and that the only defence against it was Indira Gandhi's strong leadership. Rajni Kothari told me later that 'the carnage which followed this about-turn by the Congress was not confined to Punjab and Kashmir, because India's democratic polity itself fell victim to it'. The ultimate irony was that although Indira Gandhi herself was not a religious bigot – in fact she had once been a secularist to the core – she was an irresponsible politician whose basic shortcoming was an absence of permanent values.

Since all this had the makings of a major conflagration, I had a meeting with a group of friends towards the end of October 1983 to discuss developments. I had prepared a paper to form the basis of our discussions, at the end of which we agreed that the best thing would be to try to get it published as a newspaper article, with all our names as co-authors. But who would publish it? Many of the major newspapers were less than keen to give coverage to the Sikh point of view. Fortunately George Verghese, editor of the *Indian Express* – the most extensively read English daily nationwide – was, unlike some of his counterparts, impeccably correct and non-partisan in his editorial policy. I went to see Verghese and asked him if he would publish the article. He read it, agreed with what we had to say and ran it over four columns of his editorial page. (Our twelve names appeared as its authors!) It was extremely well received in Delhi, Punjab and elsewhere. We had underscored 'the irony of the Punjab crisis: that the State's demands are seen as Sikh demands', and pointed out that if the Akalis articulated the demands and the Union government acceded to them – which it should, since they were just – would the Sikhs alone benefit from that? Clearly not. All the people of the State would. The Sikhs, after all, were only 60 per cent of Punjab's population!

What were the demands? To begin with, that Chandigarh should be made the exclusive capital of Punjab. As it was built to compensate the state for the loss of its 'legendary capital Lahore', it was unfair to treat it as a Union Territory and make Punjab and Haryana share it as their capital. And, surely, the demand for redrawing Punjab's boundaries, a fair division of river waters and greater State autonomy was not made for the benefit only of the Sikhs. We also pointed to the damage that invidious comment and irresponsible terminology ('extremists', 'terrorists', 'fundamentalists') in government pronouncements and media reports were doing to communal harmony. They were inflaming passions and encouraging violence. 'The responsibility of the authorities is to catch culprits, not to create conditions which lead to the aggravation of crisis-prone situations.'

Take the case of the demand for greater autonomy for the States, on which the media and the ruling party really went to town. All that the Akalis demanded through the Anandpur Saheb Resolution was that the federal principle should be observed in the nation's governance. The document asked, among other things, for the redefining of the central and state relations, decentralisation of powers, and respect for the principle of state autonomy as provided in the Indian Constitution. Though all these lie within the framework of the Constitution, the document was luridly described as a secessionist demand!

In any event Indira Gandhi and her Congress party had other things in mind. Bemused by its Machiavellian plan for Punjab, the government was pushing the Akalis towards an eclipse at the hands of the forces it had helped assemble against them. The public now saw Bhindranwale as the dominant force and the Akalis as lacking the fire and passion that Sikhs so admire. Their stature had been diminished by trying to negotiate with New Delhi and coming out empty-handed each time. Bhindranwale's trigger-happy followers, on the other hand, were taking the law into their own hands. Militancy was in the air. And it was allowed to take root because it suited the Centre's purposes – and the media's thirst for news that damned the Sikhs. Bhindranwale's sporadic following of emotionally surcharged people fired by his rhetoric and zeal, with no state-wide, cadre-based political party at the grass-roots level, got all the coverage; whereas the Akalis, who had all of these, were mocked for their moderation. An old, well-established party, which had long been a part of the Indian political scene, was deliberately subverted for short-term political gains.

Finally, as the fateful 1984 dawned, the Akalis decided publicly to burn a page of the Indian Constitution, in a symbolic protest. Some of us, convinced that this would play into the hands of the government and further alienate the Sikhs from the rest of India, flew to Amritsar to dissuade Harchand Singh Longowal, then head of the Akali Party. Lt. General (Retd.) J.S. Aurora, Air Chief Marshal (Retd.) Arjan Singh, Ambassador Gurbachan Singh and I undertook the mission, the highpoint of which was our memorable meeting with this unusual man.

We had taken an early morning flight from Delhi, and when we reached the venue of our meeting there were several thousand Sikhs on the grounds in front of it. Those were stressful times, and the tension in the air was palpable. We met Longowal in a spartan room on the first floor of a building on the periphery of the Golden Temple. A man in his early fifties, he was dressed in spotless white clothes with a blue turban and a flowing beard. He had the serene expression of a man confident of his own strength, not riven by a hunger for the spoils of office. While other heads of parties aspired to political office with all the trappings of power – and profit – he did not. During the hour and a half we spent with him, explaining in detail why even a symbolic burning of a page of the Constitution would be an ill-advised step, he listened carefully, without trying to score points. Putting his own view across, he elaborated on all that had preceded their decision to take the step they were about to take. Each time the Akalis had accepted New Delhi's offer to negotiate in good faith, Indira Gandhi's government had scuttled the talks on one pretext or another. They had now run out of patience with this game of hide-and-seek.

We listened patiently to his lucid presentation of the events that had brought matters to their present pass and explained why we could not see the logic of the present move. Neither would it lead the contending parties out of the impasse nor could it be called a creative response to a complex situation. Nor indeed would the cost of such a protest be balanced by the benefits from it. We urged him to reconsider the decision.

He agreed to try to recall the five senior members of the party who had left incognito for Chandigarh and Delhi to carry out the assignment, but doubted if he would be able to do so in time. In fact, with less than two days left, it could not be called off, and all five were arrested and sent to jail, including Prakash Singh Badal who was Chief Minister of Punjab during the years Indira Gandhi was out of office.

It was to embarrass his coalition government that Bhindranwale had been given such prominence. He had confidently moved into the precincts of the Golden Temple in mid-December, 1983. He had lived on the periphery of its environs till then, affording the government ample opportunity to arrest him without violating the sanctity of the shrine. But his arrest was not on the cards. He and the Golden Temple were to be incinerated as evidence of New Delhi's determination to hold the country together at any cost. The fact that the Sikhs had never threatened to break up the country was beside the point.

As the countdown to the final denouement began, I made one more attempt to avert the impending tragedy, this time by interceding with Indira Gandhi. I met her at her residence on March 9 and we talked about Punjab for over an hour. I doubt if I have ever argued with such intensity and passionate conviction as I did that evening. I told her that the general reading of the unfolding events was that some sort of a decision for an assault on the Golden Temple seemed to have been taken. Bhindranwale had established himself on the *Akal Takht* (the Almighty's throne), which in importance ranked next only to the Harmandir, and it was feared that his intemperate pronouncements would provide the justification for a military operation against the fountainhead of the Sikh faith. I urged her to bring all the wisdom and statesmanship she possessed to avoid that.

At this she lost some of her cool. She turned on me and testily enquired what made me imply – as others were implying also – that she was bent on violating its sanctity by ordering the army in. I assured her I was ready to leave that very minute if she found what I was saying irksome, as I wished neither to waste her time nor to tax her patience. She apologised for being short with me, and I said that that in itself was a breakthrough of sorts since she was not known to say sorry too often. She took it good-naturedly. Then she asked: 'Why don't you take the initiative to talk to the Akalis and bring them round to negotiating with us and settling the crisis once and for all?' I said I wasn't terribly keen on it, that I preferred writing on politics to being a gladiator in the political arena. But, when she insisted, I finally agreed to give it a try, although my instinct told me it was already too late. She sent an aide to call the Cabinet Secretary, the country's highest-ranking civil servant, and, when he was shown in, gave him a summary of what we had discussed and said every assistance, if needed, should be extended to me. I told her I would like to keep this initiative low-key, would request Gurbachan Singh to come with me and would report to her within a week. She agreed. I could never have imagined, as we said goodbye, that it was the last time I would see her alive.

The following days were very hectic for us. We met the top leaders of the Akalis who had been jailed in Delhi and Chandigarh; had extensive conversations with Longowal on the phone; got his concurrence on the modalities of the settlement – as we had of the jailed leaders earlier; and on March 15, six days after my meeting with the Prime Minister, we met the Cabinet Secretary at his house and told him all that had transpired. We said we were confident of an outcome acceptable to both sides. He was visibly pleased and said he would set up a meeting for us with the Prime Minister the next morning.

It all seemed too good to be true – which it was. The next morning, P.C. Alexander, a senior civil servant who was the head of the Prime Minister's office, telephoned Gurbachan, whom he knew well, and asked him to call to see him. He asked him not to tell me for the time being of their meeting. Gurbachan found this unacceptable, since I had brought about his involvement and he was not about to do anything behind my back. Alexander then agreed that I should be informed, and suggested that he invite us both with a few friends to dinner, when he would take me aside and explain things. After his meeting with Alexander, Gurbachan came to tell me about it, though I declined to go to the dinner. According to Alexander, the government wanted our initiative to be kept on hold, in view of another development which was taking place. We learnt the nature of that development from the newspapers: Longowal was to be arraigned for a speech he had given over a year earlier! They had certainly dreamt up a deft way of achieving their dual aim of sinking our initiative and antagonising the Akalis still further.

Gurbachan and I, in carefully retracing the steps we had taken over those few days of intensive diplomacy, were convinced that the Cabinet Secretary's affirmative response at our meeting was not put on for our benefit. Even he was not fully in the picture of what was going on. The only conclusion possible from the subsequent torpedoing of our initiative was that the ruling party did not want us to succeed. And the method of ensuring that was to present us with a *fait accompli* in the form of a warrant against Longowal. We weighed in the balance the possibility that Alexander, with his sense of self-importance, may have scuttled things on his own, but rejected it since he was aware that I knew the Prime Minister and had undertaken the mission at her request. To make certain, I called her personal secretary, R.K. Dhawan, for an appointment with her. He promised to set it up for the very next day – as he had always done in the past – but obviously he was not, at that stage, in the know about what was going on, because I never heard from him again.

There was little doubt now about who was directing the tragic play in Punjab, in which reconciliation did not figure. The stage for the final act was set. The Golden Temple was without doubt being used as a sanctuary, and an armed assault on it would have the sanction of large segments of the country. It would glorify the government and the ruling party: show them as conciliatory, but also unflinching in dealing with a troublesome minority. It mattered little if this theme of using the imaginary threat of a minority to get the support of the majority was an old and familiar one.

No objective assessment of Jarnail Singh Bhindranwale's role can overlook the fact that he not only allowed himself unwittingly to serve the dubious political purposes of the ruling party, but in the process endangered the lives of thousands of Sikhs everywhere without a specific plan, purpose or goal in sight. Moreover he did what no Sikh guru had done in the past: he placed the supreme emblem of Sikhism in the direct line of fire. Inevitably Indian artillery and armour, rejecting other options for flushing the militants out of the Golden Temple, mounted a frontal assault on it at the beginning of June. Tanks rumbled over the marbled walkway around the holy pool – in the centre of which stands the Harmandir – brought the Akal Takht within the sights of their guns, and blew it apart. Although the outcome of this unequal contest was never in doubt, when the determined resistance finally ended, Bhindranwale and his followers lay dead; the blackened ruins of the altar of the Sikh faith provided testimony to the savagery of the attack, and Sikhs everywhere bowed their heads in sorrow and anger.

The wantonness of the attack, and its timing, were also in character. Hundreds of original manuscripts, some written by the gurus in their own hand, were reduced to ashes, as were copies of the Granth Sahib and relics revered and treasured over the centuries. The timing of the military action was set flagrantly for the week during which the anniversary is observed of the martyred fifth guru, Arjan Dev. Over 2,000 men, women and children – innocent pilgrims – died during the action: part of the crowd which had converged on Amritsar to honour his memory.

I was abroad in June 1984, but I can identify with those who had come with pride and goodness in their hearts on a cherished pilgrimage to find their life ripped apart by their country's firepower. The journalist Pranay Gupte, in an article in the *New York Times Magazine* of September 8, 1985, suggests that 'the Indians had not apparently taken into account the fact that hundreds of Sikh pilgrims had crowded into the Golden Temple's courtyard to commemorate the martyrdom ...'. Can one really believe that Punjab and New Delhi, saturated with men from every intelligence agency in India, could have *overlooked* this centuries-old anniversary?

Gupte was moderate compared with other overseas journalists, like Ved Mehta of the *New Yorker*. His biased reporting, in a long article 'Letter from New Delhi' in the January 19, 1987 issue, outdid most others. He opened the piece on Punjab with the words 'The problem of the Sikhs ...' showing himself at ease from the outset with the proposition that the Punjab crisis was the problem of the *Sikhs*. The rest flowed effortlessly:

> Sikh extremists began to murder Hindus (in Punjab) and burn their houses and shops ... there have been daily reports of Sikh extremists rampaging through Punjab, killing Hindus ... People ask: 'If the government cannot make the Hindus in Punjab safe in a preponderantly Hindu country, how can it protect other religious and ethnic minorities?' ...
> ... Sikh extremists are indulging in excesses like those of the followers of Ayatollah Khomeini in Iran. ...
> ... In July, 1985, Rajiv (Gandhi) concluded an accord with Longowal in which he acceded to many of the political demands of the Sikh extremists ... (he had) parleyed with a private citizen and extremist almost as if he represented a government. ...

There was a great deal more of such stuff: in fact 393 lines of it, out of which, in a brave attempt to balance the report, was this sentence of two and a half lines: 'Some Hindus, especially the fundamentalists, have committed such excesses themselves.'

As for accuracy, there has not been a single Hindu-Sikh riot in Punjab till today; no concerted killing of one community by another. The one positive aspect of the otherwise distressing Punjab scene is the fact that the Sikhs have not held their Hindu neighbours responsible for the misdeeds of the Congress party. If Mehta had spent time on carrying out his journalistic responsibilities more conscientiously, he would have found that 80 per cent of the victims of all alleged militant killings in Punjab over the last few years are Sikhs. As for his assertion that Mrs Gandhi was encouraging religious toleration, she did nothing of the sort in Punjab. His bias in comparing Sikh 'excesses' with those of Khomeini's followers was unbecoming, as was the tone of his reference to Longowal, whom he described as 'an extremist'. If one man were to be singled out in Punjab for his moderation and courage in those critical days – as the very signing of an agreement with Rajiv Gandhi proved – it was Longowal. But such details cut no ice with Mehta, who even viewed the state's insistence on more river waters – Punjab, as it happens, is India's granary – and for Chandigarh, as *political demands of the Sikh extremists*. His ultimate gaffe was in suggesting that 'the extremists, for instance, had been clamouring for control over Chandigarh, a city that seemed to hold a certain exotic glamour for them, because it had been designed by the French architect Le Corbusier'. The extremists wouldn't know Corbusier from a carbuncle and are not enamoured of Chandigarh. Nor have they ever asked for it. It is an Akali demand.

In contrast to this trite, bitter reporting, was Salman Rushdie's informed and perceptive commentary on Indira Gandhi's assassination in the London *Times* of November 1, 1984:

> The wind was sown in Amritsar: now, perhaps (and it would be good to be wrong) the whirlwind ripens ... One of the saddest aspects of the growth of communalism (in India) has been that, at times, Mrs Gandhi's Congress party has seemed to be going out to get the Hindu vote. That she was willing to sacrifice the Sikh vote by her attack on the Golden Temple ... may be seen as evidence of this; and it came all the more depressingly from the leader of a party whose electoral success has always been based on its reputation as the guardian of minority groups' rights and safety.

The irrepressible editor of *The Times of India* and writers in the other dailies – more in keeping with Mehta's genre – kept up a steady flow of invective, each wave more inflammatory than the last. All of which was summed up rather well by Dipanker Gupta, of the Centre for Social Systems in New Delhi's Jawaharlal Nehru University. In his view even liberal thinkers 'feel that they are somehow being cheated by the sheer prosperity and the confidence of the Sikhs ... (and that) to be a Sikh was to be economically prosperous, independent and enterprising; and that is why many bleeding-heart liberals are not sure whether they should bleed with the Sikhs or not.'

*

Vengeance was in the air and it took its terrible toll on the morning of October 31, 1984, at 9.18 a.m. Its victim was Indira Gandhi, shot down by her two Sikh bodyguards as she walked on the flower-lined footpath which connected her residence with the office. I was in bed with fever that morning when my secretary, Indrani Mehra brought me the news. I knew deep within me that the whirlwind would follow and the communal fires banked by wayward politicians, religious bigots and media propagandists, would forever change the nation's social and political landscape.

I asked Indrani to call Jagjit, Gurbachan and Arjan and suggest that we meet that afternoon to discuss what we could do to keep things calm. We agreed to make our position on what had happened very clear: that we could not condone assassinations as solutions to political problems. I asked Brigadier (Retd.) Sukhjit Singh, a highly decorated army officer and scion of Kapurthala State, to join us. We met in my house at 3.30 and agreed to issue a press release which said in part:

> No society, least of all a society like ours with its long traditions of spiritualism, scholarship and humanism, can allow black deeds of murderous folly to destroy its civilised fabric. We condemn in un-equivocal terms the dastardly attempt on the life of the Prime Minis-ter, Smt. Indira Gandhi, to which she tragically fell victim. We consider such an act, and what it is likely to trigger off, a grave threat to the country's integrity and unity … We condemn in the harshest possible terms all those who feel that co-existence between the com-munities is not possible, or who will use such occasions of tragedy and national trauma to sow further the seeds of communal hatred …

We went over all the assumptions, assessments and analyses of the likely spin-offs from the tragedy. Interestingly enough, Jagjit Aurora doubted if a crime by two Sikhs could mean that all Sikhs were in danger. I felt it could. Given the backdrop against which the tragedy had occurred, a conflagration in which Sikhs would be at the receiving end was more than likely. One of the steps we decided to take was to call on President Zail Singh, to make him understand how important it was to prevent a backlash against the Sikhs who lived outside Punjab. We arranged to meet him next day at 12.15 p.m.

It was 6.30 p.m. by the time Arjan left, and he was followed soon after by Jagjit and Sukhjit. But within ten minutes all three were back. Arjan had been flagged down by a car less than 500 yards from the house, and the people in it were decent enough to tell him that crowds were on the rampage further up the street and it would be wise to turn back. The other two had had a similar experience. They had seen a Sikh-owned taxi in flames, which a passing crowd had set alight. The 'seeds of communal hatred' were beginning to sprout.

Well before our meeting with the President next day, we had come face to face with a brutal fact: that if the earlier incidents against the Sikhs were spontaneous, the disturbances which engulfed the Capi-tal now were part of a larger plan. Its goal, which came to light later,

135

was the subjugation of the Sikhs through large-scale massacres and state-sponsored terror, and for it to succeed the pogrom would be allowed to proceed unchecked for three nights and four days.

We assembled in my house on the morning of November 1 to drive to a meeting which would prove a charade from the very start. The setting itself, Edwin Lutyens's monumental palace, designed for the Imperial Viceroys and set in 250 acres of landscaped gardens, was far removed from the Indian reality unfolding around it. I was reminded of the words (were they mocking our mission?) carved on the Jaipur column that stands on the palace grounds:

> In Thought Faith
> In Word Wisdom
> In Deed Courage
> In Life Service
> So may India be great.

These were once described as a 'noble epitaph for British rule and fitting counsel for the future masters of India'. Another line, recording the consistency with which each of these virtues has been ignored by the new 'masters' of Independent India's destiny, should be added to update it as an appropriate epitaph for the Republic, whose President's 'wisdom' and 'courage' we were about to experience.

The next hour in the study was as surrealistic as something dreamt up by Salvador Dali. Opening the discussion, I emphatically spelt out for Zail Singh the violence which was overtaking the Sikhs throughout the city. He, as President, was morally and constitutionally bound to put an end to it.

He said he did not have the powers to intervene.

We were momentarily silenced by this astounding remark.

'You mean to tell us', I said, 'that if the nation is going up in flames and people are being butchered in the streets, you have no power to stop the anarchy and bloodshed?'

There was no answer.

When we suggested he speak forcefully to the new Prime Minister, Rajiv Gandhi – whom he had sworn in the previous evening after side-stepping several procedures and proprieties expected of the President – he said he would do so in the next three or four days because he wanted to 'give him some time'.

'Blood is being spilt on the streets and you want three or four days to talk to the Prime Minister!'

He relented and said he would have a word with him that afternoon.

136

But he did not.

We told him to go on the air, use radio and television and make a stirring plea for sanity and balance.

He nodded glumly (but did nothing). When Jagjit asked him whether the Army would be called in to restore order, he said he was not in contact with the Home Minister, P.V. Narasimha Rao (India's current Prime Minister), and suggested that Aurora should talk to him! It was like a bad dream. When we asked him how he would feel if any of his family were in such danger as Sikhs are all over Delhi – we did not know then that they were being massacred in many other states and in the trains as well – he did not answer. Nor did he respond to our suggestion that he should call all the Chief Ministers and heads of the Union Territories who had arrived in Delhi and tell them that he would take the most serious view of any transgressions against the Sikhs in their states. He did not do it.

I told him that even as we sat talking, crowds everywhere were whipping up a frenzy with the slogan *khoon ka badla khoon* (blood for blood) and that he should demand that the police put a stop to it. The slogan-shouting continued unchecked for days.

As we were leaving, an aide told him that the Home Ministry had decided to call in the army. This was another one of the many lies we would hear at the highest levels of administration.

I returned home to find an urgent message from I.K. Gujral, an old friend and brother of the painter Satish Gujral, asking me to ring him back, which I did. He told me not to let Jagjit drive back to his house – which was quite near his own – because there was chaos on the streets. No Sikh was safe on them. He said he was coming over to work out a plan of action. (Gujral wrote in his diary that night: 'Delhi is burning. There are reports of trains arriving with corpses – it is like 1947. General Aurora spent the night with us. The hero of 1971 could not sleep in his own house in Delhi.')

Over lunch that day Gujral, Aurora and I decided to go and see the Home Minister who in the Indian Cabinet is in charge of the police, the intelligence agencies and the maintenance of law and order. We found him at home at 3 p.m. looking impassive and seemingly without a care. In its own way this meeting too was an uncanny replay of our earlier experience with the President.

We asked him if the army was being called in.

'It will be here in the evening.'

'How is it being deployed?' asked Aurora.

'The Area Commander will meet the Lt. Governor for this purpose.'

Aurora suggested the setting up of a Joint Control Room to coordinate the army and police actions, with Rao monitoring events from hour to hour.

'I will look into it.'

Anyone who has dealt with any government functionary in India should know what that means! We knew. The Army was not called till the night of November 3. Had it been given charge of Delhi on the first day, 3,000 Sikhs would not have died, nor would their homes, shops, factories, taxis, trucks and places of worship have been set to the torch, under the indulgent eyes of the administration and a partisan police force. The killings took many forms. Large crowds would seize individuals, pour kerosene or petrol on them and burn them alive. Another variation was to put tyres soaked in petrol around the necks of victims, who were held down by crowds while the tyres were lit with burning torches.

Early on the morning of November 2, Romesh Thapar and Rolf and Jeanné Gauffin, the Swedish Chargé d'Affaires and his wife arrived and said they had come to take me to the Swedish Embassy. 'It is unsafe for you to stay in your home,' Rolf told me. But though I was touched by their concern I refused.

Rajni Kothari, a respected political scientist (and not a Sikh), writing of those five days, recorded that women were 'forced to witness in full the torturous methods – pulling out of limbs and eyes, tearing off hair, beards being set on fire, piercing of bowels and kidneys with sharp weapons – through which their menfolk were put to death. Ivan Fera, who has reported on this aspect the best, sums it up well: "certain images had to be burned into the psyche".' (*Lokayan* 3/1, 1985)

Writing in the same issue of *Lokayan*, Raj Thapar said: 'You can't call the killers *homo sapiens*. It has to be another mix. Because nowhere in the world has it happened quite in this way. Hitler organised mass-killing, but kept it away from the population, training the monsters separately, in a long unending chain of command.' She continued:

How did a train arrive at Sunlight Colony station and disgorge its population of monsters, who burnt and killed and mauled and maimed at breakneck speed and then got on to that waiting train, which set off as the job was completed? Who gave the orders for that train, who brought those men, who equipped them?

Or how was the train stopped at Shahdara station and Sikhs pulled out and slaughtered? They say the station platforms were littered with the symbols of our savagery, up from Madhya Pradesh across the vast Indo-Gangetic plain, all the way to Bokaro ...

6. The Eighties: The Bloodied Landscape

And what of the Sikh view? In another article in *Lokayan* Darshan Singh Maini observed:

> In Mrs Gandhi's case, the entire state machinery was shamelessly used, particularly during the last few years of her life, to create a halo of destiny and 'divinity'. Here was a pure politician who would be Saviour and Goddess! .... And since she had assumed all the airs and trappings of a 'goddess' in the eyes of the common person, her assassination brought into play all those lethal impulses and mean-nesses of the spirit that go with a charismatic politics divorced from vision .... The mob and the leader had achieved a union of dark energies and wills. A whole river of Sikh blood was deeded for the 'ceremony' of immersion.

But the deed was done. The blackout of the collective conscience of elected officials, administrators, police, editors and bigots of every religion and persuasion will long haunt the country, even if the guilt of those who masterminded the killings leaves them undisturbed. The blood on Delhi's streets had yet to dry and the spirals of smoke were still rising from half-burnt bodies when glib explanations and justification ('It was the peoples' grief and anger expressing itself') started coming in.

Sukhjit and I went to see the President again on the evening of November 6 – this time to seek his intervention in bringing the criminals to book and to ask for help for the victims. It was like talking to a non-existent person. 'Meanwhile,' as Maini put it, 'Sikh homes and hearths across the length and breadth of this great land remained cold and unlit, the Sikh hearts in torment and travail. And all this, my countrymen, during the blood-stained Presidency of a Sikh!'

We fared no better with the Home Minister, who in seven years would become the Prime Minister of India. Gurbachan and I went to see him on the morning of November 10, on the same mission that had taken Sukhjit and me to Zail Singh. The niceties were main-tained, tea was served, the appropriate expressions of concern were adopted, but the outcome was no different from the uncaring and unfeeling response of the President.

Contrast this response with the alacrity and concern with which the government acted immediately after Mahatma Gandhi's assassi-nation and you get a better idea of how India's politics have been criminalised since then. In 1948, All India Radio had delayed the announcement of the Mahatma's death by almost three-quarters of an hour to give the government time to deploy the security forces to contain a backlash, in case his killer was a Muslim. From the Governor-General downwards – Mountbatten was still in office – everyone had moved swiftly to contain any possible violence.

In 1984 the state-owned TV network helped raise the level of hostility against Sikhs by mesmerising viewers with pictures of crowds demanding blood for blood after the news of Indira Gandhi's death – the blood of *all* Sikhs, as it turned out. And this was done under the auspices of H.K.L. Bhagat, the Congress Minister for Information and Broadcasting, against whom accusing fingers for his complicity in the killings – quite distinct from his role as the broadcasting minister – have been pointed by several enquiry commissions. He has been protected by successive Prime Ministers and still continues as a senior functionary of the Congress party!

*

On the evening of November 2 a few friends who had come to cover Indira Gandhi's funeral, among them John Fraser of Canada's *Globe and Mail*, Shyam Bhatia of London's *Observer* and Joseph Lilyveld of the *New York Times*, were with me when news was brought that my farmhouse and the one next door that I had helped Rasil build, had been burnt down. A mob with barrels of oil had come in trucks at around eleven in the morning and, after ransacking paintings, wall-hangings, prints, ceramics and over five hundred books, had poured kerosene over the furnishings and woodwork and set everything alight in two gigantic bonfires. When I went there three days later I could see in the burnt-out hulks of the buildings extensions of the lengthening shadows which were falling over India, and it suddenly seemed pointless to pretend that life could go on as before. We sold our properties soon after that.

Not everyone had decency and goodness torn out of them in those days of India's shame. My friends Rajeshwar Dayal, the former Foreign Secretary, and his wife Susheela had dropped in to see me a couple of days after Indira Gandhi's funeral, wondering how they could show their concern at the injustice done to the Sikhs. Their most significant contribution, I told them, would be to persuade the government to set up an impartial commission of enquiry to identify those who had planned and directed the killings. If this was not done and the guilty were allowed to go unpunished, militant Sikhs would wreak a terrible vengeance for the crimes. It was clear by then that several Congress MPs, party officials and field workers had gone around putting markings on Sikh homes and businesses to facilitate the work of the mobs. A partisan police force had allowed the atrocities to be committed, while other government agencies and dealers had supplied thousands of barrels of kerosene – always in short supply in India – to help the arsonists with their job.

Rajeshwar Dayal understood it all. And he worked hard at it. Failing to get the government to enquire into the killings, he helped set up an independent Citizens' Commission with a former Chief Justice of India as its Chairman and former Commonwealth, Home and Defence Secretaries and himself as members. The report of the five-member Commission was a damning indictment of the 'masters' of modern India. Interestingly, when the Commission's members wished to talk to the Home Minister, P.V. Narasimha Rao was not available. Nor was he when, after the report's compilation, they wanted to present it to him in person. His arrogance towards them, who had done more for India than he, was appalling.

*

Rajiv Gandhi's actions also lacked foresight and conviction in the weeks and months following the November massacres. Even before showing a similar discourtesy to members of the Citizens' Commission by refusing to meet them, he took no note of the report on the killings, *Who Are the Guilty*, compiled by the People's Union for Democratic Rights and the People's Union for Civil Liberties. Members of these groups had with exemplary courage waded into the thick of the disturbances, recording the complicity of the Congress functionaries, the deliberate dereliction of duty by the police, the cruelly calculating way in which elected and administrative officials had ignored the phone calls and personal warnings of these two bodies. They were men and women of substance: lawyers, academics, journalists and civil rights activists. Not one of them was a Sikh, and those who had responded to the crisis had done so as human beings in an inhuman situation. But their report was ignored by the Prime Minister. The President of the Delhi Congress Committee went a step further. She called it a 'pack of lies' and warned those who had prepared it. They ignored her.

On November 19 Rajiv Gandhi rationalised the killings at a huge public rally in which he made the astonishing statement that 'when a big tree falls the earth shakes'. Whoever wrote it into his speech did him a disservice and he himself was not perceptive enough to strike it out. Before the December 1984 General Elections the massive advertising campaign of the Congress party brazenly provoked anti-Sikh feelings. This unethical, ill-advised and crude campaign was cleared at the highest level. But even if Rajiv Gandhi was unaware of its thrust, which he could not have been, he should have stopped it after the first item appeared. He did not. To add to the disgust and anger of the Sikhs and other right-thinking people, some of the Congress leaders who had been named in *Who Are the Guilty* were not only given Parliamentary tickets to fight the elections but were made Ministers in Rajiv Gandhi's Cabinet.

The most extraordinary policy decision that seemed to have been secretly taken by his government was to discourage the judiciary and law enforcement agencies from identifying and punishing the guilty. Eight years and four Prime Ministers later, ten persons have been convicted for the murder of 2,733 people (these are official figures) – with the prominent ones named in *Who Are the Guilty* deliberately left out. They – the politicians, police officials, administrators and pliant judges – have been rewarded instead.

For a brief and exciting period of his Prime Ministership, Rajiv Gandhi redeemed himself. In a statesmanlike move he signed a historic Memorandum of Settlement with Harcharan Singh Longowal on July 24, 1985. It was a magnificent bid to bring Punjab back from where the unprincipled politics of the time had taken it.

I met Rajiv Gandhi two weeks before the Punjab elections. When Rajni Kothari and I called on him at his office in the South Block of the Secretariat – another one of Lutyens's monumental buildings – it was crawling with gun-toting security men. The ante-rooms were crowded but we were taken to his secretary's room – next to his own – and were shown in within a few minutes. He looked fit and at ease but soon went over the top when we brought up the subject of the guilty men of 1984. Two of them, known to have led the mobs during the massacres, had recently been shot dead by Sikh militants, and with this on his mind Rajiv Gandhi turned on Kothari and said angrily:

'I will hold you responsible if any more killings of this kind take place.' (Rajni Kothari as the President of the People's Union of Civil Liberties had jointly published *Who Are the Guilty*, which had named the two who had been killed in retribution.)

'If the Sikhs are still in India, Mr Gandhi,' I intervened, 'it is because of men like Rajni Kothari and others who showed impartiality and integrity during those days of November.' I also said that it would be a good principle to hold the killers and the colluders responsible for the crimes and not those trying to expose them.

Things settled down after a while and we made suggestions which would strengthen the detente the Accord had ushered in. We said that Punjab's governor, Arjun Singh, a former Chief Minister of Madhya Pradesh who had with rare tact and skill made the pact possible, should stay on as governor for another year to ensure its implementation. Since he had earned nation-wide praise for it, he would have a stake in ensuring its success. We also suggested that several major industries should be established in Punjab for channelling the energies of its hardworking people into more constructive pursuits, especially since the mechanisation of farming had left an increasing number of strapping young men with little else to turn to. As an adjunct to this, we stressed the need for a major institute in Punjab which could train its people – who already have an aptitude for technical innovativeness – into industrial designers. We mentioned a whole range of other possibilities as we were convinced that merely to luxuriate in the aftermath of the Accord would be counterproductive. People had to be convinced of the new dynamics at work in the State.

None of these suggestions were realised. The governor was transferred out of the State within weeks and just about every other possibility was ignored. The oppressively opinionated circle of advisors around Rajiv Gandhi took over, and the Accord was effectively killed. Though it was a mistake on Rajiv Gandhi's part to hold the elections to the Assembly so soon after the Accord (against the advice of Longowal), he showed decorum and restraint throughout the period prior to the polls on September 25 by preventing official machinery from being misused to favour the Congress. The Akalis' convincing victory was an endorsement of the electorate's approval of the Accord. After formation of the Ministry and with hopes for the future beginning to rise, things began to unravel. The Centre's shifting embrace now encompassed other ideas which had more to do with undoing the Accord. And they succeeded. Rajiv Gandhi was neither shrewd enough to see through the machinations of those around him, nor possessed of the staying power to implement what he had initiated. The resulting disenchantment led to a resurgence of militancy and terror which continues to this day.

*

My own recollections of that evening of July 24 are vivid. I had just returned from abroad and was still a bit jet-lagged when there was a call to say that Longowal, having signed an agreement with Rajiv Gandhi a few minutes earlier, was on his way to see me. He arrived with several aides and the first question he asked was if I had heard of the Accord. I said I had and I was proud of him. But, I told him, there were dark forces which had a vested interest in the continuation of the armed struggle in Punjab, and their hostility to the agreement would pose a threat to his life. To begin with, the end of militancy would mean that the security and intelligence agencies would no longer have the vast unaccountable funds to which they were accustomed or the sweeping powers they enjoyed at present. The functionaries of the ruling Congress party too – including the Sikhs in it – would resent the Akalis coming to power. The vengeful Sikh militants who had not forgiven the attack on the Golden Temple were in no mood for an Accord with the Centre either. But the danger, I felt, was greater from the former than from the militants.

Concerning elections in the State, I urged him not to agree to a snap poll; to take at least six months – he had only just been released from jail – to re-establish his hold on the party before entering the fray. With the respect he commanded, that was all the time he needed to restore his links with the people; to assess where the dangers lay; to see where hostile elements, including government agents, had infiltrated the organisation. He was of similar mind and suggested I help him draft the letter to the Prime Minister. A few days later I bought a Gurmukhi typewriter, had the letter to Rajiv Gandhi typed, giving the reasons for delaying the elections and sent my close aide, Col. Thanwar Singh, to Punjab, for Longowal's signature. I also sent him a pen I had bought at Harrods in London, along with a note expressing my hope that many historic documents would be signed with it in the coming years. Sadly Rajiv Gandhi was unable to see the logic behind the postponement of elections – he was influenced as always by minions around him rather than by his own instincts – and they were announced for the third week of September.

On the evening of August 20, George Verghese rang up to tell me that Longowal had been assassinated.

Some of us went to the press two days later to say:

> The nation has once again paid the price for ... the wholly miscon-
> ceived and opportunistic decision to ram an election through a state
> so full of fear, tension, intimidation and terror. It is responsible for the
> killing of Longowal ... (who) himself had opted just three days earlier
> for elections in February or March ... Yet those who sit in Chandigarh
> and New Delhi ... took the decision to force the elections ... (stressing)
> that its intelligence agencies had given the assurance that there was
> no danger from the extremists ... will these intelligence people be
> taken to task for their misleading reports? ... Equally, the government
> must identify and expose before the public those, either in the Con-
> gress hierarchy or any other, who masterminded from Delhi or
> Chandigarh the killings in Punjab including the killing of Longowal.

No one was ever arraigned for the murder of this man who had dared to reach out for a peaceful settlement in Punjab.

144

6. The Eighties: The Bloodied Landscape

In 1985 Harji Malik and I jointly edited a book of essays, *Punjab: The Fatal Miscalculation*, which placed the entire Punjab problem in perspective. In the opening essay, 'The Distorting Mirror', I analysed the appalling role played by some of the national dailies, through their distorted coverage of the unfolding Punjab crisis. We dedicated the book to Harchand Singh Longowal, because of his single-minded concern to lead Punjab back from the brink to which the unprincipled politics of the time had taken it.

*

In his remaining years in office Rajiv Gandhi, a decent young man, happily ensconced in the family he adored, absorbed by his love of flying, photography and a few close friends, became the victim of both his mother's dynastic ambitions and the labyrinthine atmosphere of the office he occupied. Neither his experience of life, nor his temperament nor his political talent had equipped him to judge the slick advice he was offered by the self-serving men around him. The alacrity with which such courtiers gravitate to persons in power, and the extent to which they will go to ingratiate themselves, seems ingrained in the Indian character. A hangover, perhaps, from the days when, for most, survival depended on servility.

It is not too difficult – if one begins to take dynastic attributes seriously – to make the transition from innocence to omnipotence. Sadly, Rajiv Gandhi soon made this transition. It was sad for the nation too, because it would pay a bitter price – as would he – for his inability to see through the imprudent advice on which he took two momentous decisions: Sri Lanka and Kashmir.

Sri Lanka, an island nation of 16 million, separated from the southern tip of India by 22 miles of the Palk Strait, has a population of Buddhists and Hindus of which 12.5 per cent (about two million) are Tamils. The Tamils are concentrated in the northern and eastern regions – across the narrow water that separates them from the 55 million Tamils of the southern Indian state of Tamil Nadu. Historically, the powerful Buddhists have never trusted Hindu India because of her frequent invasions of the island, and its Tamil minority figures in that mistrust. Minorities inevitably bear the brunt of majority chauvinism, and Sri Lanka was no exception.

The Tamils, resentful of job discrimination, lack of educational opportunities, denial of equal language status and second-class status as citizens, protested peacefully for almost three decades, beginning in 1948. In 1983, as with many such movements in recent times, violence overtook the more acceptable forms of protest and the Tamils ambushed and killed thirteen Sri Lankan soldiers. In savage retaliation the Sinhalese massacred 600 Tamils in Colombo. This killing spree rent the country apart and, as the situation radicalised, a charismatic rebel leader, Velupillai Prabhakaran, forged his Liberation Tigers of Tamil Eelum (LTTE) into a deadly insurgency group, championing the implacable Tamil will for an independent homeland in the island's north-eastern regions.

The Sri Lankan army's ruthless efforts to destroy the Tamils made them even more violent and efficient. While Israeli and Pakistani intelligence experts assisted the Sri Lankans, India provided the Tigers with funds, arms, training and transport. By 1987 the island's self-assured President, Junius R. Jayewardene, who had been confident of eliminating the 3,500 Tigers – against Sri Lanka's 50,000 military – was ready to pass the burden of taming the Tamils to someone else. India, foolishly, took on the burden.

Completely ignoring the ironies, contradictions and contending demands of the situation, a few wilful men around Rajiv Gandhi literally led him to his death by persuading him to intervene militarily in Sri Lanka and that too through *a massive show of force*. As if India did not already have her hands full with Punjab and a looming crisis in Kashmir! The agreement he was persuaded into signing with Jayewardene in Colombo in August 1987 was a victory for the wily President and a defeat for New Delhi's mandarins who agreed to a pact which required India to: enforce a ceasefire within forty-eight hours; disarm the rebels within seventy-two hours; expel from India those Tamils who opposed the pact; ensure Colombo's compliance with conditions like general amnesty for the rebels, equal status for the Tamil language, autonomy for the Tamil regions and much more.

No attempt was made to draw lessons from the American and Soviet experiences in Vietnam and Afghanistan. Or from other insurgency movements in which well-equipped and well-trained military forces had come to grief in an unequal war. The upstarts around the Indian Prime Minister were more interested in selling him the idea of the glory that would be his if he emerged as South Asia's youthful peacemaker and hence its hegemonic master. He was offered a vision of himself as a man of iron will, resolute enough to act when action was called for and with a powerful military to back his decisions. The underside of the venture was given short shrift: that a surrogate war in an alien setting against seasoned, battle-tested, do-or-die guerrilla forces, mistrustful of both Colombo and New Delhi, was fraught with danger and would inevitably boomerang on India! Even more infair to the military were the politically motivated constraints under which it was expected to operate.

New Delhi did everything to increase the Tigers' mistrust. Compulsively, as it had in Punjab, it supported rival Tamil groups in the classic imperial strategy of divide and rule. As an intelligence official in New Delhi put it, 'the idea was to reduce the dominance of the Tigers since the other groups were under our control and this ensured that the interim administration and the provincial council have more people who would abide by Delhi's directives'. There was a startling similarity with Punjab, Kashmir and other disturbed Indian states: the obsession with wanting *people who would abide by Delhi's directives*.

As it was bound to, India's blunder backfired; and when the Indian forces finally withdrew after two and a half years a monumental bill had accumulated for this misadventure and the Indian army lost over 1,200 men. India had been pushed into a no-win situation detrimental to the morale of the armed forces, and her intervention had alienated both the Sri Lankans and most of the island's Tamils. It also increased the lurking danger of a separatist Tamil movement in Tamil Nadu, where brute force is being used by Jayalalitha Jayaram, the autocratic Chief Minister, against sympathisers of the LTTE. Her actions were condoned by the P.V. Narasimha Rao government in New Delhi because it needed the support of her party's twelve members in Parliament!

*

Almost 2,000 miles from the southern tip of India and the seas which wash its shores, another crisis was building up in a valley ringed by snow-covered mountains of the country's northern-most reaches. Through a cruel convergence of circumstance and chicanery, 1987 would also be a fateful year for the beautiful state of Jammu and Kashmir (J&K), where New Delhi's unprincipled politics had destabilised the largely Muslim-dominated, but remarkably secular and peaceful, Kashmir Valley. To the corruption condoned by Nehru from 1953 to 1962 had been added over twenty years of Indira Gandhi and her son's manipulations and misrule, aimed at getting – and keeping – the state's Congress party in office. Their paranoia for personal power had finally, perhaps irretrievably, alienated Kashmiri Muslims.

The Valley's rage reached boiling point after the brazen rigging of the 1987 state elections. While earlier dissent was manageable, the Centre's contemptuous disregard for democratic norms that year

147

was the final straw, coming as it did after the dismissal of the duly elected Farooq Abdullah ministry (formed by the opposition National Conference Party) in 1984 and the installation of the thoroughly corrupt G.M. Shah. The Kashmiri Muslims' bitterness at the denial of their right to honest elections soon crystallised into armed militancy and a demand for secession. The subsequent inducement to Farooq to join a coalition government with the Congress destroyed forever the credibility of New Delhi, which from then on was considered the principal enemy of the Kashmiri people.

Characteristically, New Delhi's reflexive response was to blame this crisis too on external forces: a perennial standby for its continuing political mismanagement. But an inconvenient question remained unanswered. If internal stability and the solidarity of the population with the rest of India remained unaffected by three wars with Pakistan, what went wrong in the eighties? Why did these people who in the past had rushed to inform India's security forces of Pakistani infiltrators suddenly turn against the country? Was the Muslim strain flawed as well? Or did that unseen 'foreign hand' create this crisis too?

Instead of correcting the obvious shortcomings in its administrative, economic and election practices in the State that so long had irked its people, New Delhi inducted massive military and paramilitary forces into Kashmir. For added effect, it did away with the legislature and electoral politics, imposed President's Rule under which a Governor appointed by the Centre rules through extraordinary powers given to him, and began cutting a bloody swathe of state terror across the Valley.

There was also another, a hidden, dimension to the growing bitterness in the Valley. This had to do with the increasing toll of lives that anti-Muslim riots were taking all over India, often with the connivance of the police and political parties. As the number of states in which outbursts of violence grew – Uttar Pradesh, Bihar, Madhya Pradesh, Maharashtra, Karnataka, Assam – it ignited a mood of religious resurgence in the Valley's Muslims which the Mullahs and others of their class were quick to exploit. Even as the orientation in India's favour changed, New Delhi – bemused by the muscle of the armed forces it had fielded there – seemed oblivious of the danger.

Not that there were no other options open to it. It could have worked at strengthening the emotional integration of the State's people with India. Sheikh Abdullah, the Kashmiri political leader and father of Farooq Abdullah, had pointed the people in India's direction. He had favoured the Indian connection rather than the Pakistani, because he respected Gandhian ideals and the democratic promise of India. The earlier Kashmiri confidence could have been restored by avoiding electoral malpractices and letting the State run its own affairs. But the improprieties increased through the eighties. The greater regional autonomy which the State was promised under the Indian Constitution – an expression of India's intention to respect Kashmiri identity – was negated at every turn. In the end the Kashmiri Muslims got just one message: they were the colonised whose subservient status was repeatedly underscored through New Delhi's arrogant disregard of their identity and self-respect.

As the insurgency in the Valley increased and its once creative people took to the Kalashnikov, tourism revenues nose-dived and popular discontent spread. At precisely this point hopes for a settlement were raised with Rajiv Gandhi and his Congress party's defeat in the November 1989 elections and the swearing-in of V.P. Singh as Prime Minister. Singh came to office with a formidable reputation as a clean man – a rare species in Delhi's political wasteland. But he proved a chronic waffler – indecisive and inchoate, altogether inadequate to the task of keeping one-sixth of the world's population on course. He did little about Punjab and Kashmir – which he was quick to visit after the elections and just as quick to neglect after that – and the hopes he had raised remained unfulfilled. If anything, they aggravated the existing resentments because the disappointments which come from shattered hopes are even more corrosive. And his inaction was seen as further proof of an untrustworthy Centre.

*

Against the lengthening shadows of India's social and political degradation, rays of hope were provided by the turn her economy had taken. The shackles binding it were loosened during the Rajiv years and more pragmatic policies ushered in. Greater incentives for industrial growth, liberalisation of terms for foreign tie-ups and decontrol of many sectors had encouraged the forces of competition and led to a dramatic spurt in industrial output. There was also a growing diversity of goods produced: from turnkey projects, heavy machinery, chemical plants, railroad locomotives, carriages and other ancillaries, aircraft, ships, oil-drilling equipment, thermal plants, tractors, automobiles, electronics, military hardware, rocketry and missiles to an incredible range of consumer goods. The latter catered to the increasing demands of an emerging middle-class which had reached 150 million by the end of the decade. Its flagbearer was the Maruti car. Made largely with Japanese collaboration

149

and generous help from the government – which owned the plant – it symbolised the coming-of-age of the Indian yuppie.

But the poverty of the have-nots was the dark side of this picture. As India's growth rate rose from 3 per cent in the previous decades to 7 per cent in the eighties, the number of Indians living below the poverty-line continued to be almost a third of the total population because of growing income disparities and increasing poverty due to virtually no trickle-down of the new prosperity. Inevitably the nutrition also worsened. To take calorie-intake as the yardstick, the income-levels of people below the poverty line are so inadequate that they are unable to provide for even a daily intake of 2,000 calories per capita, which is far below physiological levels needed. By the end of the eighties around 300 million people lived on the wrong side of this line.

My friend Dr C. Gopalan, an internationally recognised authority on nutritional research and President of the Nutrition Foundation of India, feels that the main reason for undernutrition in millions of poor households is not so much 'the lack of food at the overall national level, but the fact that the income levels of households, which represent over 30 per cent of the population, are so low that they just cannot command access to food in quantities necessary to meet their basic nutritional needs'. He sees it as a 'cruel paradox' that while the nation has sufficient stocks of food grains at the national level, large segments of the population suffer from undernutrition through grossly inequitable distribution.

The self-centred preoccupations of the three different Prime Ministers during the eighties did nothing to decrease the number of the deprived, whose distress was in no way alleviated by the new economic upsurge, the booming stock markets, the escalating demand for consumer goods or the expanded industrial base. Because the wealth generated was stashed away in the vaults of the rich, or wasted on non-priority projects promoted by elected officials or invested in projects which pandered to the consumerist tastes of the new India. Winston Churchill once remarked in a radio speech in March, 1943, that 'there is no finer investment for any community than putting milk into babies. Healthy citizens are the greatest asset any country can have.' In 1987 a Unicef report on hunger stated: 'In the last two years more children have died in India and Pakistan than in all 46 nations of Africa put together.'

The uncaring mentality of the political decision-makers is cruelly symbolised by the extravagant advertising on state-owned television and radio that mocks the masses with seductive invitations to try the latest flavours in ice-creams, chocolates, soft drinks and the rest. No passing thought is given to the feelings these ads evoke in the undernourished, anaemic, semi-starved people who daily watch or hear the virtues of these products.

The ruling class in India, unwilling to allow itself the luxury of being distracted by such distortions, did itself proud in the eighties. While Indira Gandhi had an austere bent, Rajiv Gandhi showed no such weakness. During his official trips abroad, a Boeing 747 jet would be requisitioned from Air India and another kept on hold, while the airline was left to its own devices to deal with disrupted schedules. This mindless extravagance and self-indulgence was reported by Sunil Sethi, one of India's finest young investigative journalists. His piece 'Air-India's New Maharaja' in the November 14, 1987 issue of the *Sunday Mail* told it all:

> ... The report on the outfitting of the flight runs into 61 pages with annexures. Its contents would bring a blush to the cheeks of the most dollar-demented NRI ... leave alone serve to enhance the image of a head of government whose country is reeling from a year of the bleakest drought. Two Boeing 747s out of the carrier's fleet of ten were laid off commercial flights for the period of nearly a month wreaking havoc on international flights. A Boeing 747 from Middle East Airlines and a smaller aircraft from Cargolux were hired at the approximate rate of US$5,000 per day to replace these two aircraft ... the Prime Minister's flight was sent to London in order to be specially outfitted for the Prime Minister's impending use while Flight AI-2 stood on stand-by duty throughout the period ...
>
> ... A double-bed, with an electronically controlled headrest was installed in a bedroom, swivel chairs with special off-white coloured headrest covers adorned the twelve-seater conference room and seven sets of specially imported table cloths ... were airlifted to cover the Prime Minister's dinner table in his VIP cabin. Turkish towels in pastel shades from Singapore, white bedsheets and pillow covers from ....

Sethi's piece inspired my first and only attempt at painting. It started with a visit from Nicola Feakes, wife of the Australian High Commissioner, who dropped by one morning in October 1987 and insisted I do a painting for an auction of artworks she had planned for funding a hospital.

'Impossible,' I said. 'I have never painted in my life.'

'Why don't you try? Many of the others who have agreed are not artists either. There will be a spontaneity in these exhibits, something different. Especially since persons like you will be expressing themselves in a medium different from the one they are used to.'

She mentioned the names of several persons who had agreed, and

I felt if they could do it so could I. Never having held a paint brush in my life, I was wildly toying with the idea of a few frenzied splashes of colour on a large canvas – when Sethi's article appeared. That was it. It had a photograph of the Gandhis walking up the gangway of an Air-India jumbo and below it a cut-out of a menu which read: 'Brunch Menu Specially Created for the Prime Minister's Flight.' Then came the Air-India logo and after it the line: 'The Prime Minister's Special Flight.'

I cut this part of the page out and made it the centerpiece of a collage on which I arranged cuttings from newspapers and magazines showing the stark contrariness of Indian society. Below cones of dripping ice-creams was a tearsheet of the parched, drought-stricken earth; pictures of emaciated children with vacant eyes and empty begging-bowls were placed next to elegantly-attired men holding cut-glass decanters of cognac against the backdrop of richly panelled walls; rows of bloody and battered bodies after an orgy of violence were juxtaposed with a beautiful woman in a bikini lying in the sun on an Indian beach with a background slogan: 'In India it's Magic'. Part of a magazine cover was slapped on with the words 'Defence Scandal – Who gets the Kickbacks?' In the middle of the collage was a big letter 'G', tilted to show its imbalance, and around it and from top to bottom of the canvas I drew a bold outline of India in crimson. I then had it framed and called Nicola Feakes to come and collect it.

She almost passed out when she saw it. There was the question of protocol, of diplomatic niceties, of possible embarrassment and mis-interpretation if such a 'work' were to be displayed – no matter for how worthy a cause – in an ambassador's residence. But she rallied, and the fact that Edmund Hillary, who was then New Zealand's High Commissioner in India, bid for it did much to make me think momentarily of a possible career as an artist. I confess to being sufficiently moved by my 'artistic expression' to get a friend to outbid Hillary on my behalf, and I ended up owning it.

*

Of India's many political parties, the Bharatiya Janata Party has consistently stood by its single-point programme of Hindu rule over India – for Hindu nationalism. Known by different names in the past, it took on its present incarnation in 1980. Its militant wing – in a sense its parent body – has been the Rashtriya Swayamsevak Sangh (RSS), two of whose more fanatical members shot Mahatma Gandhi dead in January 1948 for his pro-Muslim leanings. M.S.

Golwalkar, the principal ideologue of the RSS, had even before Independence visualised post-Independence India as a Hindu nation, so the RSS has kept the BJP's actions and ideological commitments under constant audit.

Now, towards the end of the 1980s, the presence of these two on the Indian political scene was for the first time perceived as a threat to the mainline parties. What opened the way for the BJP was the cynicism with which Indira Gandhi had played the religious card in Punjab and alienated the ever-trusting Kashmiris. If the head of the Congress party, who was also Nehru's daughter and inheritor of his and Gandhi's secular spirit, could make such a cynical pitch for the Hindu vote, the BJP was more than willing to come out of the closet. It was better at the game; had more experience of it. And this time there would be no holds barred. The stage was now set to make Lothian's prediction come true: *The mass of the people will still, I think, respond to religious feelings once they are stimulated for political purposes.* So far the masses hadn't, but the BJP was set to ensure that they did.

Congress misrule had helped militant Hindu resurgence. Twelve out of twenty-five Indian states had been under President's rule at one time or another during the eighties, with their legislatures dismissed or suspended and the states ruled at the whim of the Centre. Those who still believed that Indian democracy was alive and functioning, ignored the symptoms of creeping fascism which other more perceptive observers could see. The extraordinary powers government had acquired through acts, ordinances and amendments to the Constitution, combined with their unscrupulous use in the form of illegal detentions, torture, killings through faked police encounters and increasing disregard of fundamental human rights, had helped create a climate of counter-terror in which physical assault, indiscriminate massacre and contempt for the laws had become commonplace. India did not stumble into violence and terror. These catastrophes were courted. People were led to the slaughter by their perverse, power-obsessed leaders who were bent on providing proof of Amiel's observation that 'institutions are worth no more than the men who work them'.

The 1989 general elections saw the BJP come of age. Its representation in parliament rose from two to 88 seats: a spectacular victory for the naked face of Hindu revivalism for which the Congress had opened the doors. As the decade – with its more than 4,500 incidents of communal clashes, violence and killings, and the growing resonance of the appeal to replace the mosque at Ayodhya with a temple dedicated to Lord Rama – drew to a close, the BJP's emergence spelt greater instability in the nineties. If the experiment with a coalition government had failed in the seventies, and the Congress rule in the eighties had created deep and dangerous fissures, the BJP's brand of Hindu nationalism threatened the nation's unity in the nineties. There was no let-up in sight.

Who could the people turn to for a stable government? The coming years should provide the answer to this and to the larger question: can India's democratic institutions and her unified Republican entity survive through the nineties? Or will inconsequential men, unable to envision a deserving future for her, because they lack a larger vision themselves, end up destroying the promise of a free India? Would Indian sanity, wisdom, moral values, perseverence and persistence be able to prevail over such men?

What helped to sustain me through this disgraceful decade was the book I had started to write on the Golden Temple. I felt, that since the ultimate tragedy of the deceitful politics which had preceded the events of 1984 was the manner in which this supreme emblem of the Sikh faith was placed at the centre of an unseemly controversy, its magnetic hold over the hearts of millions of Sikhs had to be documented, so people could understand the influence it exercises over Sikh minds and the role it has played in the evolution of their faith.

I did not want it to be just another book, but one which established a context – provided a backdrop of events which had ravaged the Indian subcontinent before and up to the 15th century, when Guru Nanak and Sikhism were born. It must portray the mood, temper and persecutions of those times, the baptism by fire of a people who were not militant to begin with but were led into militancy through the tyranny of capricious rulers, who survived against amazing odds to establish their own empire in the North.

The book had to show how all facets of the Sikh personality were shaped by the fountainhead of Sikh inspiration, their Golden Temple. 'They came to it with untold wealth or a handful of flowers; to seek the blessings of the Gurus or in gratitude for blessings already received; to offer homage to the martyrs who gave their lives for this hallowed shrine, or to pray for the privilege of sacrificing their own lives for it ... or they came for the sheer joy of seeing it calm and serene in the early morning light as they immersed themselves in the immortal pool.'

I wanted to write a book which would provide readers with the very essence of this faith. Especially since Sikhs continue to be provoked by the attribution to them of crimes they have not committed, by the denial to them of justice and by sly and invidious forms of discrimination. Even though my narrative would end in 1925 and would have nothing to do with contemporary events, it must show through historical analogy the futility of tyrannical persecution, especially since the will to resist such persecution is ingrained in the Sikh character.

When *The Golden Temple* was published at the beginning of 1989, to gratifying reviews in India and abroad, the editor of the *Indian Express* asked me to contribute a piece explaining what had made me write it. It appeared on May 15, 1989, and though I had expressed concern about the events which could overtake the country in the next three years, I was surprised at the extent to which these concluding lines would prove tragically prophetic, thanks to the new breed of Indian politicians:

> Sikhism was born as a synthesis of – and a movement of reconciliation between – the two great religions of Hinduism and Islam. It is time again for reconciliation and not loud and unrestrained political rhetoric, if bloodshed and carnage – which will eventually destroy the country – are to be avoided.

Chapter 7

The Nineties: The End of the Dream?

In our country the lie has become not just a moral category but a pillar
of the state.
Alexander Solzhenitsyn, *The Oak and the Calf*

Your light illuminates the Kaaba and the temple,
Then why am I caught differentiating between the two.

Ka'abe mein but-kade mein hai yaksan teri zia,
Mein imtiaz-e dair o haram mein phansa hua.
Allama Mohammed Iqbal, *Bang-e-Dara*

Though the eighties proved to be the most violent decade since
Independence, hopes for a more stable nineties were also quickly
shattered during the brief Prime Ministership of V.P. Singh. Sworn
in on December 2, 1989, this former Congressman had held the
Finance and Defence portfolios in the Rajiv Gandhi government
before joining the Janata Party. The Janata Party's impressive showing in the 1989 elections, though a vote against the misdeeds of the
previous government, was also a vote for Singh's honesty and secular credentials. He believed in the right of all faiths to coexist in the
larger religious mosaic of India, and yet this is where the unending
paradoxes of the Indian mind again manifested themselves. Lacking
sufficient strength in Parliament, Singh formed the National Front
government with the assured support of the reactionary and mili-
tantly Hindu BJP. So the picture which emerged was of a secularist
dependent on communalists for his stay in office.
How long could this last?
Clearly, the question was very much on Singh's mind. And even
though he considered himself adept at managing contradictions –
among his outside supporters were the Left parties too – the strain
of managing the rather creaky alliance began to tell. At this point the
picaresque side of his personality took over. In a sudden move to
prop up his waning popularity, he sprang the recommendations of
a ten-year old Commission on an unsuspecting public. It was obvious to everyone that the timing and suddenness of this move had

less to do with improving the lot of the underclasses – which is what the Commission's report was about – and more with bettering his own chances of surviving in the Prime Minister's chair.

It is an accepted strategy in India to appoint enquiry Commissions to get round contentious issues. By the time they finish enquiring passions have cooled, and their reports are quietly filed away. And so it was with the Mandal Commission report which had been gathering dust since December 1980. It had recommended that reservations – which till then had meant government jobs reserved only for the untouchable castes and the tribals – should be increased by 27 per cent to include 'other backward' castes. The definition of these was also broadened. If implemented, this would in some cases almost double the percentage of government jobs reserved for the backward classes. Singh would increase his electoral support through new vote banks thus created, and with the Muslims and other groups already in his favour he would no longer need the BJP's support. He would emerge as the caste constituency's new messiah.

But, through an astonishing oversight or miscalculation, he underestimated the explosive nature of intercaste tensions which were already on the boil, with the frustrations and resentments of 'upper' caste hopefuls seeking employment in a limited job market. No sooner had he announced his intention, than these tensions exploded across the nation, and in a bizarre and unthinkable form of protest students doused themselves in oil and died fiery deaths in public places. Almost three hundred persons died through self-immolations and street battles, and hundreds were disfigured for life. Within a matter of weeks the country was left with another deeply divisive legacy which carried its own poison of anger and bitterness into the mainstream of an already disturbed nation. It also brought Singh's government down in November, 1990 – after a mere eleven months in office.

The opportunistic aspect of his bid for the backward-caste votes aside, was he justified in placing centre-stage the need to help the underprivileged castes? He certainly was. For millions in this category live below the poverty line. But is reservation of jobs for them, on the basis of caste, the logical way of improving their lot? After all, countless people in the higher castes too live in poverty and break their backs chasing hard-to-come-by jobs made scarce by long years of restrictive economic policies. There is a school of thought in India which argues with equal justification that economic criteria must be the basis for reserving jobs: that the economically underprivileged – to whichever caste they belong – must have a claim on jobs.

The entire reservations-debate sidelines the critical importance of merit, and the only enduring way of ensuring merit is through better education. But if the underprivileged do not have access to good educational institutions even after forty-five years of Independence, how do they acquire merit? Shouldn't the emphasis then be on investing in such institutions so that all castes and classes can get a good education? And get jobs on merit after that? Instead of taking this course, several state governments have introduced a particularly distasteful and odious policy of 'capitation fees' by which admission in certain colleges can be had if parents pay fees for the entire duration of their studies in advance. Where would impoverished families find several hundred thousand rupees for just one member of the family? The result is a nightmarish situation in which the privileged can give their children a good education and get them in line for good jobs while vast numbers, disillusioned and angry, unable to afford education or compete for jobs, look to reservations or take to the streets. The social environment denies them educational opportunities through which to prove their merit and potential.

Neither Singh nor his predecessors tried to change this social environment. For each of them, politics was an end in itself. The power, patronage and privileges were not worth risking in futile attempts at righting centuries-old wrongs. Even if the personal inclination of some of India's Prime Ministers favoured change, it was not allowed to come in the way of politics. Politics was the art of the possible, and since they could not see themselves effecting social dislocations on the scale needed to pull India out of her medieval past, they left things alone. This was V.P. Singh's problem too. Instead of opting for structural changes, which as a man of integrity he should have done, he tried for political mileage by adopting allegorical positions. And, like his predecessors, he relied on rhetoric. In India rhetoric has to be experienced to be believed. Its momentum carries the orator along and in time leaves all contradictory evidence behind, developing a life and lore of its own. It manages to provide its own underpinnings of moral justification, ideological integrity and much else, but, as Singh discovered to his cost, this was not enough to keep him in office. And when the knife was finally turned, the hand holding it was the BJP's.

*

Fearful of the distinct possiblity that Singh would actually corner the backward-vote bank, the BJP, with cold and ruthless intent unmatched even by India's unprincipled political standards, decided

159

to outdo him by openly and provocatively courting the Hindu vote. For which the Muslims would have to pay with their blood. It placed in the eye of the storm – which it was aware would hit the nation with primal fury – a mosque built in 1508 to honour the first Mughal Emperor Babar. The BJP announced its intention of demolishing this 464-year-old Babri Masjid and building a temple in its place, since a temple – so it claimed – had been destroyed by the conquering Mughals to build this Masjid at Ayodhya: a temple, moreover, which had stood on the exact birthplace of Lord Rama. But some of India's most respected historians, including Sarvapalli Gopal, Romila Thapar and Bipan Chandra of the Centre for Historical Studies at Jawaharlal Nehru University, disagree. They doubt whether present-day Ayodhya is the one mentioned in the epic poem *Ramayana*. They maintain that in this elegantly rendered work the personalities, places and events are largely fictional, and, unless there is evidence on the ground to prove their existence, these cannot be accepted because 'very often historical evidence contradicts popular beliefs'. King Rama, according to Valmiki who wrote the *Ramayana*, was born thousands of years before Ayodhya was inhabited, since no archaeological evidence of it exists. The only settlements at the disputed site – of extremely simple, primitive materials which do not tally with the sophisticated palaces and structures described in the *Ramayana* – date from the eighth century BC whereas Lord Rama was said to have been born thousands of years before even the *Kal Yuga* (fourth age of the aeon, according to Hindu cosmology) which began in 3102 BC.

The BJP was unmoved by these arguments – as was its militant associate, the Vishwa Hindu Parishad (VHP), which had spearheaded the campaign for the mosque's demolition. They were not interested in historical and archaeological evidence. What excited them was the rubric of political opportunity, the stirring up of Hindu sentiments and the siphoning off of votes from the biggest vote bank of them all. What came next was straight out of a Hindi potboiler movie. The BJP's President, Lal Krishna Advani, announced that, starting September 25, 1990, he would undertake a 10,000 km journey from Somnath, the great Hindu pilgrimage centre on the west coast, to Ayodhya. After travelling across several States, the massive procession of assorted vehicles would reach Ayodhya on October 30. In the lead would be an airconditioned Toyota truck, made to resemble Lord Ram's *rath* (chariot), only this one – converted to provide all the necessary comforts for Advani – turned out to be a surprisingly incongruous-looking *rath*: a parody enacted by these latter-day charioteers of a great epic in Indian mythology.

7. The Nineties: The End of the Dream?

The *rath yatra* (or journey of the *rath*) was an unqualified success from its sponsor's point of view. All the sister-organisations, the BJP, RSS, VHP, ABVP (student wing) and Bajrang Dal, had geared up to shake the country to its very foundations. And they did their job well. Every inflammatory slogan along the 10,000 km journey extolled *Hindutva* (doctrine of Hindu hegemony), the temple at Ayodhya and India's impending return to her Hindu roots. Each speech was an open threat to the Muslims – and other minorities – inviting them to pay heed to the new wave.

Within days of the *rath yatra* Uttar Pradesh, where over 138 million people live, and where Ayodhya is located, became a battlefield with Hindu-Muslim riots raging in the towns, cities and countryside including the state capital Lucknow. 'Never since Partition has Indian society been polarised so strongly along communal lines,' observed Coomi Kapoor, a seasoned newspaperwoman who travelled across the State to assess the damage for her paper. 'Even the chant *Jai Siya Ram* has taken on the menacing tone of a battle-cry rather than a slogan of religious devotion.' The killings spread across the other volatile regions of the country, reaching all the way to the south. The figures of persons killed: shot, stabbed, bludgeoned, burnt or thrown into the rivers could not be accurately tallied, given the gruesome ways men devise to kill each other.

When the indecisive V.P. Singh finally had Advani, his erstwhile 'ally', arrested, just before his juggernaut could roll into Ayodhya, the BJP withdrew its support to the government, plunging India into political uncertainty.

*

The man who emerged as Prime Minister was Chandra Shekhar. He too had once belonged to the Congress and was one of its 'Young Turks' – a small splinter group which wanted the party to have a more socialist orientation. Later, he had left and stayed on the fringes of political power except for a brief period in the seventies as chairman of the Janata Party which had displaced Indira Gandhi in March 1977. But even then he had not held any executive office. With less than fifty of his own men in Parliament, in a house of over 500 members, he now offered to form the government with the outside support of the Congress party. This unusual arrangement was accepted by President R. Venkataraman, who felt that the alternative of holding nationwide elections in the surcharged atmosphere could end in chaos.

During the brief period he was in office (from November 1990 to

161

June 1991) Chandra Shekhar performed surprisingly well. He was a down-to-earth politician whose democratic instincts and aversion to the authoritarianism of the Gandhis and the chronic waffling of V.P. Singh could have done much to restore normality in Punjab, Kashmir and Assam, had he stayed in office longer. But there were many things working against him. He was totally dependent on the support of other parties and there was continuing opposition, even from his allies, to any breakthroughs he may have achieved. They realised that his success would make it difficult for them to dislodge him, especially as they were less interested in restoring normality in the troubled border states and more in getting back into power. Within months the Congress was plotting to oust him, as there were many around Rajiv Gandhi who wanted to see him toppled at the earliest opportunity. It epitomised the tragedy of men like Chandra Shekhar who, lacking their own support-base, are forced to compromise on vital issues. One of the issues on which he compromised – at considerable cost to his credibility – was when he postponed presentation of the government's annual budget to Parliament on February 28, 1991. He agreed to it at the insistence of the Congress but did serious damage to his standing as a result.

I met him after he became Prime Minister, mainly to talk about Punjab and point out to him the perversion of the previous administrations which had refused to hold elections to the State Assembly since 1985. They had ruled the State by coercion. Thousands of Sikhs were in jail for years without trial, many of them being tortured mercilessly. Countless eager, intelligent, hopeful and virile young men had been killed in cold blood by the security forces, with the killings made to appear as casualties of armed encounters. Yet those who had instigated the killings, instead of being placed in the dock, had been elevated to exalted positions from where they could mock the victims' near and dear ones. I told him that even De Klerk of South Africa had appointed a judicial commission to investigate death squads of the South African security forces, and the British army had tried and sentenced officers and soldiers guilty of crimes against the Irish. Yet the Indian government had still to sentence a single security official for excesses against the Sikhs in Punjab. The central issue in Punjab now was: can a people be denied the right to elect its own government for more than five years?

He was straightforward and sympathetic during the hour or so we talked, and what came through clearly was that he wanted to do the right thing by Punjab. Even though he had started his brief tenure by arresting several of Punjab's Akali leaders, he had soon released those arrested and met a cross-section of Sikh leaders from Punjab.

7. The Nineties: The End of the Dream?

He said he would have no hesitation in meeting the militants if they accepted his invitation to come and talk to him. He guaranteed them safe passage. He also promised to hold state elections and, true to his word, scheduled them for May 1991. But, in keeping with the dubious traditions of Indian democracy, the Congress party dislodged him in March, and though the President asked him to continue as a caretaker Prime Minister till June his was clearly a lame-duck government from then on.

He made one mistake. He postponed Punjab's May elections to June: which meant that they would be held towards the end of his term in office. And of course they were not held till February of the following year because the Congress, in keeping with its pathological aversion to doing the constitutionally correct thing in Punjab conspired – through the Election Commission – to have the State elections called off on the last day of Chandra Shekhar's Prime Ministership, so that they would be held during the governance of whoever succeeded him, which, of course, would be the Congress. The Prime Minister was not even informed of the postponement by the Election Commission!

*

Tragically, a month earlier, on the evening of May 21, 1991, an explosion near Madras had killed Rajiv Gandhi as he campaigned in the general election in which he had hoped to come back to power. Even though the LTTE (which many are convinced was created by New Delhi) denies its complicity in his killing, there is evidence to suggest that it masterminded it. The bitter irony lies in the fact that the LTTE, one of several movements trained, armed and supported by a Congress government, in time became too big for it to control. And so, in a sense, the Congress party itself paved the way for the assassination of first Indira Gandhi and then her son, Rajiv Gandhi.

If Rajiv Gandhi's killing was a senseless act, what followed was equally so. Within hours of the news of his death mobs, which are kept on call to coerce or kill with impunity those whom the Congress sees as its adversaries, tried to burn down the house of an Opposition MP, roughed up many other people and shouted inflammatory slogans against the current and the previous Prime Minister. Even though the violence in the wake of Rajiv Gandhi's death was in no way comparable to the violence against the Sikhs following Indira Gandhi's assassination in 1984 – that was an altogether different game being played out – it would have got out of hand if the government of Prime Minister Chandra Shekhar – a non-Congress

163

government, as it happens – had not made sure that the police did not dishonour itself as it did in 1984. It also called in the army without waiting for the disturbances to spread and a difficult situation was handled firmly and impartially – in marked contrast to the way Rajiv Gandhi and his government had allowed the killing of the Sikhs to continue for four days.

The long-term implications of the lumpenisation of Indian politics are even more sinister, because other political parties have followed the Congress lead by mobilising their own bands of hoodlums for scoring political points – not in the legislatures but in the streets. The BJP – India's main opposition party in Parliament – would prove it to devastating effect before the end of 1992.

*

With Rajiv Gandhi gone, P.V. Narasimha Rao was sworn in as Prime Minister. A veteran Congressman, he had held just about every ministerial portfolio under the Gandhis, before which he was Chief Minister of the rich and populous Southern state of Andhra Pradesh. On coming to New Delhi he was in turn the Minister of Home Affairs, External Affairs, and Human Resources Development, proving – with rare consistency – his singular ineffectiveness in each. This was possibly because he created no waves, did what the Gandhis told him, and took only those decisions he was directed to take. This had worked well and he saw no reason to doubt its efficacy for staying on in power, because, while others had come and gone at the whim of the Gandhis, he had been a sort of Forever-Rao – pliant, resilient, enduring, indecisive and ineffectual.

When he moved into the office of Prime Minister some people said, rather optimistically, that he was the kind of low-key person needed to restore the nation to an even keel. They felt we had had all we could take of the pyrrhic politics of his predecessors – with the exception of Chandra Shekhar – and it was time we had a more level-headed person, even if he was somewhat wooden, doleful and uninspiring. These expectations were belied to some extent by the way he allowed the Punjab elections to be scuttled – a sleight-of-hand which was carried out with skill and a complete unconcern for the proprieties. But most of Punjab's Sikhs, faced with militancy on the one hand, a sadistic police force on the other, and a customarily undependable Congress government in New Delhi, took it with stoic calm. They had become wiser about the ways of New Delhi, and they had the grit to see adverse situations through.

Rao surprised everyone by bringing in Dr Manmohan Singh, a

brilliant economist, as Finance Minister and giving him a free hand to liberalise the Indian economy, to a degree which had been inconceivable in the past. Multinational corporations were encouraged to set up plants in India; steps were taken to simplify complex government procedures; exchange rates were pegged at more realistic levels; rationalising of tax structures was promised; and various incentives were offered for higher exports, exchange earnings and increased productivity. The gradual privatisation of state enterprises was also announced. Given the rising graph of external borrowings, it was accepted that the only way to get out of the vicious circle was to deregulate and liberalise the economy. This made sense. But it also meant that battle would be joined on many fronts: against a powerful bureaucracy reluctant to give up its arbiter's role, against the ideologues of the *laissez faire* era, against the advocates of planned development, and against those sectors of the industry which had thrived under protectionist policies. The labour unions would also mount an attack, as would opposition parties, since opposition to the government had become an end in itself, not a means of monitoring its performance. Although there was an undeniable and very real danger of a sell-out to the mega-corporations and financial institutions of the West, firm steps to get the economy moving again had been overdue.

But with so many battlefronts to impede the economy's forward thrust, the question most people were asking was: would Rao be able to stand up to the strain of it all – especially as he also needed the support of the Left and other parties who disapproved of his economic policies? He was an unlikely warrior and there were grave doubts about his staying power. People feared that he would be overcome by battle-fatigue before it came to the crunch; that he would sacrifice the head of his able Finance Minister to appease his foes. Fortunately Singh was unfazed by the constant sniping at him. This was the first political office he had ever held and he did not see it as an only lifeline to his survival. Respected in financial and economic circles in India and abroad, he had – given his qualifications and standing – all the confidence needed to go about implementing the reforms with aplomb, without permitting a politician's insecurities to deflect him from his course. In this case Rao had picked the right man for a difficult job.

*

The moves Rao made on Punjab were quintessentially Congress. After he had scuttled the elections in the state once, he announced that they would be held in February, 1992. No one was impressed.

People had heard it before. In the past the BJP had been completely opposed to them because the very idea of the Sikhs coming to power made them queasy, and the Congress had felt the same since they had no chance of winning either. The Left parties had also concurred. But this time the Akalis sprang a surprise: they would not contest! Every time they had geared up for elections in the past the polls had been called off, and they had just about had enough. They would only contest if the Centre conceded some of Punjab's demands before the elections, as a gesture of its good intentions.

Sensing shrewdly the attractive possibilities offered by the Akali refusal, which could be exploited to his advantage, Rao arranged for a rumour to be floated that he was seriously thinking of offering 'a package' to Punjab as proof of the Centre's decency and goodwill. The Akalis let it be known that if the offer made sense they would be prepared – despite the undependability of the Congress – to revise their decision. Having got them nibbling at the bait Rao and his partymen, without wasting time on questions of political morality, began preparing for the elections. There was a chance – just that one exciting possibility – that the Congress might edge past the contestants, non-contestants and others and win this non-race. If it won – and why wouldn't it since no one worth the name was contesting? – Rao's minority government could gain some badly-needed seats in Parliament.

But wouldn't such an election be farcical? Of course it would. But why should that matter? What about the anger of the people and, if the Akalis boycotted the elections, wouldn't that create tensions, lead to violent incidents? So what was new about that? And there were always those two tried and tested democratic options to fall back upon which are so favoured by India's politicians: arrest the Opposition leaders *en masse* and call in the army as a massive deterrent. India's massive deterrence is not of the crass kind with which John Foster Dulles threatened the Communists in the fifties; India's political leadership has devised its policy through its own ingenuity and for its own people.

In yet another replay of the theatre of the absurd, I found myself again calling on the Prime Minister, this time P.V. Narasimha Rao, whom I had met in 1984 when he was Home Minister. I was convinced our meeting would serve no useful purpose as I had observed him before at a time of crisis, but I was persuaded by my ebullient friend Ram Jethmalani, a brilliant criminal lawyer and MP, who felt that we should try and bring Rao around to conceding some of Punjab's demands so the Akalis could contest the polls. I agreed out of a writer's curiosity, rather than any hope of succeeding in our mission.

*

We met the Prime Minister on January 21, 1992, and though he was generous with his time his generosity ended there. We urged him to rise above the prejudices, passions and conflicting interests which had brought Punjab to its present pass. We said time was running out on reconciliation but creative leadership could succeed even at this late stage. The larger national interest would be ill-served if the Akalis abstained from the elections, so he should persuade them by announcing the transfer of Chandigarh to Punjab, referring the river waters dispute to the Supreme Court and promising greater autonomy not just to Punjab but to all States. If he announced this package, we would do our best to persuade the Akali leadership to withdraw its boycott.

He responded by telling us in some detail about his honesty and integrity: the days and nights he had spent poring over the various options in Punjab; his helplessness in the face of the pressures on him; his promise to find a political solution within weeks of the elections. He asked us with folded hands to carry this pledge to the Akalis. As for making a gesture before the elections, he hoped we would understand why he could not make it. We of course couldn't. It was all of a piece: the same bland phrases, the promises he had no intention of keeping, the obliviousness of the costs involved. At one point he came up with an amazingly abject remark: 'Mrs Gandhi could do many things which I cannot. She had broad shoulders, I am only a small man.'

So much for creative leadership.

When we stood up to leave, I gave him a piece of paper on which I had written a few lines before leaving for our meeting. They were from Barbara Tuchman's book, *The March of Folly*: 'If the mind is open enough to perceive that a given policy is harming rather than serving self-interest, and self-confident enough to acknowledge it, and wise enough to reverse it, that is a summit in the art of government.' He read it, folded it carefully and put it in the breast pocket of his jacket. That note, I have a feeling, met its nemesis the next time his coat went to the cleaners.

Driving back home after this non-event, Jethmalani suggested we go to Chandigarh and try and bring the Akalis around ourselves. I told him I had had my fill. The Akali leaders had been very co-operative during my earlier meetings with them – especially when I

167

tried to mediate at Indira Gandhi's request – but their attitudes had hardened; they felt the Centre was not interested in the state's stability but in destroying their legitimacy. But Jethmalani was not easily put off. With his own unstated goal of establishing some sort of political foothold in Punjab very much on his mind, he was adamant that we go together. We drove to Chandigarh the next morning, and our first call was on Prakash Singh Badal, Punjab's former Chief Minister and leader of one of the two mainline Akali groups. After an hour and a half of intense exchange of views with him and his aides, we went to see Simranjit Singh Mann. This former police officer is the head of the other major Akali faction. He had resigned his commission in the police in protest against the 1984 assault on the Golden Temple, and had been arrested on trumped-up charges soon after. For five years the government had used every means to break his will, including torture of the most malevolent kind which had left him permanently scarred. He was just as suddenly released in 1989, without any of the charges against him ever being proved in a court of law. He had returned to a hero's welcome in Punjab and had entered its political life with considerable élan.

After a long conversation with him and an overnight stay in Chandigarh, we had breakfast the next morning with V.N. Narayanan, Editor-in-Chief of Northern India's leading daily newspaper, the *Tribune*. A Tamil Brahmin himself, Narayanan's coverage of Punjab had maintained an admirable objectivity which contrasted sharply with the mischief-making editorials on the Sikhs by most of his contemporaries in Delhi. After getting his assessment of the current situation in the state, we drove to Patiala, about 50 miles away, to talk to Gurcharan Singh Tohra, the patrician chairman of the Shiromani Gurdwara Parbhandak Committee, a powerful apex body which oversees the religious affairs of the Sikhs and their institutions. A politician to the core, he is the only one among the Sikhs wily enough to outwit a conclave of Brahmins without unduly straining himself.

The more than two hours we talked with him were fascinating both for what he had to say and for his compelling way of saying it. Then it was back to Delhi, and this time it took over eight hours of a gruelling drive, which was not made easier by the many military and police roadblocks on the way; New Delhi was clearly at war with its own people. But even this was nothing compared to the BJP's *rath yatra*, which we had run into on our way to Chandigarh. These *rath yatras* had caught the fancy of the BJP's mandarins, because the man who had taken over from Advani as the party's head promptly launched on one of his own, leading – in a silly-looking contraption

7. The Nineties: The End of the Dream?

– a motley collection of vehicles all the way from Kanyakumari on India's southern tip, to Kashmir in the far North. The aim of this exercise, he had announced with a straight face, was to knit India together. It ended comically with an Indian Air Force helicopter airlifting him on the last leg of his journey. (Why the Centre was keen to help him keep his rendezvous in Srinagar, which was aimed at provoking the Valley's Muslims, is yet another of those cruel paradoxes India is plagued with.) Days before he had nearly unravelled our plans as we tried to ease past the enormous traffic jams caused by the hysterical knitters who were keeping him company.

The question now was: where do we go from here? We had to be certifiably insane to ask the Prime Minister to reconsider his position. But what might work was if Nikhil Chakravartty, the highly respected political writer and President of the Editors' Guild of India, spoke to Rao. They were friends and Rao respected his judgment. So I rang Nikhil the next day and he dropped by for a drink that evening, which gave Jethmalani and me plenty of time to cover events with him. Nikhil agreed that our visit had opened up an opportunity which should not be squandered but, since Rao's calling was politics, his own interests would come first and the rest later. Nonetheless he would talk to him.

True to his word, Nikhil called the next day to say that the Prime Minister would be very interested to be briefed on our Punjab visit and would I write him a letter setting things down in cold print? This I did on January 23:

> Our conclusion at the end of this visit reinforces the urgency of the appeal we made to you on January 21: you must, Prime Minister, rise above the influences at work within the Government of India and your party, which have prevented a solution to the Punjab problem until now. The situation there is very grave, and the attitudes of the Akalis and many other thinking people have hardened against the government. New Delhi is seen as unprincipled, vacillating and undependable, with which the Sikhs cannot deal as equals ...
>
> One of the things which came out clearly during our talks was the Akalis' genuine concern about the rigging of elections. This is nothing new in this country. Their fears that elections may not be free and fair can be legitimately entertained, because militancy is not the only threat to free elections. Government can and should announce suitable measures to create confidence ...
>
> Another resentment expressed was against the possible misuse of Article 356 (by which a duly elected State government can be dismissed by the Centre) of the Constitution. The Tamil Nadu precedent has not gone unnoticed, where even the Governor was opposed to supersession of the State government. Yet the deed was done. ...

169

Your government is [also] bound politically and morally to carry out the promises made when the Rajiv-Longowal accord was reached. Some of these promises can be carried out forthwith before the last day for nomination. You must not permit their fulfilment to be vetoed by politicians of your party. You must act as a national and not a party leader at this critical juncture ...

I urge you with the utmost earnestness possible, not to fail the country in this hour of crisis. Because, by rising to your full stature as the Prime Minister of a great Republic – in which one sixth of the world's people live – you will save its unity, continuity and integrity. ...

A year and a half has passed and there is still no reply! I have to admit I am not disappointed, and in this lies Rao's strength: he does nothing and you learn to expect nothing from him. Although this can be a restful attribute in a leader of an idyllic little island with, say, a population of a thousand, in a volatile, human cauldron of almost 900 million, inaction and intransigence can prove apocalyptic, as we were about to witness.

And so the elections were held, the Akalis abstained and the Congress – with no opposition worth the name – romped home on only ten per cent of the vote. It took twelve parliamentary seats in the Lower House and gained seven more in the Upper through this charade, giving a much-needed boost to Rao's minority government. The Congress formed the ministry in the State, installed a clone of a Chief Minister, who promptly announced that Punjab's was a law-and-order problem and that was the way he intended to approach it. The state's police chief was only too willing. And the figures of those killed, tortured or detained without trial – innocent or guilty – climbed steeply. Government communiqués took to announcing the liquidation of another 'top militant with 1,000 killings to his credit', but no names of the thousand he had killed were ever announced.

Rao's lack of wisdom – aside from his reluctance to tackle political crises with the necessary seriousness – also lay in presuming that, because he had strengthened his power base through several adroit moves, his political instincts were infallible. Things never quite work that way. The intangibles which influence tidal moves in politics are not always in the politician's control. And in December of 1992 such a destructive wave overtook Rao and the nation, the ultimate irony being that it was not the Sikhs who were at the centre of this epic disturbance but his co-religionists and the politicians of his ilk who mobilised rampaging mobs – as Rao's Congress had done in 1984 – to set the country aflame.

*

The BJP and its many associates had viewed the *yatra*-inspired killings in 1990 as a propitious sign. They saw them as vindication of an electoral strategy which had turned religious intolerance into a virtue – which with cruel intent had raised to a frenzied pitch the intense dislike of large numbers of Hindus for the Muslims: all carried out with the virtuous aim of honouring Lord Ram. This surge of anti-Muslim hysteria was waiting to be translated into a landslide of Hindu votes for the BJP. It had worked before, as the party's electoral triumphs of 1989 and 1991 proved. While in the first its parliamentary strength had risen from 2 to 88, in the second it increased to 119. The time was now ripe to go for the jugular of political power and rule India. For that the BJP needed at least another 150 seats in Parliament, and so the period till the next elections had to be used well. If it meant the ripping apart of India's tranquillity, traditions, resilience and stability, so be it. Power comes to the hard-headed, not to those squeamish about murder and mayhem.

The BJP and its web of interlocking organisations knew they had hit a gold mine in the Babri Masjid dispute, and they were not about to let it go. The idea of righting this historic wrong – whether real or imaginary – appealed to an increasing number of people and, as the stridency of the demand for the masjid's demolition and the building of a Ram temple in its place increased, so did communal tensions. The Muslims, incensed at the fraudulent case that was being made at their cost – against a centuries-old structure – vowed to oppose the move. Which made the BJP, VHP and Co. happy: they could use this further to aggravate the prejudices, hates and blind beliefs of their followers. What added to their combativeness was that India's biggest State, Uttar Pradesh, was now ruled by a BJP government which was confident that its administrators, police and intelligence agencies could be made to do the party's bidding, or at least look the other way when the elected representatives were breaking the law.

As the new aspirants to power manipulated the militant spirit of the Hindu masses, the man already in power – instead of providing 'creative leadership' in the face of the crisis – tried to talk his way round it. And since talking is India's national sport, the idea was enthusiastically received. Everyone now got into the game with much fanfare. It started with slanging matches in Parliament. Rao held talks with the holy men of Hinduism, and the Centre entered into discussions with the State's Chief Minister and with the Opposition parties. Hindu and Muslim leaders tried negotiating with each other, and the National Integration Council met to hear its members. More than 100 officially-recorded meetings were held. Even those who had nothing to do with it were drawn into the dispute; the Allahabad High Court for one, and then the Supreme Court. The Prime Minister was in his element because he loved talking his way out of a dispute, not necessarily resolving it but sending the contestants into a catatonic state induced by the sheer scale of the discussions held.

But this time Rao had met his match. While a self-satisfied Prime Minister was convinced that his endless meetings and the Supreme Court's directive to the BJP-VHP combine, asking it to conduct only a symbolic ritual next to the masjid, were paying off, the BJP, under cover of negotiations, was ready for an audacious showdown. It knew that Rao felt he was on top of things; his inaction had helped him in the past, and he saw no reason why it should not do so now. This psychological block is just what the *Hindutva* forces were about to exploit.

*

The fateful day was December 6, 1992. The first assault on the barricades around the masjid began at 11 a.m. This was soon followed by waves of hysterical, hate-filled men trained and readied for the purpose, and within minutes the chief of police and the head of the district administration gave up all pretence of trying to control the situation. By 4.49 p.m. the 464-year-old Babri Masjid had been razed to the ground in the presence of L.K. Advani, the 'moderate' past President of the BJP whose *yatra* had triggered off the 1990 round of bloodshed. Also present were his successor, Murli Manohar Joshi, who had set out to 'knit' India, several MPs, administration officials and an impressive number of Indian and foreign media persons. And of course the 200,000 and more screaming and slogan-shouting people who had been brought from all over India by the votaries of *Hindutva*.

Historian Gyanendra Pandey's comment on what happened (it appeared on the front page of *The Times of India* on December 10) captured the essence and significance of that event:

Ayodhya, on December 6, gave us a glimpse of a Raj whose culture would be defined by a lumpenised, urban, male youth, ironically called a Kar Sevak [voluntary religious worker]. A Raj with no room for dissent, or difference of opinion, or even of appearance. All those who did not brandish lathis [wooden staves] and bricks, scream victory and dance for joy as the work of destroying the mosque commenced, were threatened by the votaries of this 'new India'. Journalists – practically the only 'outsiders' on the spot – young and old, men and women, foreign and Indian, were abused and man-handled. Those with cameras had their cameras snatched, smashed, broken into smithereens with lathis, and stamped upon. Those with tape-recorders or just pen and pad suffered similar treatment a while later. Many journalists were beaten unconscious (and at least one, a foreigner, was danced upon while he was in an unconscious state.) A woman reporter was stripped. All this on the ground that journalists 'always' present facts in a 'distorted light' ....

[Some] images ... well represent the moment. The image of an uncouth Murli Manohar Joshi, clenched fist raised in egotistical salute ...

Twenty-five to thirty Muslims, chiefly older men with a few women and children, the only ones of the 250 or so inhabitants who had stayed on ... asking what they had done wrong to deserve this isolation and terror 45 years after Independence.

In a single revealing, disgusting move the disguise had come off and the BJP and its associates had shown their contempt for things which men of honour – even politicians – set store by: the country's Constitution and its highest Court; the pledged word; peaceful settlement of disputes; honest governance; and concern for human life.

*

This ominous deed brought India face to face with the dangers facing her: the realisation, for instance, that men in high office – like the Chief Minister of India's most populous state – could openly mock the directives of the Supreme Court. Despite his assurance to the Court on November 27 that the mosque would not be touched until the Court had given its final decision, rehearsals for its demolition had been carried out under state protection. At the time of the final assault the state police refused to intervene. When four battalions of the Centre's Rapid Action Force (RAF) were summoned, the Chief Minister had them stopped. As the first dome of the structure came crashing down, the RAF was wheeling around to go back to its camp.

The conduct of the law-makers was no better. Their raised ringside seats provided the MPs of the BJP, VHP, Shiv Sena and Bajrang Dal with an uninterrupted, grandstand view of the masjid, and as the three huge domes fell, one after the other, these latter-day heroes, eyes welling with gratitude at the divine opportunity afforded to avenge historic wrongs, cheered and hugged each other to celebrate their 'victory'. Over a dilapidated structure, as Advani crudely called it.

Such is the stuff India's political leaders of today are made of.

The most disgraceful conduct was of the police and administration officials who were present to protect the masjid. P.A. Rosha, who has held very senior and sensitive posts in thirty-four years of police service, calls it 'a black day in the life of the Indian Police when it let the entire world see it abdicating its responsibilities'. In a conversation with me a few days later, he said: 'Once the system has made up its mind to have a pliable police which helps it in the misuse of authority, rather than a professional force committed to uphold the rule of law and accountable to the institutions established for the purpose, it is the beginning of the end of democracy.' No matter how many orders are issued by a Chief Minister 'they cannot', according to Rosha, 'absolve the police of its statutory responsibility to protect life and property and to bring the offenders to book. In case of deliberate inaction, it would be liable for dereliction or, what is worse, abetment.'

No less despicable was the behaviour of the District Magistrate, the senior official present at Ayodhya. Film clips show the man and his aides, happy and relaxed, watching the surging crowds make their ascent to the top; the police walking away; the expertise with which the domes were scaled and then brought down. The officials sit through it, drinking tea, smoking, stretching lazily in the winter sun, laughing and occasionally cheering. It was such good fun. The District Magistrate (reports say) stirs himself briefly to summon the Rapid Action Force but, when the battalions are still two kilometres away, asks them to return to base on the Chief Minister's instructions. This was the conduct of a member of India's prestigious administrative service, inheritor of the traditions established by men who administered India with fierce independence, imbued by the spirit of their service. He had come a long way from the description of a civil servant provided by A.D. Gorwala – himself an Indian member of the Indian Civil Service (ICS) through which Britain ruled India: 'The young man imbibed standards, sometimes without even being told. Automatically he learned there were certain things one did not do. However awkward the circumstances ... however grave the consequences to oneself ... one did not lie. In all emergencies it was one's duty to stand firm ... In all one's dealings, the rule must be probity.'

The vicious attacks on media persons, who had converged on Ayodhya, were another preview of the future. They were set upon in front of Members of Parliament, political leaders and law-enforcement officials. The physical violence did not stem from the whims of

7. The Nineties: The End of the Dream?

the hoodlums, or because they were aware of which news had been presented in a 'distorted light' in the past, nor did they know anything of the journalists' duty to document facts in words, pictures and on film. The 'minders' of the mobs orchestrated the attacks. The press, which 'lives by disclosure', had to be stopped from telling the truth about the planning which had preceded the mosque's destruction, or about the administration's culpability, or about the politicians' glee.

*

The BJP and its associates – aspirants to the pinnacles of political power in New Delhi – took less than six hours to disown parliament, the judiciary, the civil service, secular traditions and freedom of information. But what of those already in power? Consistent with his past record, the Prime Minister's conduct before December 6 and in the days after clearly aggravated the crisis. Equally it is not true to say that he was unaware of the plans to destroy the mosque, or that he could not have ordered central forces to throw a protective ring around the structure. According to Rosha 'the Constitution empowers the central government to station its para-military forces anywhere in the country, even though "Public Order" and "Police" are state subjects'.

How did Rao respond to the news of the demolition? It took him six-and-a-half hours to get his Cabinet to meet and discuss the crisis. By which time there was nothing left of the mosque. Why did it take so long, asked a BBC interviewer? 'We were monitoring ... asking the UP government to make use of the forces available to them ... we were watching, but they would not say yes or no to our demands.'

Rao could have dismissed the State government even before December 6. This he did not do. He dismissed it *after* the event. According to him it would have been unconstitutional to do so earlier. This is far from the truth. The Intelligence Bureau – India's topmost intelligence agency – had been monitoring the situation in Ayodhya from November onwards and the Prime Minister had been warned of the mosque's impending destruction. In anticipation of the holocaust that was bound to result, Rao had sufficient grounds under the Constitution to supersede the government. The Centre had, in fact, sacked dozens of state governments on the flimsiest of grounds in the preceding eighteen years. Nor was the dismissal of the two BJP governments in Rajasthan and Himachal Pradesh, after December 6, constitutionally correct, considering that what had taken place was in Uttar Pradesh and they had not openly encour-

175

aged the massacre of the Muslims in their States. But the BJP government of Madhya Pradesh – which was also dismissed after the demolition – was certainly culpable, with gruesome killings taking place even in Bhopal, the capital of the State. There was every reason to sack it.

But despite the justification and constitutional authority, Rao did not suspend the Uttar Pradesh government. Why? Was there more to it than meets the eye? A growing body of opinion in India feels that deep inside he is sympathetic to the *Hindutva* doctrine, approves of the BJP's brand of nascent Hinduism.

Even after the State-sponsored vandalism the putting up of a make-shift structure on the site of the former mosque and the placing of Hindu idols in it could have been prevented, since it was bound to become the centre of a new controversy. Rao helped to increase the existing bitterness by saying that he would build a new mosque to replace the old. It was just what the BJP wanted. They dared the government to touch the idols, or rebuild the masjid. The Prime Minister then made yet another astonishing move: he arrested L.K. Advani, Murli Manohar Joshi and others, *after* it was all over. And with it he turned the mounting revulsion against their vandalism into a wave of sympathy. He restored their spirits by placing a halo of martyrdom on them. Instead of isolating them politically, he made heroes of them. He is too much of a politician to have done all this unwittingly.

These moves too placed the Muslims at the receiving end. Even though they had no hand in Rao's announcement to reconstruct the mosque, or in the arrests, the proponents of *Hindutva* pointed an accusing finger at them, holding them responsible for just about everything: for being an 'appeased minority'; for the attitude of the 'pseudo-secularists' (i.e. all those who opposed the BJP); for being Muslims. The propaganda of hate was unbelievable. My friend Saeed Naqvi, a Muslim himself and a political commentator widely-acclaimed for his incisive writings, suggested a way out for the Muslims: 'First, get out of the firing line. The mosque is now a rubble. A 464-year old structure cannot be resurrected. Desperate politicians want to keep the issue alive. Let the secular forces and others join battle. Let them build the mosque or not build one. Muslims as Muslims must keep out of it.' This was sound advice since now the coming fight will be between secular Indians and the Hindutva fanatics. The Muslims should do nothing to weaken the secular forces because, as Naqvi correctly points out, Indian Muslims in any event are 'an inseparable part of the secular State'.

*

But no one who witnessed what followed the demolition on that December day, would believe that India is a secular State. The epicentre was again Ayodhya, with the difference that it was not a heritage structure this time but Muslim households in Ayodhya and its twin city, Faizabad, which were attacked. No sooner was the masjid destroyed than the crazed mobs turned on the Muslims – killing, pillaging, torching homes, terrorising men, women and children. Every Muslim home in Ayodhya was destroyed. Mosques were attacked, even the graves vandalised. The aggrieved and not the aggressors were savaged. By the next day frenzied communal violence had gripped large parts of India. Hardly a state escaped and Punjab was among the few in which there was no violence. Maharashtra topped the list in numbers killed (over 200), most of them in Bombay, once the most civilised and best-administered of Indian cities. Bombay's police force added to its degradation through its blatant anti-Muslim bias, wantonly killing them – in the name of quelling the riots – by aiming at the abdomen, rather than in the air first, and then at the feet, as laid down in police manuals. Around 90 per cent of the people killed died in police firings!

Delhi was no better. Its police behaved as it did in 1984: in a thoroughly partisan manner. Of the properties worth millions which were destroyed, 99 per cent belonged to the Muslims. Almost all those killed were also Muslims, again most of them by police bullets. The collusion of the police and the killers was well-documented, the most damning being by Sampradayikta Virodhi Andolan (SVA) on behalf of the People's Movement for Secularism. Its report, compiled by academicians, lawyers, doctors and social workers had this to say of the police: 'They signalled to the mob to move ahead and exhorted them saying *aage badho; aag lagao; loot lo* ('Move on, burn, loot'). As for the constant refrain of temples being burnt, 'none of the major temples that we visited in the area [Seelampur in East Delhi] seemed even minimally damaged; and all three important mosques of Seelampur bore signs of varying degrees of attack'. Its most revealing findings relate to the extent to which Congress political leaders connived at the murderous assaults on the Muslims. This was also borne out by the findings of the People's Union for Civil Liberties. 'The events of December 11 cannot be described as a "riot" between members of the two communities. It appears like a well-planned police operation, joined by some BJP/Congress activists and local *goondas* [hoodlums], which was singularly targeted on the Muslim residents of the Timber Market and Kabutar Market localities of Welcome Colony.' Although Delhi's death toll was less than Bombay's, the pattern of the killings in the nation's capital did not say much for the central government's secular credentials, or for the Congress Party's non-communal postures in public.

Segments of India's population sank to sordid levels in many parts of the country in those grim days of December. In Surat, Gujarat's second largest city, about 200 km north of Bombay, Muslim houses were locked from the outside and set alight with their occupants still in them; a group of women were stripped naked, then gang-raped, while others recorded the scene on video cameras; both men and women were hacked to bits and their bodies thrown into huge bonfires. The police mostly stayed away for the first few days of this violence, which took over 200 lives.

Eyewitnesses said that in ill-fated Bhopal, seat of the state administration, frenzied mobs indulged in an orgy of brutality which exceeded even Surat. The bloodthirstiness of the *Hindutva* forces was given rein by the BJP ministry. According to a front-page report in *The Statesman* (December 30, 1992) the State Governor had, in a top-secret communication to the President and the Prime Minister on December 8, held the State government primarily responsible 'because of the political leadership's overt and covert support to the associate communal organisations'. He had written that 'serious reports of either police indifference, or callousness, or inadequate presence and even police indirectly fuelling the riot frenzy and mob fury have been received from a large number of organisations, that met me yesterday'. The Governor also recommended that the Centre 'dissolve the State legislature forthwith'. An ever-helpful Prime Minister took a week to do so, by which time the carnage was over. People again wondered whether it was only his habitual irresolution which had prevented him from saving countless human lives.

What the casualty figures of over 2,000 dead in the eleven most-affected states showed was that the systematic subversion of the civil service and police and the near-absence of political morality, had finally come to haunt the country: a spectre brought on by the reckless, mealy-mouthed, goose-stepping politics of the BJP and its associates, aided by a secretive and complacent Prime Minister and his Congress colleagues.

But paradoxically the nationwide violence after the tearing down of the Babri Masjid also showed that a way out of the impasse could be found if the civil services played their statutory role in the country's governance, as provided in the Constitution. This ray of hope was provided by the exemplary conduct of those members of India's administrative and police services, who resisted the wayward pressures of the politicians during the critical days of December. In Lucknow, the scene of earlier communal conflicts, two men saved the day: the District Magistrate, Ashok Priyadarshi, and the Senior Superintendent of Police, D.N. Sambal. It was the same in several other trouble spots in the State. In Khurja, a young woman Sub-Divisional Magistrate, Dimple Varma, prevented the outbreak of violence. Nor was violence allowed in Bijnore, a chronic trouble centre. In Ayodhya itself a young woman, Anju Gupta, an Assistant Superintendent of Police on duty on December 6, charged into a crowd with a wooden stave and saved the lives of two news photographers who were being mercilessly beaten. In Indore, Madhya Pradesh, which had exploded in a welter of bloodshed after Advani's *rath yatra*, the lid was kept firmly down by the Commissioner, Vijay Singh. In Bhiwandi, 80 km from Bombay and one of the most communally volatile towns with a grim record of killings, not a single incident took place because of the brilliant handling of the situation by its ranking police official, Gulabrao Pol. There were many such instances across the nation.

It is difficult to appreciate the role of the executive if its importance as one of the four pillars of Indian democracy is not kept in mind. It is bound by the laws – just as the judiciary and legislature are, and to an extent the press by its own rules – and not by the capricious and corrupt demands of the politicians. But many in it connived at the erosion of their own pivotal role in upholding the rule of law, of which citizens' rights are an integral part. Their role is to protect these rights, not trample on them. The executive, in a democratic system, derives its authority from the Constitution and the laws which flow from it, and so its primary accountability is to these institutions, rather than to the politicians in power.

But partly because they lacked backbone and integrity, and partly because the politicians gradually overwhelmed them by their unprincipled and bullying ways, many members of the executive gave in. Transfers of officials with each new ministry, favouritism, uncertainty of tenure, punishment postings and other forms of needling added to their demoralisation. And with the loss of morale, the ability to perform their duty conscientiously also suffered. Which suited the politicians fine, making it easier for them to bend the more pliant and self-seeking members of the services to their will. The pity of it is that the different branches of the executive offered no collective resistance to these inroads into their authority, because the politicians also knew how to play the divide-and-rule game.

If the executive is able to assert itself, which it is empowered to, and the way towards which was shown by many of its upright constituents during the holocaust which overtook the country, it is still possible to correct the politicians' misconduct. It will not be easy, but nothing is. What will make it difficult is the extent to which the executive has been influenced by the appeal of *Hindutva*. There is enough evidence to show that by touching on the sensitive nerve of Hindu self-assertion, the BJP has won many adherents in the services to its cause. The question is: will they continue to uphold the Constitution, which the BJP and its associates have been treating with scant respect? Fortunately, countless others in the permanent executive reject the vision of an India conjured up by the fevered minds of the *Hindutva* ideologues. It is their sane and even-handed approach which can prevent communal bloodshed and chaos.

George Woodcock once quoted this poem to me in which W.H. Auden affirms his faith in the future of Europe when it was reeling under the onslaught of invading armies in 1940. While George had quoted it in the context of the work of Kabliji Hospital, because it gave him similar cause for hope, for me hope in the future now depends on the integrity of those upright men and women who are trying to safeguard the fabric of Indian society:

> *Defenceless under the night*
> *Our world in stupor lies;*
> *Yet, dotted everywhere,*
> *Ironic points of light*
> *Flash out wherever the just*
> *Exchange their messages:*
> *May I, composed like them*
> *Of Eros and of dust,*
> *Beleaguered by the same*
> *Negation and despair,*
> *Show an affirming flame.*

The 'affirming flame' in India too is visible everywhere, even amid the profanities, violence and the detestable propaganda of the religious fanatics and power-hungry politicians. It can be seen in the Hindus and Muslims who reached out to each other in those critical days. In the balanced writings of editors and columnists. In the outrage of rational people, repelled at the turn of events. In the restraint of states like Punjab, Tamil Nadu, Bihar and Orissa. And even though the odds are mounting, these 'points of light' spell hope.

7. The Nineties: The End of the Dream?

*

But India's strange subconscious urge to self-destruct cannot be underestimated, considering how often we have, in defiance of logic and sanity, chosen the road to certain disaster. Is there a psychological explanation for our collective death-wish? Have our myths, rituals, symbols, superstitions, illusions and esoteric beliefs helped to shape and exalt a frame of mind – a mental structure – which enables it to ignore the obvious and tragic consequences of our actions?

There is a poignant immediacy to these questions as we face the inconsistencies and self-betrayals which have dogged us for centuries. As our ingrained divisiveness again encourages forces which could lead to India's disintegration, much as the unending internal conflicts of the past had once led to subjugation and humiliation. What happened to those shared and passionate convictions – whose stirrings we had first experienced in college – which made us believe that India's full flowering would come after the departure of the British? They, after all, were aliens who could never do for us what we could for ourselves. We were so confident then of substituting for their imperial arrogance our concern for the dignity and well-being of every Indian.

It is almost thirty years since we lost our brief war with China, a major setback to our self-esteem, as a euphoric anticipation of victory was turned into defeat through political gamesmanship; by egocentric, meddlesome politicians unversed in the conduct of wars. In a curious way we managed to find this reassuring too, seeing it as a one-of-a-kind event we had to experience: painful, humiliating, but helpful since nations learn from their mistakes. To soften the bitter after-taste of the defeat, we blamed it on the Chinese: their perfidy and undependability. If we learned one thing from it, it was how to find scapegoats to take the blame for our errors, our misgovernance. The 'foreign hand' would become a part of our political vocabulary, a constant, handy, dependable abstraction to which we could attribute just about anything. The alienation of entire states – troubled by the Centre's policies and prejudices – could be blamed on a foreign hand. If Western powers armed Pakistan, it was seen as a conspiracy of the foreign hand to destabilise us. And even when our own evil, homegrown, religious bigots fanned Bombay's second wave of massacres – within a month of the December 1992 killings – we attributed it to a foreign hand.

What about the drift from our earlier ideals – from the time when respect for the laws was mandatory, when proprieties and probity in public life were observed? Surely a foreign hand could not have helped us subordinate the nobility of our freedom struggle to self-seeking politics? We took many other steps without prompting by outside powers: the surrender to linguistic jingoism which continues to leave a gory trail as the reorganised States seethe discontentedly over territory, river waters and jobs; the failure to overhaul the administrative system because we liked exercising power from the top – as in the colonial days – with no participatory role for the people below. The lack of a trickle-down effect from economic and industrial growth did not help either. We clamped the Emergency too through our own innovative genius, substituting a dictatorship for democracy, and putting to rest democratic aspirations by yearning for dynastic rule. Since dynasties and dictatorships need massive funds, we successfully tried our hand at corruption on a matching scale; by amending the statute more than seventy times to make it easier to keep people in place, by eroding the judiciary and the executive, by encouraging state terrorism, and by using religion to usurp the majority community's votes.

Neither Pakistan, the Western powers nor other foreign hands had anything to do with any of this. We did it all on our own.

But what of the future? It holds the dismal prospect of a stand-off between the sclerotic Congress and the BJP with its network of associate organisations. The Congress, divided, corrupt, devious, culpable and conspiratorial, the others conditioned and controlled by the obsessed and brooding mandarinate of the Rashtriya Swayamsewak Sangh (RSS) whose ideologue, M.L. Golwalkar, in *We or Our Nationhood Defined*, spelled out his vision of India in perfectly unambiguous terms. 'The foreign races [i.e. non-Hindus] in Hindusthan must either adopt the Hindu culture and language, must learn to respect and hold in reverence the Hindu religion, must entertain no idea except [their] glorification ... must lose their separate existence to merge in the Hindu race, or they may stay in the country wholly subordinated to the Hindu nation, claiming nothing, deserving no privileges ... not even citizens' rights.' In his view those who did not share these ideals were 'either traitors and enemies to the national cause, or to take a charitable view, idiots'.

In the same unabashed vein he had drawn admiringly on Nazi Germany's purification methods where 'foreign races' were concerned. 'To keep up the purity of the race and its culture, Germany shocked the world by purging the country of the semitic race – the Jews. Race pride at its highest has been manifested there. Germany has also shown how well-nigh impossible it is for races and cultures having differences going to the roots to be assimilated into one united whole, a good lesson for us in Hindusthan to learn and profit by.'

The RSS-BJP group has not temporised over Golwalkar's vision of a 'purified' Hindusthan, nor relented in its efforts to realise it. In the sixty-eight years since the RSS was founded in 1925, it has worked with tenacity, industry and uncompromising zeal till its offspring, the BJP, now stands on the threshold of political power. And if it wins the next elections, it will finally be in a position to reshape India as Golwalkar would have liked it. It has embraced *Hindutva*, or the doctrine of Hindu hegemony, in much the same way as the Nazis adopted *Deutschtum*, or pronounced German nationalism, as representative of their nation's social and political goals.

The prospect of the BJP coming to power is not a reassuring one, considering the amount of blood it has helped shed, its discriminatory and manic political goals, and the use of the big lie as a major instrument of political strategy. The culture it will usher in will not be very different from what the fascists imposed on Germany. Equally grim is the mental makeup of the BJP's top leadership, and of its associates it will have to share power with. L.K. Advani, for one, who helped place the Babri Masjid in the eye of the storm and sees himself as a future Prime Minister. Although he is the leader of the Opposition in Parliament, his statements show an astonishing disregard for the truth. He started saying publicly years ago – in speeches, in interviews, on camera and elsewhere – that Muslims had destroyed over forty Hindu temples in the Kashmir Valley. Yet George Verghese, who investigated this allegation on behalf of an RSS-run institute, reported that not one temple was destroyed (though a few were slightly damaged), and that simply because security forces had been billeted in their compounds. The attacks were against them, not the temples. But the brazen lie aimed at increasing hostility against the Muslims continued to be repeated *ad nauseam*. As were other distortions.

Foremost among these is that, given their birth-rate, Muslims will swamp the country in the coming years. The census figures for 1971 and 1991, however, tell an altogether different story: the percentage of Muslims to the total population in these twenty years went up from 10.7 to 11.4, a 0.7 per cent increase! As for the simmering resentment over the right of Muslims to have four wives and the Hindus only one, 5.8 per cent of the Hindus practised polygamy as against 5.7 per cent of Muslims. Equally revealing is the truth behind the false charge that the Muslim population is exploding because they are opposed to family planning. An all-India survey by the

Operations Research Group shows that Muslim couples practising family-planning methods rose by 11.5 per cent between 1980 and 1989 as against 10 per cent for the Hindus. Another dishonest charge against them is that they are an appeased lot. One certainly would not believe it from the figures of placements in jobs, per capita incomes, literacy rate – especially among Muslim women – and other indicators.

But Advani is not distracted by facts. Nor does he think much of the pledged word – as his public speeches showed during the mini-*yatra* to Ayodhya which he took in December 1992. In Varanasi, on December 1, he said: 'We do not want to destroy any masjid or make a mandir ... *Kar seva* (devotional service) does not mean *bhajans* and *kirtans* (religious songs); we will perform *kar seva* with shovels and bricks ...' Later, in Azamgarh: 'We want peaceful *kar seva* but the Centre is creating tension.' In Mau, December 2: 'All *kar sevaks* will perform physical activity ...' On the same day he urged the crowd at a public meeting 'to take a plunge and do not bother whether the Kalyan Singh (UP's Chief Minister) government survives or is dismissed'. On December 3, in Gorakhpur: 'I never said such a thing [about shovels and bricks being used].' Back in New Delhi on December 7, after the mosque had ceased to exist he claimed: 'Both I and the UP Chief Minister did all we could to prevent the destruction, but what actually happened was that we could not gauge the intensity of the people's feelings over Ayodhya.' An odd statement, considering the extent to which he had gone to whip up people's feelings. Nor do film documentaries show his colleagues doing much to stop the demolition. The Chief Minister was not even present there.

Since the BJP's leadership is clearly inspired by its ideologue's admiration for Nazi Germany, a look at how their role-models handled the 'purification' programmes can be instructive. The Pulitzer prize-winning author John Toland, in *Adolf Hitler*, describes what took place on the afternoon of November 9, 1938, when orders for the first nationwide wave of anti-Semitic violence – the Nazis were more circumspect then – were given. '[Hitler] conferred briefly with Goebbels before boarding his special train. Goebbels returned to the meeting to announce that ... the Fuhrer had decided that if the riots spread spontaneously throughout Germany they were not to be discouraged. The party leaders took this to mean that they were to organise demonstrations while making it appear that they had nothing to do with them.' The 'spontaneous' killings, burnings, lootings and desecration of the synagogues later that night (the Crystal Night) have become recorded history; the truth could not be kept hidden. Historians in India too will, undoubtedly, sift, analyse and investigate the mass of evidence to record the extent to which the Babri Masjid's demolition and massacre of the Muslims that followed was spontaneous. The truth of this vandalism will also be chronicled.

The BJP and its associates are not unaware of the damage which honest documentation can do to their cause, and the assault on journalists at Ayodhya was only a precursor of what came later: vicious attacks on Hindu and Muslim editors and reporters who dared to criticise the votaries of *Hindutva*. Many were subjected to a barrage of hate mail and filthy phone-calls – from which their families were not excluded – while the properties of others were looted and burnt. Still others were badly beaten, and two reporters of a Bombay evening paper were knifed. The onslaught on the media brought into clear focus the BJP's preferred method of dealing with exposure, dissent and free thought. Given the proclivity of its leaders to lie and its intolerance of dissent, Alexander Solzhenitsyn's description, 'In our country the lie has become not just a moral category but a pillar of the state', would be most apt for India if and when the BJP comes to power.

With freedom of expression out of the way, next on the list would be the right to life and property. The extent of the BJP's concern for the sanctity of life was self-evident in the early nineties. Less so the role that property mafias – perhaps in collusion with the *Hindutva* forces – played during the turbulent months of December and January. The reports from most major cities had to do with real-estate – with the sordid greed of property-owners, developers, politicians, slum-landlords and hoodlums-for-hire who saw in the communal violence an opportunity to rid the slums of slum-dwellers and free the land for redevelopment at astronomical profit. It was not greed or social inequity which was responsible for the urban violence in Bombay, Delhi, Calcutta, Kanpur, Ahmedabad, Surat or elsewhere, but Advani's 1990 *yatra* and the Ayodhya demolition. The cities were then left – by the BJP, Shiv Sena and their associates – to the mercy of the developers who could profit from the situation. The carefully organised January riots were a brazen example of state terror, directed against people of a different religious persuasion, and combining with it a class war by the propertied mafia against Muslim slum-dwellers. Some Hindu shanty-dwellers also lost everything, but as in the case of reprisals against journalists these distinctions matter little in the new order being advocated for India. In the case of Bombay it will be the Maharashtrians only who will be eventually spared the violence and, in due course, only certain castes among them ...

*

It certainly seems a very long time since those days when I established my magazines in Bombay and crusaded for urban sanity and civic grace. Of course I wrote about politicians manipulating zonal laws for their personal profit and advantage, but even in the worst doomsday scenario I could never have imagined the cold and calculated cruelty with which Bombay would be debased by its own people.

What then of the future? It is unrealistic to expect a new or even an existing political party to contest and win an election and be dedicated to running a clean government and restoring respectability to the political process. But an individual who can mould, influence and inspire a party, whose concerns and responses are rooted in people's recent experiences and urges, can make the difference. Some see in this the danger of an emerging dictatorship. I do not. The many checks and balances which exist will make this very difficult. The major Opposition-ruled States, for one. It is also highly improbable that the armed forces will support such ambitions. It is worth remembering too that men like Nehru and Shastri were able to mobilise people behind them because of their open-handed and clean governance, because they were respected. And not because they were dictatorial.

People are again waiting for a person of quality, with resolution, courage, fortitude and drive, to provide India with dynamic leadership. The outrage of vast sections of the population – at the shenanigans of the *Hindutva* forces and the support they received from the Congress – stood out as another 'affirming flame' at a time when everyone was asking the question: how will the coarsening political culture and disregard for decencies affect the future of Indian society? India is not a land of inconsequential achievements. The monumental treatises produced here, based on epic journeys of the Indian mind in its unending quest of knowledge, are unique. As are her humanistic traditions, architecture, dance, music, sculpture, painting, crafts, and myriad other creative expressions which came effortlessly to a naturally gifted people. Equally impressive are her present achievements in agricultural breakthroughs, industrial growth, diversity of manufacturing, entrepreneurship and innovation. Each testifies to the potential of our people. But the question that remains unanswered is: will the manic nature of the politicians' mind-set destroy India's larger promise? Will the in-built, self-defeating constraints of some sections of orthodox Hindu thought keep India from honouring her economic, social and human rights commitments?

An interesting perspective on this possibility (Chidananda Dasgupta, 'Ayodhya agitation as class war', *The Times of India*, January 4, 1993) views the Ayodhya outrage as part of a class war launched by privileged sections of Hindu society against India's democratic Constitution. To them the Babri Masjid, being Islamic, symbolised the enemy, but it was also seen as an irksome reminder of India's democratic secularism. And 'to the traditionally privileged Hindu, the idea of democracy is equally abhorrent. He is simply not prepared to accept the equality of all human beings irrespective of caste, creed and sex, because it hurts his self-interest. If people of all classes have to be accepted as his equal, he loses his right to exploit the castes lower than his own.' Dasgupta then looks at those 'modern' Indians who went to Harvard and elsewhere to get their MBAs, and wonders, 'Did that modernise their minds?' His conclusion: 'Not necessarily ... the idea of the equality of all human beings remained anathema to most of them.'

Since a 'privileged Hindu' can be anyone in the trilogy of top castes, Brahmin, Kshatriya or Vaishya, 'the BJP combine's war upon the Constitution is being waged on behalf of (these) three Hindu castes'. A comparison can be made with Japan to show how a staunchly traditional nation, controlled by a powerful oligarchy of *daimyo* and *samurai* (territorial lords and their noble warriors) broke from an isolated, inward-looking existence to become one of the world's great powers. This decision was taken in 1868, during the Meiji Restoration, by a few key members of the Japanese elite determined to oppose Western dominance by modernising Japan. Of course the feudal order bitterly opposed the transformation, but it was compelled to yield before Japan's national interest. The Japanese veneration of the state and the ethos of discipline, honour and valour overcame their resistance to change.

In India the Hindu oligarchy is 11 per cent of the total population (it roughly equals her Muslim population). Not surprisingly hundreds of millions of untouchables, tribals and others – since they themselves are exploited by this privileged hierarchy – are unmoved by its insecurities. And they are even less enthused at being represented as a part of the Hindu fold, which the BJP is keen should appear bigger than it is. Nor do they share the upper castes' antipathy to the Constitution because it still holds hope for them, the disadvantaged, who have been denied their rights for millennia and for whom

187

the existing liberal, secular Constitution is more promising than a future Hindu Rashtra (rule). Thus the underprivileged too, by standing up to these uncaring forces, are showing yet another 'affirming flame' to a beleaguered India.

*

It seems incongruous to talk of human rights when even the right to life is losing its meaning. But it was not always so, because upstanding men and women who inspired the framers of our Constitution, had a different vision of India. And its opening lines affirm the Republic's resolve to secure for its citizens:

Justice, social, economic and political;
Liberty of thought, expression, belief, faith and worship;
Equality of status and opportunity; and to promote among them all;
Fraternity assuring the dignity of the individual and the unity of the nation.

That was forty-three years ago and we have, since then, amended the Constitution 71 times. (The Americans have amended theirs 26 times in 206 years.) We have come a long way from those days when our goals were invested with a sense of purpose, a moral vision which saw exciting possibilities ahead. That vision was overtaken by a nightmare of legislative amendments which made a mockery of civil liberties and human rights. For instance, the 59th Constitutional Amendment operative from March 30, 1988, authorised the suspension of the fundamental right to life and liberty! Interestingly, this provision was in effect virtually confined to Punjab. (Repealed from January 6, 1990, by the 63rd Constitutional Amendment.) One of the many lethal acts is the Terrorist and Disruptive Activities (Prevention) Act (TADA) which was enacted in May 1985 and given even more odious powers in 1987. It poses a grave threat to every single individual in India. Its provisions are bizarre and it provides many pretexts for people to be arrested, detained without trial and killed by the security forces. Unbelievable as it seems, a person innocently buying a magazine can be picked up under TADA because information in it is 'likely to assist the terrorists' and so he becomes guilty of abetting terrorism. TADA is being used to detain people indefinitely all over India.

Section 21 of this Act demolishes the internationally accepted basic concept of justice, namely the presumption of an accused's innocence until he is proved guilty in a fair and open trial. The obnoxious statute now reads: *'the Designated Court shall presume, unless the contrary is proved, that the accused had committed such offence.'*

An equally excessive piece of legislation, the Armed Forces (Punjab and Chandigarh) Special Powers Act, 1983, gives 'any commissioned officer, warrant officer, non-commissioned officer ...' the right in disturbed areas (which Punjab and Kashmir were declared to be years ago!) to destroy shelters from which armed attacks are likely to be made and to arrest without warrant a person on suspicion that he is *about* to commit an offence. In other words, a citizen's home could be razed to the ground because it was *likely* to be used for an armed attack against the state. The real crunch lies in the stipulation that no person whose rights have been thus abused under the provisions of this Act, can institute any legal proceedings against those responsible without 'the previous sanction of the Central Government'. The Courts do not figure – except when they decide to intervene in their discretionary writ jurisdiction conferred by the Constitution.

This legislation was one of 30 Punjab-related Acts and Constitutional Amendments enacted between 1983 and 1989, whose specific aim was to terrorise the Sikhs. The effect of these – to all intents and purposes – was that there was one basic law for Punjab and another for the rest of India. Government armed itself with still further powers for Punjab through the 67th and 68th Constitutional Amendment Acts of 1990 and 1991. Yet it is the Government of India that has projected Sikhs as terrorists worldwide, while encouraging State terrorism at every turn.

In a report on the escalating human rights abuses in India ('Might vs. Right', January 18, 1993) *Time* quotes this remark by an Indian army officer: 'When we torture the Sikhs in Punjab, they can hold out for weeks, and they will die before they tell us a thing. But when we torture these little Kashmiri boys, they break down on the first day and blab everything.' Its distasteful, patronising tone about Kashmiris aside, what makes it possible for such statements to be made with assurance is the extent to which the forces have been empowered under this Special Powers Act.

In April 1992, after the unprincipled arrest under TADA of Justice A.S. Bains, a retired High Court judge and Chairman of the Punjab Human Rights Organisation, some of us took the matter to the Supreme Court, questioning the Constitutional validity of this Act and seeking to have it struck off the statute book. We used Justice Bains's detention as illustrative of its gross abuse by the government. The others who joined me in the petition were N.K. Mukherjee, former Cabinet Secretary and Governor of Punjab, R.S. Narula, former Chief Justice of the Punjab & Haryana High Court, Inder Mohan and Rajni Kothari. My friend R.S. Sodhi, a distinguished lawyer and a man deeply concerned at the social and political trends of our times, filed the petition. When he appeared before a Justice of the Supreme Court on the morning of April 26 and requested an order on the petition, he was told that since the Chief Justice was not in town, the matter would have to await his return. Subsequently too no pressing desire was apparent to end the uncertainty surrounding the unjust incarceration of a former High Court Judge, or to adjudicate without delay on an outrageous piece of legislation. Our petition, as it happened, was the only one before the Supreme Court which challenged the Constitutional validity of TADA, right from the preamble to its last section. And yet it remained unheard. Nor is it being considered by the Constitution Bench while dealing with the Constitutional validity of TADA. Why? Sodhi doubts if the petition will ever be heard. It is not surprising that people in India are beginning to doubt the highest judiciary's professed concern for human rights.

In marked contrast to this unfortunate lack of urgency was the alacrity of the response of two other legal institutions. Within five days of his arrest, the first of the two reports I wrote appeared in *The Pioneer* on April 8. The very next afternoon the Bar Association of India passed a resolution deploring the 'inhuman and humiliating treatment meted out by Punjab state authorities to a former Judge of the High Court' and called upon 'the Home Minister of the state of Punjab to explain publicly why Justice Bains was handcuffed and maltreated following his arrest under TADA'.

Equally impressive was the stand taken by the Geneva-based International Commission of Jurists which aims at defending the rule of law and full observance of the Universal Declaration of Human Rights. Its Secretary-General wrote to the Indian Home Minister on April 16, expressing the Commission's concern at 'reports of the arrest and inhumane treatment of a former judge of the Punjab & Haryana High Court, Mr Justice A.S. Bains, on April 3, 1992 ... (and) that Justice Bains was handcuffed and maltreated following his arrest under the Terrorist and Disruptive Activities (Prevention) Act 1987 (TADA) and was not produced in Court when his writ of habeas corpus was heard. We urge that Justice Bains be treated humanely and be granted full legal safeguards while in custody ... In conformity with international norms guaranteeing freedom of expression and association, we respectfully urge that Justice Bains be immediately and unconditionally released.'

My friend Fali Nariman played a key role in the prompt response of these two organisations to the outrage against Justice Bains. The judge was released on bail much later, but not before the Government of India had made its point to human rights activists: keep off, or else!

This is not very surprising, considering Prime Minister Rao's own stand on human rights which has been amazing, to say the least. He came up with a breathtaking charge against human rights organisations, dutifully endorsed by several of his partymen, officials and Indian diplomats abroad, made obliquely – which is how he prefers it – in a speech to the National Integration Council. He suggested that these organisations were more concerned with the rights of terrorists than with those of the victims. This was a clever but unbecoming attempt at not only deflecting attention from the government's own excesses, but also projecting human rights activists as defenders of antisocial elements. His charge was false, because such groups have consistently condemned – through the media, seminars and such – the violence which flows from insurgencies and militancy. No right-thinking person condones acts which are viewed as unwarranted assaults on the lives and properties of innocent citizens, but that scarcely means that, because terrorists trample on the rights of people, the state is absolved of its constitutional obligation to respect and protect the rights of *all* citizens.

Human rights concerns in democratic countries all over the world are always – and only – directed at the ever-present possibility of excesses by the state and its agencies. Those who break the law do not cease to be human beings. They continue to have the right to be given humanitarian treatment according to the Universal Declaration of Human Rights, 1948, and the Covenant on Civil and Political Rights which was adopted by the UN General Assembly on December 16, 1966 and came into force on March 23, 1973. India, a signatory to the Covenant, ratified it in 1979. According to its provisions, the state cannot arbitrarily arrest or detain individuals; the law must treat *all* human beings alike so far as their basic rights are concerned, and appropriate punishment can only be awarded by a fair and impartial judicial tribunal, after an open trial.

The implication of the Prime Minister's extraordinary statement is that it is for the police or armed forces to decide who is a terrorist and whom they should arrest, detain, torture or shoot dead; that such persons can be presumed guilty even before they are tried. Many of the more sadistic elements in the police no doubt find the PM's stand very agreeable, although saner Indians are dismayed at this attempt to match criminal acts with lawless acts by the state. The most troublesome aspect of Rao's astonishing stand is the extent to which it is conditioning people's minds into accepting the arbitrary exercise of state power, and the violation of human rights, as an inevitable spin-off of the times. His attempt deliberately to confuse the issue is helping to coarsen people's sensibilities.

What Rao says has to be judged against the backdrop of these observations by Justice R.S. Narula, whose entire life was spent in upholding the majesty of the law: 'There are now more killings by our police in one year than there were in 150 years of colonial rule. Deaths due to torture in police custody are continuing unabated and unwept despite the public outcry of Human Rights Organisations.' As for those who profess to govern – or misgovern – from New Delhi, 'the policy of the present government appears to convey to the people: *our dear citizens, we will beat you, maim you, even kill your boys, but we will not allow you to protest.*' To sum it up in his words, 'Freedom of conscience and freedom of expression, indeed!'

*

It doesn't seem very long ago when I awoke to the captivating, sunlit world of my childhood – when old honoured virtues had a place in people's lives. Yet it was another era. The conversation in our home was not hate-filled against people of different religious faiths. Religion exalted my parents' lives, they were fulfilled by it, so there was no room left to run other religions down. When Hindu, Muslim or Christian friends came to call, they were welcomed. My parents valued their friendship, and admired them for their warmth, wit and wisdom, for their learning and integrity and genial ways.

Nor can I conceive of another physical setting I would rather have been born in, or which could have given me as much as Delhi did. She gave me her architectural gems to marvel at, her great buildings, her cultural uniqueness, the untamed landscape which stretched all around her, rich in flora, fauna and wildlife. Her gracious parks with majestic structures from the Lodi and Mughal periods, reminders of India's long, rich and textured history. They often resonated to the sound of *mushairas* (poetry soirées), music and dance – events which were also frequently performed in the gracious homes of the Walled City where Delhi's old merchant families lived.The residential complexes which would swamp New Delhi – and to which they would move – were years in the future. But during my boyhood they resided in the graciousness of their old mansions. And I was transported to another world when my school friends from those families took me visiting.

We did not refer to the centuries-old buildings around us as 'dilapidated structures', we were not even allowed to etch our names on their weathered walls, much less visualise their outright destruction. What was impressed on us was that our heritage, in its many-faceted forms, was our teacher and deserving of respect. The magnificent buildings we saw, whichever way we looked, had to be admired for the aesthetics, craftsmanship and skills which went into their making. They could also – if we wished to hark back – remind us of those times when we were subjugated, not because the conqueror was stronger, but because of our own internal weaknesses. It was never implied that, to regain our manhood and sense of self-esteem, we had to tear those buildings down.

My mother taught us Sikh history at home, when the valorous deeds of men and women and the indelible imprint they had left behind were often discussed. Only exemplary and courageous leadership, we were told, could inspire those who were led into battles against tyranny. And if the tyrant's authority had to be challenged, it should be done openly, when he was around to pick up the gauntlet thrown down at him. And in full awareness of the consequences involved. Heroic men did not use crazed mobs to massacre innocent men, women and children, nor did they wage wars against empty buildings centuries after their builders had departed this earthly existence.

That I live in an entirely different era from the one I grew up in, is brought home to me in many ways. When I see the once gracious streets of Delhi – which people used even as the British Viceroy drove past – emptied of *all* traffic now because the Prime Minister is due to pass: a democratic leader hemmed in by gun-toting guards, looking menacingly out of every window of a long cavalcade of cars. Not one out of a succession of several Prime Ministers has found this grotesque. These insecure men who seem frightened of their own shadows do not at all resemble the leaders I had read of and admired; men who did not cower behind their security personnel while conniving at the killing of thousands of their countrymen. In today's India, not only those in power but Opposition leaders, bureaucrats and various other categories of inconsequential men are also attended by armed guards all the time and at the state's expense. Uniformed men with machine guns, chaperoning their charges everywhere, have come to symbolise Delhi. An appropriate form for rulers pathologically obsessed with safeguarding their own lives even as others are being incinerated alive.

Somewhere along the road to that promised land which Gandhi and Nehru had inspired us with when we were students, we took the wrong turning. Into unfamiliar territory. And imperceptibly the journey became less inviting as darkness closed in and the murderous milestones told us that the bloodied trail we were travelling on would lead to the final destruction of the hopes we had nurtured over the years.

In another abrupt transition to the present I see in a cartoon in *The Pioneer*, by my friend Sudhir Dar, a child learning about present-day India: A for Ayodhya, B for BJP, C for Communalism, D for Demolition ... More disturbing is what I read next to it, how school textbooks *were* actually made to include, during the eighteen months the BJP was in office in Uttar Pradesh, a new version of Indian history: that the Aryans did not migrate into India from central Asia, but were her original inhabitants. It certainly fits, because in the BJP's pantheon of inspiring literature *Mein Kampf* occupies an honoured place and according to it 'every manifestation of human culture' is clearly and 'almost exclusively the product of Aryan creative power'. The Aryan issue aside, if the BJP had its way I may not even know which country I belong to. One of its propagandists – they are a hardworking lot – has now come up with this weird but priceless gem: rename India 'Hindudesh' (land of the Hindus). But why? Because it will solve the majority and minority problem once and for all since everyone will have Hindu written on his passport! And all nationals of our renamed land will be called Hindus. *Voilà!*

There is much more of the same. India's struggle for independence, according to the BJP, began 2,500 years ago, and the greatest leader of the struggle against the British was Keshavrao Hedgewar, who founded the RSS in 1925! Confusing? But then there it is. The Qutab Minar, a marvel of engineering which rises to a height of 242 feet and was started in AD 1200 to celebrate the annexation of Delhi by Qutb-ud-din, the Afghan general, is now credited to the Hindu king Samudragupta who ruled in the fourth century! And so on.

I had been led to believe that education meant being informed – not disinformed – and that it was odious to lie. But when lies become a cornerstone of the State – as they have today – and are unselfconsciously told, by men in and out of power all the time, then we have certainly travelled downhill steadily from where we started on that profoundly moving night of August 14, 1947, when we jostled and milled outside Parliament House, with the wildly cheering, celebrating, emotionally-charged, impassioned and misty-eyed men and women as they awaited the midnight hour for India to be free – when Nehru got up and told the world that India's moment had come:

7. The Nineties: The End of the Dream?

Long years ago, we made a tryst with destiny, and now the time comes when we shall redeem our pledge, not wholly or in full measure, but very substantially. At the stroke of the midnight hour, when the world sleeps, India will awake to life and freedom. A moment comes, which comes but rarely in history, when we step out from the old to the new, when an age ends, and when the soul of a nation, long suppressed, finds utterance ...

I could not know then, as I set out to keep my own tryst with destiny, that what lay ahead was a rendezvous with renegades – with corrupt, criminal men who would exploit India's promise for their profit, willingly instigate nationwide massacres in their blind pursuit of political office, and wrest for themselves the powers which had to be shared with the other regions and States of the Union. Even though that rendezvous would end my age of innocence, I cannot help but feel that some of it has lingered on. Why else would I continue to believe that despite what we Indians have done to ourselves, since those long ago decades of hope, we might still overcome our self-destructive urges?

Mahatma Gandhi put it this way:

Today the Hindus and the Muslims are clinging to the husk of religion. They have gone mad. But I hope that all this is froth, that all the scum has come to the surface, as happens when the waters of two rivers meet. Everything appears muddy on top, but underneath it is crystal-clear and calm. The scum goes to the sea of itself, and the rivers mingle and flow clear and pure.

It is to be hoped that the scum which is clouding our vision and promise will also be washed away. I feel that our damaged social and political fabric can be repaired. But when I talked about it with a friend, his response was surprisingly vehement: 'Why must we always end on a positive note? Must we continue to live with our illusions for the sake of psychic – and moral – survival?' He has a point. Yet life without hope, faith and optimism is unappealing. If you love your country, you cannot turn away on seeing her dragged back into the dark ages just as the world readies itself to move into the next century. Only a sense of the positive can sustain the will to fight medievalism.

At times of crisis people are reassuring; they say that India will survive. I agree. She has survived for millennia and will in the future too. But in what form? As a proud, republican nation? Or a number of warring states perpetuating the chronic conflicts which so often brought her to grief in the past? In the face of the present threat optimism is made even more difficult by the priorities of men aspiring for political power: they want first to build nuclear weapons before doing anything to lessen the poverty and privation of India's teeming millions!

Chilling as these prospects are, I still believe that sane, upright and decent Indians outnumber the devious and the wayward. In that belief lies hope.

Epilogue

A S I look around, my mind goes back to those years in the thirties when I woke in the mornings to the sight of Delhi's noble monuments, the clean, crisp and invigorating air, the cared-for, tree-lined, grassy expanses and public parks. I remember the people's pride in the aesthetic merits and comfort of their city and their confidence that law and order would always be maintained. I see nothing wrong with this occasional mood of nostalgia. It helps strengthen the resolve to resist the vandals.

My memories of Delhi's Ridge are equally vivid. This extension of the Aravalli hills, one of the oldest mountain systems in India, originated over 1,500 million years ago. A hard, rocky, elevated tableland which runs through Delhi, it was carefully conserved – until we became independent – as Delhi's vital green lung. Emperor Firoz Tughluq, the fourteenth-century ruler, reserved large sections of it for game and had it extensively planted. The British, in their turn, planted thousands of trees of every variety from 1912 onwards. Even earlier, as records tell us, they planted over three thousand Neem (*Azadirachta indica*) and Babul (*Acacia nilotica*) trees from about 1878 onwards, but once a decision was taken on the construction of the new capital its afforestation was placed in the charge of William Robertson Mustoe. Great importance was also given to conserving the spectacular wild life which flourished there: blackbuck, leopard, hog deer, nilgai, jackal, hedgehog and an incredible variety of birds. My friends and I spent years exploring the Ridge when we were young. It was like being on one of those safaris in Africa which we watched wide-eyed when we went to the cinema. But the resident and migratory bird population and the marvellous wild life that once nested and roamed free are now mostly gone.

The government has built a gigantic stadium-cum-theatre on thirty-six acres of land which is larger than Rome's Colosseum and is seldom used; a wireless station complete with staff quarters; a Satellite Instructional Television Experiment centre; and many more structures of every description, along with miles of new roads. Two major parks were also developed by uprooting the undergrowth, removing the natural scrub and vegetation and endangering the ecosystem.

The forested Ridge once offered unstinting help to Delhi's climate by purifying the air, by replenishing the oxygen, by helping to cool the high temperatures of summer and by standing guard against the fury of the summer dust storms from the deserts of Rajasthan. This self-sustaining ecosystem – a proud friend and benefactor – has been grievously wounded by those it reached out to help. The sight of the Ridge bleeding to death is not only an agonising reminder of the happy days we spent there, but also of the predatory ways of man.

*

To return to the case of that much-loved and proud Delhi whom my friends and I had also courted, see how she has been laid low. Not by invaders, conquerors and interlopers, but by her own people who, cruelly indifferent to her vulnerability, are destroying her grace and charm with their high-rise walls of greed, who are polluting the air around her, poisoning the life-giving waters which had sustained her, blackening-out the blue of the sky and the shimmering stars so she can never see them again, and who have inflicted many indignities on her. She deserved better.

She is today the third most polluted city in the world. A dose of 1990 tonnes of pollutants is administered to her daily; it was 100 tonnes a decade ago. The levels of atmospheric pollution are already three times the permissible limit, and specialists agree that they will be nine times that limit in eight years. They feel that the city will be an atmospheric gas chamber by then. Among the factors responsible for the deadly chemicals which envelop her are two million automobiles, smokers who smoke an average of twenty cigarettes per head per day, the industries in and around Delhi, and the gigantic power-generating stations which loom over her. The number of motor vehicles exceeds the combined total of Bombay, Calcutta and Madras, and they kill five people every day in road accidents! In 1991 more people died on Delhi's roads than on those of the three other cities put together. The noise levels – almost ninety decibels at some places – are also taking their physiological and psychological toll.

The sources which supply her with water have been savaged too, with similar indignities inflicted on her revered and legendary companion, the river Yamuna. Twenty-four main sewerage arteries discharge human and other wastes into this river every day with an unending flow of toxic chemicals. Almost half Delhi's population of over 8 million draw their drinking water from hand pumps, traditional wells, ponds and the river – water which is never tested for its potability and the extent of water-borne diseases in it.

The decision to build high-rise buildings to demonstrate by this 'modern' urban symbol that we too have arrived, is another of the wounds inflicted on her. Aside from their inappropriateness in a setting like Delhi, there are other powerful arguments against vertical buildings: the costs involved, the use of materials produced by oil-based industries which would increase national indebtedness, the energy needs of air-conditioning, elevators, water supply, the environmental degradation. Not being an island city, Delhi has no problems of space. Yet skyscrapers are being built with a frenzy bordering on dementia. The fate of Connaught Place, the graceful two-storied, colonnaded circle of exclusive shops, is a telling example of officially-sanctioned vandalism. Brazen high-rise buildings around it, and its present rundown condition, have destroyed the quality and scale of one of the world's most elegant shopping centres.

Yet another important reason for not building high – the need to respect the existing architecture – was also completely ignored. Exquisite buildings, big and small, centuries-old relics of great walls, gateways, battlements, columns and tombs have been encroached upon by tasteless and vulgar buildings.

If these mute reminders of the past are neglected, what about the people who live here? Over 1.5 million live in slums in conditions of unbelievable congestion, with the litter of human execreta, liquid sullage and garbage everywhere and with open gutters which also serve as lavatories. And in the midst of all this – as if in parody of the principles of coexistence which India ardently espouses – are pigs, dogs, cows, cats, kites, crows, vultures, rats, cockroaches, flies and other vermin.

Since nature deals in her own way with those who violate her laws, the incidence of respiratory disorders in Delhi is twelve times the national average. The combination of atmospheric pollution and contaminated water is leading to diseases of the kidneys, liver and reproductive system in addition to higher risks of emphysema, bronchitis, cancer, cardiovascular complications and abdominal diseases. There is an element of poetic justice here since these afflictions hit both the decision-makers and those on whose behalf the decisions are ostensibly taken.

I often wonder if there is a pattern in these perverse attempts to defile Delhi, a compulsive urge to undo the magnificence of the eight Delhis which existed before we started building the ninth after Independence. Perhaps there was no conscious attempt to degrade them. And perhaps there was.

Government and real-estate developers are not the only ones to blame. Many well-off citizens joined in the plunder by getting permission to convert their villas into high-rise properties. Where the developers could not succeed with their bribes the citizenry succeeded with its influence – and of course bribes. Between them they have shamed the dignified and distinctive heritage of which any nation in the world should be proud.

Can Delhi ever regain her allure and entice her lovers back to her warm embrace? I would like to believe she can, but not as long as coarse and insensitive men oversee her destiny. Only a passionate admirer can give her back what was so wantonly taken from her.

Index

Index

KODANSHA GLOBE

International in scope, this series offers distinguished books that explore the lives, customs, and mindsets of peoples and cultures around the world.

INVISIBLE MEN
Life in Baseball's
  Negro Leagues
Donn Rogosin
Introduction by
  Monte Irvin
1-56836-085-1

BLACKBERRY WINTER
My Earlier Years
Margaret Mead
New Introduction by
  Nancy Lutkehaus
1-56836-069-X

ELDEST SON
Zhou Enlai and the
  Making of Modern
  China, 1898–1976
Han Suyin
1-56836-084-3

THE AWAKENED SELF
Encounters with Zen
Lucien Stryk
New Introduction by
  the Author
1-56836-046-0

ALONE
The Classic Polar
  Adventure
Adm. Richard E. Byrd
New Afterword by David G.
  Campbell
Facsimile of the 1938 Edition
1-56836-068-1

OF DREAMS AND DEMONS
A Memoir of Modern
  India
Patwant Singh
New Preface by the Author
1-56836-086-X

PASSING STRANGE AND
  WONDERFUL
Aesthetics, Nature, and
  Culture
Yi-Fu Tuan
1-56836-067-3

THE DESERT ROAD TO
  TURKESTAN
Owen Lattimore
New Introduction by
  David Lattimore
1-56836-070-3

OPTIMISM
The Biology of Hope
Lionel Tiger
New Preface by the
  Author
New Introduction by
  Frederick Turner
1-56836-072-X

THE MOUNTAIN OF NAMES
A History of the
  Human Family
Alex Shoumatoff
New Preface by the Author
New Introduction by
  Robin Fox
1-56836-071-1

EMPIRES OF TIME
Calendars, Clocks, and
  Cultures
Anthony Aveni
1-56836-073-8

ESSENTIAL SUBSTANCES
A Cultural History of
  Intoxicants in Society
Richard Rudgley
1-56836-075-4

To order, contact your local bookseller or call 1-800-788-6262 (mention code G1). For a complete listing of titles, please contact the Kodansha Editorial Department at Kodansha America, Inc., 114 Fifth Avenue, New York, NY 10011.